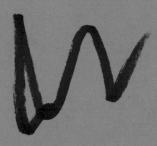

Praise for *Wiser*

"*Wiser* is a brilliant contribution to the emerging science of wisdom—how we define it, research it, and how we can intentionally cultivate it in ourselves and our society. A timely and hope-giving book as our world faces challenges that require the deepening of our wisdom as a species."

TARA BRACH
author of *Radical Compassion*

"The new science of wisdom is transforming the way we understand human potential and showing that the ancients were right: wisdom is real, wisdom is precious, and we can all be, yes, wiser. Drawing on cutting-edge neuroscience and a lifetime of research, Dilip Jeste brings the attributes of wisdom—compassion, self-reflection, humor, curiosity, and spirituality—to every page. He shows that wisdom can be developed and strengthened, and he explains how. A lot of books have made me smarter. This one made me better."

JONATHAN RAUCH
author of *The Happiness Curve*, senior
fellow of Brookings Institution, and
recipient of National Magazine Award

"*Wiser* is the readable summation and thoughtful culmination of the thought and work by Dr. Jeste on wisdom over many years. No medical scientist, to my knowledge, has been willing to tackle the expansive complexities of practical wisdom, what some may label as 'wisdom that matters,' as thoroughly as the author. Jeste takes us on a journey through the neurobiological foundations as well as the psychological and social components of practical wisdom. He artfully integrates the unique perspectives of his cultural background and a stellar career of scientific inquiry using Western methodologies. He has collaborated with and supported conversations among many scholars and has distilled these conversations into a basic handbook that will be of immense value to all who read the material, more importantly to those who are willing to grapple with this ever-expanding horizon of inquiry. That horizon is informed by science, the humanities, and wisdom itself."

DAN BLAZER, MD, PHD
author of *The Age of Melancholy* and *Freud vs. God*,
JP Gibbons professor emeritus of psychiatry and
behavioral sciences, Duke University School of Medicine

"Much has been written about human tendencies to compete, with winner-take-all rewards. Yet none of us would survive alone. The true story about humankind involves cooperation, kindness, and compassion. This lesson appears to grow stronger with age. Dilip Jeste, with Scott LaFee, details the science behind the proclivities to be concerned for the welfare of others and the circumstances that enrich it. Read this definitive account of wisdom and be wiser for it."

LAURA L. CARSTENSEN, PHD
author of *A Long Bright Future: An Action Plan for a*
Lifetime of Happiness, Health, and Financial Security;
founding director, Stanford Center on Longevity;
Fairleigh S. Dickinson Jr. professor in public policy
and professor of psychology, Stanford University

"In *Wiser*, Jeste, with LaFee, has written a compelling new book about the scientific research that takes the notions of wisdom and morally grounded reasoning out of the realms of myth and philosophy and into the bright light of modern psychology and neuroscience. From defining wisdom as an aspect of human mind and brain to explaining its psychological components and how to become wiser, Jeste, with LaFee, has produced an important and exciting new book on the science of wisdom. This is a deeply engaging book that explains clearly the science of wisdom and provides practical suggestions for wiser reasoning grounded in solid research."

HOWARD C. NUSBAUM, PHD
founding director, Center for Practical
Wisdom, and Stella M. Rowley professor
of psychology, University of Chicago

"We have never needed this book more than we need it now. It is the right book, at the right time, and for all the right reasons. Professor Dilip Jeste, with Scott LaFee, traces the scientific and sociocultural roots of wisdom, its cultivation, and its deep links to compassion and to lives well led. Not only medical and social scientists but also health and social policy makers and general readers will find insight and comfort in this volume. We need wisdom and courage for the facing of this hour. *Wiser* helps immensely."

CHARLES F. REYNOLDS III, MD
distinguished professor of psychiatry emeritus,
University of Pittsburgh School of Medicine; recipient
of Pardes Humanitarian Prize in Mental Health

Wiser

Wiser

THE SCIENTIFIC ROOTS OF WISDOM, COMPASSION, AND WHAT MAKES US GOOD

DILIP JESTE, MD
with SCOTT LAFEE

sounds true
BOULDER, COLORADO

Sounds True
Boulder, CO 80306

Published 2020

Book design by Maureen Forys, Happenstance Type-O-Rama

 The wood used to produce this book is from Forest Stewardship Council (FSC) certified forests, recycled materials, or controlled wood.

Printed in the United States

Library of Congress Cataloging-in-Publication Data
Names: Jeste, Dilip V., author. | LaFee, Scott, author.
Title: Wiser : the scientific roots of wisdom, compassion, and what makes us good / Dilip Jeste, MD with Scott LaFee.
Description: Boulder, CO : Sounds True, 2020. | Includes bibliographical references and index.
Identifiers: LCCN 2020005609 (print) | LCCN 2020005610 (ebook) | ISBN 9781683644637 (hardback) | ISBN 9781683644644 (ebook)
Subjects: LCSH: Wisdom. | Neurobiology. | Compassion—Psychological aspects.
Classification: LCC BF431 .J47 2020 (print) | LCC BF431 (ebook) | DDC 153.9—dc23
LC record available at https://lccn.loc.gov/2020005609
LC ebook record available at https://lccn.loc.gov/2020005610

10 9 8 7 6 5 4 3 2 1

To three women—my wife, Sonali,
and our daughters, Shafali and Neelum—
and three boys—grandsons Nischal, Kiran,
and Arjun—who have been doing
their best to make me wiser faster.

—DILIP JESTE, MD

To Marlee J,
marrying you is the
wisest thing I have done.

—SCOTT LAFEE

Contents

CONTENTS

PART III: Enhancing Practical and Societal Wisdom

Introduction

Seeking Wisdom of the Ages at All Ages

Wisdom is not intelligence.
It is more, much more.

TO BE SURE, we all want to be smart. We all know people who are intelligent, to whom the workings of the world come a bit more readily and easily. Smart people seem to understand complexities. They make connections, see patterns, and find solutions with efficiency and apparent ease. They are the classmates who got straight A's, the coworkers with the brilliant plan or best way to make the bottom line. They see the "next big thing" before others are even looking.

But many smart people are not happy. They appear perpetually stressed and under pressure. They may appear to care only about themselves, making you reluctant to seek their advice because you don't know whose priorities are first. You can't always predict how they will react to your request. They may smile and say, "Of course." They may become angry. They may be indifferent.

It's good (and often profitable) to be smart, but being wise is more interesting and more useful if our goal is to live a full and meaningful life. I'm not referring simply to the pursuit of happiness, which is distinctly subjective and frequently shifting. What makes you "happy" one moment or at one point in your life may not in another moment or as you age. Our notions of happiness change over time. And they are often different from others'.

Of course, happiness is a good goal. It typically accompanies becoming wiser, but wisdom is more about acquiring a deeper understanding about meaning in life, of being able to see how and where you fit into the grander scheme of things and how you can be a better person for yourself and for others. Searching for and finding meaning and purpose in life is not limited to philosophers. It is associated with better health, wellness, and perhaps longevity and definitely with wisdom. People who have a clear-eyed sense of the rational meaning in life—whatever that may be—are happier and healthier than those without it. They are also wiser.

We all know wise people. They're smart. Intelligence is an integral part of wisdom. But they are also warmhearted and compassionate. They are sophisticated, not simply or only in terms of academics or business, but in the ways of the world and of people. They are open-minded. They listen and make others feel heard. They are reflective, unselfish, and problem focused. They are willing to act on their beliefs and convictions, to do what is right, first or alone. Wise people become trusted advisers because they possess characteristic sagacity, happiness, and a calm demeanor we can rely on. They seem to instinctively know how to handle the personal problems that others find overwhelming. Wise people stand still and resolute amid chaos and uncertainty. They are different. And the rest of us would like to be more like them.

Many of the wise people you know are probably old, or at least older. Wisdom and advanced age seem synonymous. Consider the great works of legend and literature: Moses, Helen Keller and Toni Morrison, Gandalf, Albus Dumbledore and Yoda (who undoubtedly picked up a few things over his 900-year life).

"Older and wiser."

"Older but wiser."

So go the adages. We all expect wisdom to bring the fruits of contentedness, happiness, and calm, with a corresponding decline in stress, anger, and despair. But as you will see, wisdom and age are not inextricably bound.

Personality certainly plays a role. Psychologists define personality as a set of characteristic and consistent patterns of thinking, feeling, and behaving that distinguish each of us from everyone else, such as individual variances in sociability or irritability. Why are you shy and introverted while your sibling is a life-of-the-party extrovert? Why do coworkers panic over missed deadlines while you do not? Why is your boss is always angry?

Wisdom is a personality trait. The complex components that comprise and characterize it are part of the even larger and more complex set of elements that describe and define your personality.

Becoming wiser is a personality plus. But why are some people wiser, more perceptive, and more content in their lives than others? Do we have to become old to become wise as well? Can people become wiser faster? These are questions I have pursued over a long and revelatory career.

As a teenager growing up in India, I became fascinated by Sigmund Freud's books for laypeople on interpreting dreams and everyday errors in life. Freud was a neuropsychiatrist. He believed that all behaviors had a biological basis in the brain. He asserted that psychology rode on the back of physiology. Though I didn't know if Freud's interpretations of dreams and slips of tongue were accurate,

I was taken by his strong sense that the ultimate answer lay within the physical brain.

So I decided to learn more about this mysterious organ and its primary product, the mind. I went to medical school to become a psychiatrist, which was a rather odd choice in India at that time.

When I completed medical school in Poona (now called Pune), India, at age 21, the total number of trained psychiatrists in all of India—a nation of more than 550 million people at the time—was probably fewer than one hundred. Although my family and close friends did not try to deter me, I am sure they were perplexed by my choice. Perhaps some secretly suspected my sanity.

My interest in psychiatry focused on studying the brain itself. My medical school in Poona did not have a research program in psychiatry, so I moved to Bombay (now Mumbai) and did my residency under the mentorship of two pioneers of academic psychiatry in India: N. S. Vahia and D. R. Doongaji. I learned how to properly conduct simpler types of clinical research; I published several papers. But soon I bumped up against the limits of brain research in India at the time. There simply weren't enough facilities, physicians, or resources to do the kind of work I wanted to do—and so I headed for the mecca of medical research, the United States and the National Institutes of Health (NIH). After completing another psychiatry residency that was required for a license in the US (at Cornell University), I would spend several years at the NIH working on a host of psychiatric issues and questions. In 1986, I moved again, joining the faculty of the University of California San Diego School of Medicine, then and now a place of invigorating, collaborative research. It is still my academic home.

My early work at UC San Diego focused on the nature and biology of schizophrenia, especially in older people. Throughout this period, I never quite got away from my youthful fascination about the fundamental workings of the brain and its connection to wisdom.

But for a long time, I wasn't comfortable pursuing such research as a scientist. When I finally broached the idea of formally studying wisdom a dozen years ago, others, including colleagues and close friends, reacted with varying combinations of amusement, dismissal, sympathy, and maybe sometimes pity and dismay.

They told me that wisdom was a religious and philosophical concept, not a scientific one. I was counseled to not speak about research on wisdom if I wanted to avoid whispered ridicule or to successfully garner project funding. If I had been a young researcher at the time, I likely would have been persuaded to retreat in the face of overwhelmingly negative conventional wisdom. But being older and already having an established academic career, I was willing and prepared to take up the challenge.

Most of my academic and professional life has been spent seeking to understand the human mind and its condition, principally in terms of cognition and brain function across the adult life span and especially in older age. During the last two decades I, as a geriatric neuropsychiatrist, have focused primarily on the idea of "aging successfully," and what that means in terms of happiness and satisfaction, which surely rate high among most people's goals.

We tend to think of aging, particularly after middle age, as a period of progressive decline in physical, cognitive, and psychosocial functioning. For many, the graying of America represents its number one public health problem—looming, unavoidable, and alarming.

Yet there are many older people who thrive in later life. We all know of artists, writers, judges, and politicians who are active, productive, creative, engaged, and contributing members of society in important ways. At age 61 and weighing just 99 pounds, for example, Gandhi led a 200-mile, three-week march to protest the British salt tax, a major step toward India's national independence. Benjamin Franklin was 70 when he signed the Declaration of Independence.

Nelson Mandela became president of South Africa at age 76—and married Graca Machel four years later. Shigeaki Hinohara, a Japanese physician who lived to the age of 106, published multiple books after his 75th birthday. Anna Mary Robertson Moses, better known as Grandma Moses, took up painting at 76 and produced more than a thousand images before she died a quarter of a century later. Her works now sell for tens of thousands of dollars.

Older people are often happier than people half their age. In a study conducted in 2016, my colleagues and I found that the mental health of adults improved with age, even as their physical health declined. They enjoyed higher levels of life satisfaction, happiness, and well-being and lower levels of anxiety, depression, and subjective stress than those decades younger.

I believe—and it's the basis of this book—that wisdom, like consciousness or stress or resilience, is fundamentally grounded in biology. And like all other biological functions, wisdom too can be studied, measured, altered, and enhanced using modern, empirical methods of science and medicine. Saying so does not negate the role or importance of psychosocial factors in the development of wisdom. From the presence of loving parents and grandparents to attending safe schools to having a supporting network of family and friends, the world we experience shapes who we are and how we live with others within it.

Behavior and environment impact biology—and biology impacts behavior. That's a good thing. It means that each of us can increase our biologically based wisdom through various means, including behavioral, environmental, biological, and technological interventions. We can, in effect, become wiser faster.

This is a big, bold idea. It turns traditional understanding about wisdom on its head. For most of us, and for most of human history, wisdom has been considered sublime and indescribable, an accumulation of lessons learned over a lifetime. People seek wisdom, but finding it takes time, frequently accompanied by blood, sweat, and tears. Wisdom was considered the ethereal fruit and reward of aging.

But with ever-accelerating advances in science, with our growing ability to literally watch our minds at work and identify the mental mechanisms involved—down to the patterns of electrical and chemical messages between neurons that form memories—we are increasingly able to deliberately and positively alter our minds and behaviors in a relatively short period. Indeed, scientists are already able to create—and then erase—memories in laboratory animals. If we can alter the very fabric of our minds, why can't we weave in new threads of wisdom as well?

I believe we can. As we progressively understand the biology of the human brain—how all its diverse parts work together to produce the human mind—we will be able to expand, minimize, repair, improve, and just generally modify its results.

Wiser is an unprecedented guide designed and intended to help you identify, understand, nurture, and promote the behaviors of wisdom that already exist within you, the biologically based traits that the new science of wisdom posits can increasingly be measured, modified, expanded, and enhanced.

The scientific term for the only surviving human species is *Homo sapiens*, Latin for "wise man." Humans need to be wise. Wisdom has evolutionary significance, which we will explore later in the book.

Despite occasional moments of serendipity, science is usually laborious and plodding. That's a strength. It helps assure that the eventual finding or conclusion will more likely be right than wrong due to painstaking effort. Wisdom is similar. No one goes to sleep a fool and wakes up wise. Becoming wiser is a process. This book, based on the relatively youthful science of wisdom, is about how readers might speed up that process.

Perhaps in reading this introduction, you remain skeptical. That's entirely understandable and the sign of a scientific mind.

For so long, wisdom has seemed ephemeral, something cool to think about—but only to think about. Many people, scholars and scientists among them, are skeptical. I meet them regularly and routinely. They express surprise at this topic. They have doubts and questions. To them and to you, this book represents my answers and evidence. It is not the end of the discussion, but the beginning.

We need the powers and benefits of wisdom now more than ever. The need is particularly acute in times of trouble, fear, and woe, in times of war and global pandemic. In such moments, we need wisdom both in ourselves and in our leaders, because it is our collective wisdom that will lead to the betterment of humanity.

In this book, you and I will take a journey together, one that I hope will offer ample persuasive proof, but more importantly, reveal new ideas, insights, encouragement, and hope that wisdom is not a vague aspiration but something we can grasp, modify, and enhance, that the emerging neuroscience of wisdom and the understanding of how wisdom can be consciously improved promises to change ourselves and our world. I believe it can be for the better. For each of us. For all of us.

Part I

What Is Wisdom?

Here's the first rule of improvement, whether the matter at hand is installing a new sink, rebuilding a car engine, or becoming wiser: you need to know what you're working with, how it (the plumbing, car engine, or in this case, your brain) works, and how to know that what you've done is actually an improvement on the original.

Part I addresses these requirements and lays the groundwork for the chapters that follow. I recount the enduring constancy of the concept of wisdom, which surprisingly hasn't changed much in meaning over millennia, the neuroscience of wisdom (where in the brain its traits reside), and the emerging tools of science that have moved investigation and discussion beyond the salons of philosophy and into the lab.

I also discuss the intimate but not inevitable linkage of age with wisdom. Wisdom often comes with age but, to paraphrase Oscar Wilde, sometimes age comes alone. Likewise, wisdom is sometimes apparent in youth, although even in those lucky people it should increase with age and experience.

And I introduce a new, peer-reviewed measure of wisdom called the Jeste-Thomas Wisdom Index, which you can take online. It is the first measurement developed and based on the neurobiology of wisdom.

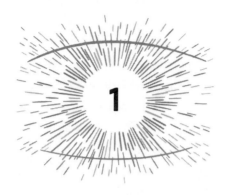

Defining Wisdom

*Of all the pursuits open to men, the search
for wisdom is more perfect, more sublime,
more profitable, and more full of joy.*
THOMAS AQUINAS

No man was ever wise by chance.
LUCIUS ANNAEUS SENECA

THE GREEK PHILOSOPHER SOCRATES, who lived twenty-five hundred years ago, is widely associated with the search for wisdom. He famously went looking for it among the citizens of ancient Athens, only to conclude that no one he met was any wiser than he (and often quite less so) and timelessly declared (purportedly according to Plato) that "the only true wisdom is in knowing you know nothing."

But Socrates was hardly alone in his penchant for pondering the nature of wisdom. In Proverbs 4:7 of the Bible, King Solomon, immortalized as an archetype of wisdom, declared it to be "the principal thing." Wisdom is a favorite subject of the Sebayt—recorded teachings dating to the Middle Kingdom of Egypt, 2000 BCE to 1700 BCE—and the Bhagavad Gita, a similarly venerable Hindu text of religious and philosophical scripture (written 400 BCE to 200 CE, but based on the Vedas, which are perhaps five thousand years old). Writers in ancient India and China ruminated on the question, from Confucius to Buddha. So too have philosophers, priests, poets, and pundits from long ago Babylonia and the Akkadian empire through the European Renaissance and Age of Reason and into modern times.

But while discussions and debates might vary somewhat over time and in different cultures and places, definitions of wisdom have tended, by and large, to be ethereal, a bit beyond our grasp. Wisdom seemed to exist on a different plane. It was thought to be rare and aspirational. You might find wisdom, live it, be fortified by it, and do wonders through it, said Hermann Hesse, who penned the 1922 novel about the spiritual journey of self-discovery of a man named Siddhartha, but "one cannot communicate and teach it."

I began my own quest to understand wisdom by asking myself: What is wisdom, really? How is it defined? How can it be measured? These sorts of hard metrics are how scientists think and assess their ideas and hypotheses, and for a long time, wisdom eluded such quantification. But that is changing as other intangible aspects of humanity—such as consciousness, stress, emotions, resilience, and grit—are beginning to be studied, calibrated, and described in deductive detail. As recently as a few decades ago, hard-core scientists dismissed these constructs as indefinable, immeasurable, and nonbiological.

"One could write a history of science in reverse by assembling the solemn pronouncements of highest authority about what could not be done and could never happen," the great American science fiction writer Robert A. Heinlein once said.

It also turns out scientists lacked the tools to say otherwise.

Today, with advances in neuroscience, brain imaging, neuro-chemistry, as well as improved methodology in behavioral sciences, serious researchers accept that *all* of these aspects of the human condition, from how we manage our emotions to our resilience and fortitude, have a biological basis that underlies or runs parallel to psychosocial factors. It's another example of the old nature versus nurture debate, except there really is no "versus" here. The development of wisdom is indisputably dependent on what happens to you in life, but there is also an equal and inextricable biological element that profoundly influences how you learn and respond to life's lessons and events.

Take, for example, resilience. Thanks to the work of investigators like Eric Nestler and Dennis Charney, both in the Icahn School of Medicine at Mount Sinai in New York, we now know a lot about the neurobiology, genetics, animal models, and molecular pathways of resilience. And what's more, we're starting to get at behavioral and biological ways to enhance this most useful of personal traits.

Swap "wisdom" for "resilience," and that's my message too.

Wisdom is a product, not only of age and experience, but also of distinct behaviors and traits, all associated with discrete but connected regions of the brain.

The Emerging Science of Wisdom

Wisdom is the result of neurons firing in specific patterns in specific parts of one or more relevant neural circuits in the brain to produce behaviors that we deem to be "wise." It is biology and behavior that make it possible to separate wisdom from platitudes.

A scientific movement to define and explain wisdom began in earnest during the 1970s when a few scientists in different countries working in disparate labs started asking what wisdom is and whether it could be measured. In Germany, a psychologist named

Paul Baltes, with his wife, Margret, and other colleagues, began developing a theory of human development with respect to wisdom, one that examined and sought to explain how people changed biologically, cognitively, and psychosocially over the course of their lives. It was the first empirical attempt to parse the nature of human wisdom based on scientific principles and approaches, and to propose specific features that affect how we think and behave over time.

Baltes and his colleagues would compile a list of key characteristics, among them that development occurs throughout life, beginning to end; that it changes in all directions and dimensions; that it is a process of growth and decline, but is also fluid and plastic; and that social and environmental factors are powerful. Ultimately, their work would become the influential Berlin Wisdom Project, and their model of wisdom would define it essentially as proficiency in the conduct and meaning of life.

The Berlin model of wisdom placed great emphasis on knowledge and cognition. It was a good start, but more was needed because wisdom is clearly much more than simply cognition. It involves emotions too.

Halfway around the world from Baltes, a young University of California, Berkeley, graduate student named Vivian Clayton was asking similar questions. Her mentor, James E. Birren, one of the founders of gerontology, challenged her to conduct a scientific search for answers.

Clayton scoured the literature of wisdom, from ancient texts to contemporary treatises, for mentions, allusions, and evocations of wisdom, developing a crucial framework for thinking of wisdom as a psychological construct. Between 1976 and 1982, Clayton published several noteworthy papers establishing important markers for the scientific study of wisdom. She declared that wisdom fundamentally has three distinct components: cognition, reflection, and compassion. They could be defined and measured by scientists.

Others picked up and expanded on Baltes's and Clayton's ground-breaking work. Among them were inspired and inspiring scientists like George Vaillant at Harvard Medical School; Robert Sternberg at Cornell University; Judith Glück at University of Klagenfurt in Austria; Dan Blazer at Duke University School of Medicine; Monika Ardelt at University of Florida; Jeffrey Webster at Langara College in Vancouver; Howard Nusbaum at University of Chicago; Igor Grossmann at University of Waterloo in Ontario, Canada; and others.

These researchers deeply probed the nature of wisdom, primarily in terms of aging, intelligence, and happiness. But a wholly satisfying understanding of wisdom remained elusive. Ursula Staudinger, a Columbia University psychologist and a leading scholar in the field, once noted, perhaps wryly, that "most empirical research on wisdom in psychology has so far focused on further elaboration of the definition of wisdom."

From Schizophrenia to Wisdom

My interest in wisdom and its relationship with aging is more tangible. And it started with an unexpected finding during my research on, of all things, serious mental illnesses.

In the 1990s, while conducting studies at the University of California San Diego School of Medicine in older people with schizophrenia, I was struck by a surprising research result.

Schizophrenia is a devastating mental illness. In essence, schizophrenia is a breakdown in the relationships between thought, emotion, and behavior. It has been described as a "cancer of the mind." Unlike Alzheimer's disease, which typically develops in old age (it used to be called "senile dementia"), schizophrenia usually manifests in adolescence or young adulthood. From that point on, the disorder tends to spiral progressively downward.

7

People diagnosed with schizophrenia develop physical diseases much earlier in life, and they generally die 15 to 20 years younger than the general population—sometimes by their own hand. Among people diagnosed with schizophrenia, an estimated 20 to 40 percent will attempt suicide, 5 to 10 percent successfully.

But while the onset of schizophrenia often occurs in adolescence or the early 20s, many patients live with this disease for decades. In my research, I was studying hundreds of middle-aged and older adults living with schizophrenia, following their lives over a long period of time. The expectation of my colleagues and myself was that most of these patients would develop dementia (Alzheimer's or another form) early, with associated decline in neurological and biological function. The conventional thinking was that life after a diagnosis of schizophrenia would be nothing but a descent into dysfunction, disease, and despair. Indeed, the original German name for schizophrenia meant "precocious dementia."

But our results were surprising. We discovered that many individuals with schizophrenia functioned *better* in later life. They were more adherent (compliant) with their medications because they had learned from hard experience that stopping treatment led to relapse and calamity. They were less prone to abuse illicit drugs. They had fewer psychotic relapses, and they were less likely to require psychiatric hospitalization than younger individuals with the same illness. With aging and continued therapy, many seemed to have become, dare I say, *wiser* about how to manage their disease, and how to live their lives. When we initially reported our findings, there was skepticism among researchers even about the diagnosis of schizophrenia in our patients.

Around this time, the movie *A Beautiful Mind* debuted, based on the 1998 biography by Sylvia Nasar of the late Nobel laureate John Nash, a brilliant mathematician who proposed a revolutionary game theory in his youth. This work led to his Nobel Prize in 1994.

Nash was among the most brilliant minds of his generation. He also had schizophrenia.

Nash was diagnosed in his early 20s and underwent multiple treatments, from electroconvulsive therapy and insulin coma to myriad medications and psychotherapy. He was often hospitalized. But these efforts seemed to have little sustained effect. Largely separated from family and colleagues, he would disappear at times, sending cryptic postcards, then return to Princeton, where he had once been an academic superstar, to wander the campus "a lonely figure scribbling unintelligible formulas on the same blackboards in Fine Hall on which he had once demonstrated startling mathematical feats."

But as Nash entered his 50s, the course of his illness changed. His symptoms eased; he began to improve, and he gained new insights into his illness. By the time he turned 60, he had ceased all treatment for schizophrenia. He returned to research and teaching, joining the faculty at Princeton. For the first time in many years, he published papers in journals. People who knew him from his young days remarked that "the John Nash we knew is back again."

He was not entirely free of symptoms. He still endured episodes of hallucinations and delusions, but he was now able to differentiate these from normal thinking. He developed new insights into his own mind. He learned how to catch himself when symptoms appeared, and instead of succumbing to the psychopathology, he would consciously seek to normalize his thinking and behavior. "I emerged from irrational thinking, ultimately without medicine other than the natural hormonal changes of aging," Nash wrote in 1996 to Harold W. Kuhn, a Princeton professor and longtime friend.

Nash's story mirrored some of our own findings in aging patients with schizophrenia. Many of these people who had suffered so badly at the hands of this insidious disease in their youth were slowly able to reclaim their mental health in later years. Even as their bodies began to decline with age, their minds were becoming clearer than they had been for decades. Was the reason the emergence of wisdom? Years later, we published a paper showing that in people with schizophrenia, the level of wisdom was associated with the level of their well-being and functioning.

If people with a serious mental illness like schizophrenia could enjoy greater wisdom and improved mental function with age, despite worsening physical health, could the same thing also occur in the general population?

By this time, I had been appointed director of the Stein Institute for Research on Aging at UC San Diego School of Medicine. With colleagues, I began studying a cohort of several thousand older adults in the San Diego community. We sent out surveys. Some study participants visited our labs; some we visited in their homes, in senior housing communities, and elsewhere. Our findings among this general population echoed the earlier "paradox of aging" we'd seen among individuals with schizophrenia: as people get older, their physical health declines, but their mental well-being and satisfaction with life *increase*. It doesn't happen with everybody, but many older adults—particularly those who take positive actions to manage their lives—become happier.

In a comprehensive 2016 published study of approximately fifteen hundred adults between the ages of 21 and 100 years, participants who felt they were aging successfully described higher levels of happiness, resilience, optimism, and well-being, even if their physical functioning was impaired by advancing age. The findings held true even after accounting for variables like income, education, and marriage. Like wine and good leather shoes, they improved with age.

A caveat: This was a cross-sectional study—a part of a multiyear investigation called the Successful AGing Evaluation, or SAGE—of a somewhat randomly selected group of adults from the community. All participants were residents of San Diego County in California.

The cohort was almost evenly split between genders, with a mean age of 66. Twenty percent had high school or less education, 60 percent had at least some college education, and 20 percent had postgraduate education. Seventy-six percent identified as non-Latino white, 14 percent Hispanic/Latino, 7 percent Asian American, 1 percent African American, and 2 percent other ethnic or racial backgrounds. Cross-sectional studies are observational. They do not differentiate cause and effect. And they reflect only insights gleaned from the targeted study group.

The counterintuitive increase in well-being with aging was heartening, but also mystifying. How can one be happy getting up in the morning if getting up in the morning also involves a host of physical hurdles, from the aches and pains of arthritis to the annoyances of an enlarged prostate to the gut-wrenching reminders that the coming day will not be occupied by family or friends who are no longer alive?

Other questions arose: Was this phenomenon merely the result of older people accepting the inevitability of age-associated losses? Or did it indicate some enhancement of brain function associated with aging? Were they, in fact, getting wiser as they grew older?

This brought me to the first and most pressing question: What is wisdom?

What Do Scientists Know about Wisdom?

The first step in starting research on a new topic is to review the existing literature so that you don't end up reinventing the wheel or retracing known ground, so that's what I did. Thomas "Trey" Meeks, who was my research fellow at the time, and I combed through the literature—specifically the voluminous PubMed and PsycINFO databases—to review all the papers that had sought to define wisdom in an empirical, but not religious or philosophical, fashion.

We found Baltes in Germany and subsequent work by other gerontologists, sociologists, and psychologists, mostly in Europe and the United States. There seemed to be a general sense that wisdom is a complex trait comprising several components.

But what components, exactly? Here, there was uncertainty amid unclear definitions. How could the scientific community understand wisdom without a common, accepted definition? So Trey and I set out to provide just that. We created a table listing all the individual components proposed by different researchers. We found that a handful of components topped the list of many of these definitions: prosocial behaviors like empathy and compassion, emotional regulation, decisiveness while recognizing the uncertainty of life, insight and self-reflection, general knowledge of life, and social decision-making.

But even as we discovered these commonalities among wisdom researchers, new questions arose. Most of these papers were written by Western scientists, working in Western labs, studying a fairly homogenous population. But isn't wisdom a cultural concept? Was wisdom defined differently in different places around the world? What about scientists in other parts of the globe whose definitions had not been published in the journals we studied? We realized that for our study to truly have value, we had to widen the scope of our inquiry. So we began searching for international experts in wisdom who had published papers or book chapters on this topic.

The process was complex and laborious, but basically consisted of rounds of surveys with experts anonymously parsing and paring statements about wisdom. It is called the Delphi method and seeks to determine an overall consensus.

Eventually, our diverse experts arrived at some conclusions: Wisdom is a form of advanced cognitive and emotional development driven by experience. It can be measured, learned, and observed. We all know people who epitomize wisdom.

Our experts concurred that wisdom does increase with age, that it is uniquely human and distinctly personal. But it isn't likely to be enhanced by taking medication (at least not at present).

Not every expert concurred on every item defining wisdom, but there was consensus on several, which proved to be quite similar to the components that Trey Meeks and I had found in our earlier literature review:

PROSOCIAL ATTITUDES AND BEHAVIORS. These include empathy, compassion, and altruism. What exactly do these terms mean? Empathy is the ability to understand and share the feelings and thoughts of another. Compassion involves translating empathy into helpful behavior. Altruism is opposite of egoism and refers to actions to help another person without expecting any external rewards. Can you put yourself in others' shoes and do you want to help those in need? In psychology, there is a concept called "theory of mind," which describes the ability to attribute mental states—beliefs, desires, emotions, knowledge—to both yourself and others. Theory of mind is essential to behaviors like compassion, where we often act out of a recognized connectedness with others.

EMOTIONAL STABILITY WITH HAPPINESS. This is the ability to maintain self-control, while preferring positive feelings to negative ones. "Anger is a brief madness," observed the ancient Roman poet Horace. Few acts are done well when driven by unthinking passions.

BALANCING DECISIVENESS WITH ACCEPTANCE OF UNCERTAINTY. The latter involves acknowledging that different but equally valid perspectives exist and that things can change, including one's deeply held thoughts and beliefs, over time and with new knowledge, experience, and insights. It means recognizing that other people may have different beliefs, desires, intentions, and perspectives and that people with different belief systems need not be considered evil or unintelligent. But while we accept uncertainties in life and diversity of perspectives, one cannot sit on the fence too long or too often. One must act when action is called for, based on the information at hand, knowing that the decision could later prove to be the wrong choice. Deciding not to act is also a decision.

REFLECTION AND SELF-UNDERSTANDING. These include insight, intuition, and self-awareness. Are you able to analyze yourself and your motivations, your strengths and weaknesses? Understanding oneself is much more difficult than people think.

SOCIAL DECISION-MAKING AND PRAGMATIC KNOWLEDGE OF LIFE. These relate to social reasoning and the ability to give good advice, as well as share life knowledge and life skills. Wisdom not shared is wisdom not gained but lost.

These, we concluded, are the bases of wisdom. However, they do not stand alone and apart from one another. Quite the contrary. They all share commonalities and sometimes overlap in surprising ways. And yet, like pillars, they are distinctly foundational to wisdom. You need all of them, albeit the levels of individual components in a person may vary.

A few years after our first wisdom survey, a fellow in my group named Katherine Bangen joined Meeks and me for a second review of the scientific literature to further refine the empirical definition of wisdom, based on novel and emerging types of assessments. The new findings largely confirmed the old. The basic components were those we had previously described, with the addition of an important new element, spirituality, and two less common components: openness to new experiences and a sense of humor.

The "science of wisdom" was maturing.

SPIRITUALITY. It should be noted that spirituality is not the same as religiosity. The latter typically refers to organized or cultural systems of belief. Religion can be and often is spiritual in nature, but its practices vary considerably in societies and around the world. Spirituality is a more universal constant, a core human belief in something larger than the individual and the society. It leads to a feeling of humility as well as comfort in going beyond the stresses of everyday life. Spirituality can include religion, but it can mean and embrace much, much more.

There was criticism of our definition from a particular perspective. Since wisdom is a cultural concept, perhaps it was viewed differently in ancient times. Maybe the Wisdom of Solomon is not the same thing as wisdom today. Our task was to become better versed with how wisdom was defined in the distant past. Growing up in India, I had learned about the Bhagavad Gita, or Gita, a 700-verse poem written 500–200 BCE and based on Yogas (practices or disciplines) that date back at least a few thousand years. With advice from a medical anthropologist at UC San Diego, my research fellow Ipsit Vahia and I conducted a study of English online translations of the Gita, searching for the words *wisdom* or *sagacity* and their antonyms, *foolishness* or *folly*. We looked at the context in which these words were commonly used, which helped us identify components of wisdom in the scripture.

For example, there is a verse in the Gita: "[Anger, desire] the Wise man's eternal foe; by this is wisdom overcast" (chapter 3, verse 39). Thus, the Gita considers equanimity to be an essential virtue. Wise people are characterized by balance: no extreme emotions, negative or positive. Wisdom implies that events of joy or sadness are treated similarly. We deemed this to be emotional regulation.

A number of verses in the Gita relate to compassion and altruism. For example, "steadfast in the yoga of wisdom, restrained and open-handed, performing sacrifice" (chapter 16, verse 1). A wise person is compassionate, says the Gita. Sacrifice for the sake of sacrifice and not for its material rewards is also an element of wisdom. We labeled this as prosocial behavior.

In a paper we published in the journal *Psychiatry*, we reported that, by and large, the components of wisdom in our literature review and international expert consensus were strikingly similar to what we uncovered in the Gita.

To be sure, there were a few differences. Love of God and lack of materialistic pursuits are stressed in the Gita, but not so much in modern Western conceptualizations of wisdom. But such differences paled in significance compared to the similarities. That was a big surprise. It suggested that the basic concept of wisdom had not radically changed across millennia or cultures. To me, this further suggested that wisdom is biologically based.

I was getting excited. We had an accepted definition of wisdom. We'd determined that this definition had remained largely consistent over time—for millennia, in fact. But the next step was going to take us even further, into the leading edge of what current science has made possible. I needed to probe the brain itself to begin to understand the neurobiology of wisdom—where these specific components live in specific regions of the brain—if I hoped to help people become wiser.

In chapter 2, we delve into the neuroscience of wisdom.

The Neuroscience of Wisdom

The supposedly immaterial soul, we now know,
can be bisected with a knife, altered by chemicals,
started or stopped by electricity, and extinguished
by a sharp blow or by insufficient oxygen.
STEVEN PINKER, *How the Mind Works*

If the human brain were so simple that we could
understand it, we would be so simple that we couldn't.
EMERSON W. PUGH, researcher,
Carnegie Institute of Technology

AS I MENTIONED IN the introduction, in my teenage years, I loved reading Sigmund Freud's popular books on interpreting dreams and everyday errors in life. Freud would begin a story with a description of a dream or a ("Freudian") slip of the tongue, then proceed to decipher its latent meaning (consistent with his psychoanalytic theories), using clues from the person's behaviors, past and present.

Thus, a bit of blundered speech purportedly revealed an unconscious thought. Someone might intend to say, "I'm glad you're here," but actually utter, "I'm mad you're here." The latter supposedly signified the speaker's true sentiment. Freud imparted a great deal of hidden meaning to these errors, and to me, his books were like reading Agatha Christie mysteries, which characteristically began with a murder from which Christie's protagonist detective would employ various behavioral and environmental clues to identify the culprit and solve the case.

But here we're talking about something beyond mere mind over murder. Freud believed that all behaviors had a biological basis in the brain. Dreams were an unconscious process to resolve some sort of conflict, usually deep within the past but precipitated by a recent event. The behavior signified stressful, competing demands of the desires of the id, driven by primal impulses, instinctive urges, and unrestrained wish fulfillment, versus the rational ego or the severe, punishing superego, shaped by society's values, morals, and expectations.

I didn't know how accurate Freud's interpretations of dreams and slips of the tongue were, but I came to conclude that the ultimate answer lay within the physical brain. My fascination with mind and brain has only increased with time.

Most of us use the words *brain* and *mind* interchangeably and in some ways, justifiably so: they cannot be separated. But the brain and mind are obviously different things. The brain is a physical object; the mind is not. The brain is composed of nerve cells, blood vessels, and tangible tissues. It has a definite shape, weight, and mass. It possesses a distinctive look and has the squishy consistency of Jell-O.

The mind is a function of the brain, the resulting thoughts, emotions, behaviors, and acts prompted by the interactions of all of those brain cells with each other and with other cells in the body—and with every sort of stimulus beyond. The mind has no shape, weight, or mass. It cannot be seen or felt by our physical senses. It is detected only by another mind.

If there is a timeless, universal understanding of wisdom—we all know it when we see it, and have through the centuries—then it makes sense that wisdom must be, in some way, hardwired into our brains. It's a basic rule of evolution: nature conserves what works. But where was the actual wiring? And how does one go about finding it?

This Is Your Brain on Paper

Every organ of your body possesses a singularity of form, but none is more distinctive than your brain, with its hemispherical halves, ellipsoid shape, and iconic, twisting bumps and grooves called gyri and sulci. Alive, our brain isn't even one color. It's pink, red, white, black, and 50 shades of gray.

The human brain is instantly recognizable, the tireless subject (and originator) of our thoughts and ruminations. And yet, it remains among science's greatest and most enduring mysteries—a riddle and enigma wrapped inside a wrinkly cortex, to paraphrase Winston Churchill. We probably know more about how stars are born than we do about the electrochemical, cellular, and molecular workings of that three-pound lump of variegated tissue perched atop our spines, most of which is water.

So how do you solve the problem of finding where things like empathy, self-understanding, and emotional control—all elements of wisdom—reside within the brain?

In a 2009 paper, Trey Meeks and I began with a simple idea. We Googled two terms: *wisdom* and *neurobiology*, which is the study of the anatomy, physiology, and pathology of the nervous system (that is, the brain and spinal cord). Our search did not turn up much that was relevant, mostly science papers published by authors named Wisdom or treatises on wisdom teeth.

It was funny, but frustrating. There was not a single article that contained both *wisdom* and *neurobiology* in the title or in its key words. We would need to try something else. So we expanded our search to include numerous terms beyond *wisdom* and *neurobiology*, adding individual components of wisdom, such as compassion, and conditions or diseases associated with a loss or the absence of wisdom's components, such as antisocial personality disorder, a condition characterized by a lack of compassion. We also added relevant scientific terms like *neuroanatomy, neurocircuitry, neurochemistry, genetics,* and other facets of neurobiology.

The revealed papers began to stack up quickly. When we looked at reports of brain imaging, neurophysiology, and other neurobiological measures that associated individual components of wisdom with specific parts of the brain, we made a surprising discovery. Again and again, the same parts of the brain showed up, most notably the prefrontal cortex and the amygdala. This suggested that these brain areas might have something to do with where wisdom lies within the brain.

But a major problem remained. While we learned more about the neurobiology of wisdom's individual components, it didn't necessarily tell us much about wisdom as a whole. How did the different components of wisdom relate to one another and how did they combine to produce this single, complex trait? Different areas of the brain have different functions, but they connect to one another in a meaningful way to create specific neurocircuits.

To better grapple with this complex topic as it relates to wisdom, we need to first get a lay of the land and a common vocabulary.

Mapping the Brain

There are a few things to keep in mind as we discuss this amazing organ. First, this guide to the brain is highly simplified. It's a primer, not a textbook. Second, though we delve into very specific regions of the brain and highlight very specific functions that occur within them, it's important to remember that the brain operates continuously in its entirety. Finally, this is a tour of a so-called normal brain: healthy and fully developed, unaffected by major disease, congenital deformity, physical trauma, poor diet or lifestyle, or old age.

The human brain consists of three main regions: cerebrum, cerebellum, and brain stem. The cerebrum has two hemispheres—right and left—each of which includes four lobes: frontal in the front, occipital at the back, with parietal and temporal in between.

The outer layer of the cerebrum is composed of gray matter—neurons and their connections, known as synapses. This is called the cerebral cortex. From the perspective of wisdom researchers, the most important parts of the brain are the front portion of the frontal cortex, or prefrontal cortex (PFC), and the amygdala. In the evolutionary history of the brain across animal species, the PFC is the most recently formed and newest region. Humans possess relatively large PFCs relevant to other species. It's basically the front third of our brains, located right behind our foreheads. Conversely, the amygdalae, a pair of small, almond-shaped organs, are found deep within the oldest part of the human brain, the limbic system, which sits atop the brain stem and is almost universally found to some degree in every animal species with a brain.

To locate where exactly the limbic system is, think about the evolutionary development of the brain as a sort of progression of balls growing ever larger as new layers and sections are added and enlarged. More primitive species have brains that consist primarily of the limbic system. There isn't much tissue, if any, devoted to higher-level functions like conscious thought. The human brain, on the other hand, is the product of millions of years of evolution and natural selection, layer upon addition upon modification and improvement made in furtherance of survival. The limbic system is still there, of course, regulating breathing and blood flow. It supports a variety of other fundamental functions, such as emotion, memory, and olfaction. But now it is surrounded by the more massive cerebrum, home to higher-level thinking, with the smaller cerebellum and hindbrain managing motor control tucked behind and underneath.

Imagine spreading a human brain flat on a table like a foldout map, smoothing all of those cortical wrinkles our brains have developed to provide more surface area and shorten distances between points. Your flattened brain would be roughly 2,500 square centimeters, about the same size as a small tablecloth. This metropolis of the mind would comprise distinct districts, a few of them housing components of wisdom.

First stop on our mind-knowing tour is, naturally, the PFC. It's an indisputably upscale and sophisticated area where prosocial attitudes and behaviors reside. These attitudes and behaviors represent the innate belief and understanding that we all strive for the common good; that when we help others, we help ourselves; that we all seek something bigger and better. Empathy and altruism are prosocial attitudes. They have deep biological roots. When we watch, smiling, as a child joyously blows out candles on a birthday cake, or choke back a sob during a poignant scene in a movie, mirror neurons in our PFC are firing in the same patterns as those in the person we are watching. People with greater unconscious somatic mimicry have higher ratings of self-reported altruism. When they say they feel your pain, they really do—at least in their head.

Obviously, human empathy and altruism are more complex than just neurons in one person's brain firing in unison with those in another person's. With some exceptions, we are all governed by our ability to understand the emotions, intentions, beliefs, and desires of others, especially when they are not the same as our own. I intuit what you're thinking because I assume your mind works similarly to mine, though we may come to different conclusions. It enables me to understand, explain, and predict others' mental states and behaviors. Without it, there is no social connection, no chance to be wise.

Also located in the PFC and in the nearby neighborhoods of the anterior cingulate cortex, posterior superior temporal sulcus, and temporoparietal junction is our second stop: the homes of social decision-making and pragmatic knowledge of life. These admittedly wonky phrases fundamentally describe what each of us knows about ourselves, about others, and about how to deal with life's ever-changing conditions and problems. These are the "facts" we use to get along while getting ahead, like understanding implicitly that a crying child or grieving widow need comfort and consolation, not a sharp rebuke or disdainful snort.

In the PFC and nearby in the dorsal anterior cingulate cortex lives the third major component of wisdom: emotional regulation or homeostasis. The latter word is another way to say balance. Our bodies—indeed every aspect of the universe—seek homeostasis, a relentless drive toward stability. Our physical bodies do this constantly, every moment, tweaking internal conditions to achieve a desired equilibrium: sweating when we're too hot, shivering when we're too cold, signaling thirst or hunger when we need water or food.

It's no different psychologically. There is no wisdom in instability. If you're always angry or consumed by negative emotions, you cannot behave wisely. Buddhaghosa, a fifth-century commentator, once wrote that holding on to anger is like grabbing a hot coal with the notion of throwing it at someone else. You're the one who's going to get burned. The yin and yang of emotion and cognition, of feeling and thinking, must be balanced. There are good reasons and occasional value in being angry or envious, but such emotions must be skillfully managed to a wise purpose and end. Likewise, it's nonsensical to be perpetually giddy or blindly optimistic.

Let's linger for a moment in a specific section of the PFC called the medial prefrontal cortex, with side trips to the posterior cingulate, precuneus, and inferior parietal lobule. These are the regions of the brain where we find the fourth major component of wisdom: reflection and self-understanding.

The ancient Greeks had a saying: *Gnothi seauton.* Know thyself. Perhaps no other element of wisdom is more universally recognized. Reflection—the fixing of thoughts on a particular topic with careful consideration—is foundational to wisdom. It's hard to imagine our popular archetypes of wisdom, people like King Solomon, Abraham Lincoln, Elizabeth I, or Martin Luther King Jr., acting without thinking, without weighing consequences. No one knows what Solomon looked like, but you can see the ravages of hard thought and harder decisions in the face of Lincoln and hear them in the emotionally charged but reasoned language and exhortations of King. Rash wisdom is an oxymoron.

In the PFC and tucked just beneath in the anterior cingulate cortex is the place where awareness of life's uncertainties resides, where we learn and accept new thoughts and beliefs based on new knowledge, experience, and insights, where we hone our tolerance and acceptance of others. There can be no empathy, compassion, connection, or bonding without tolerance. Tolerance of diverse or even contrarian views is no less important to wisdom than self-reflection or prosocial attitudes. It is the ability and the willingness to look at life, people, and situations from multiple perspectives without disdain or immediate condemnation. The world is not black and white, but multihued, like your brain. There may be a right way to go and a wrong way to go, but you won't necessarily know which path is correct if you haven't considered all the options.

Also in the PFC, along with the anterior cingulate cortex and orbitofrontal cortex (which gets its name from its location immediately above the orbits in which the eyes are located) lies our last stop: the ability to behave and act despite acknowledgment that life is uncertain and ambiguous.

Sometimes there is no right way to go. There are always limits to knowledge. "Everybody is ignorant," said Will Rogers, "only on different subjects." The fact that we cannot know everything, that we cannot foretell our futures, can be profoundly unsettling. For every door that closes, another may open, but what if it's an elevator shaft? Sometimes we choose not to look before we leap or hope we'll grow wings on the way down.

My UC San Diego colleague Ajit Varki and his coauthor, the late Danny Brower, made that point quite compellingly in their 2013 book *Denial: Self-Deception, False Beliefs, and the Origins of the Human Mind*. They explained that approximately one hundred thousand years ago, something changed in the human mind. As we developed new cognitive skills and behaviors that set us apart from other animals, we began to reflect more deeply on the meaning of life, which very quickly developed into a frightening awareness of our own mortality. To assuage those fears, humans evolved the unique ability to deny reality. We became the ultimate risk-takers, choosing to ignore even science-based facts if it allowed us to more blithely pursue life, liberty, and happiness. Even death was irrelevant—or at least ignored.

Wisdom helps us cope. Wisdom means being aware that nothing in life is guaranteed (except that life is finite), and that means we must use what time we have as wisely as we can.

There are two other parts of the brain that don't directly relate to our discussion, but that still have a profound influence. In each hemisphere of the brain, folded within the lateral sulcus (that deep crease visible on the sides of the brain where the frontal lobe seems to flop over the parietal lobe) is a portion of the cerebral cortex called the insula. You have two insulae (plural form), one in each hemisphere. They are involved in consciousness and diverse functions linked to emotional homeostasis.

The other part of the brain is the hippocampus—a pair of small, seahorse-shaped structures located in the medial temporal lobe, deep within the brain. The hippocampi are primarily known for their roles in consolidating information from short-term memory to long-term memory and for spatial navigation, but in reality, their influence is much greater.

When you get a whiff of perfume worn by a former crush or experience déjà vu in a place you've never been before, it's your hippocampus at work pulling out or pulling together distant or disparate memories. The hippocampus is not really a part of the wisdom neurocircuitry, but its functioning (that is, normal memory) is indispensable to wise thinking and wise behavior.

Bumpy Skulls and What Lies Within

Today, we understand and have broadly localized different components of wisdom to different areas of the brain, keeping in mind the caveat that various parts of the brain tend to work in concert, but the road to this moment was long and winding, marked by wrong turns and dead-ends.

Two names stand out in that journey: Gall and Brodmann.

One was a fraud; the other a pioneer.

Franz Joseph Gall was born to Roman Catholic parents in Germany. He was intended for the priesthood, but as the medical historian Erwin Ackerknecht would later write, Gall's primary passions in life were "science, gardening, and women."

So, in the year 1777, the 19-year-old Gall could be found not in a seminary but in medical school, studying under the tutelage of Johann Hermann, a comparative anatomist who believed that men and apes were closely related. It was not a widely held view at the time. Charles Darwin's evolutionary masterpiece *On the Origin of Species* would not be published until 1859.

Gall was an intent observer. In his medical studies, he noticed that many of the brightest students had prominent eyeballs and concluded that this could not be purely coincidental. Hermann and other mentors had emphasized the importance of natural observation, and in his first job at a lunatic asylum in Vienna, Gall took keenly to the task, scrutinizing the "insane," most notably their skull sizes and facial features.

A notion formed in Gall's head. He began collecting human and animal skulls and wax molds of brains in order to study their cranial contours in comparison to characteristic behaviors associated with animal species or with a deceased person. For example, he looked for telltale indicators—shape or weight—that might reveal the carnivorous compulsions of a feral cat. Or the larcenous tendencies of a well-known robber, recently executed. By 1802, Gall had managed to collect, by hook or crook, approximately 300 human skulls and 120 plaster casts.

Gall concluded that different and localized regions of the cerebral cortex—the outer surface of the brain that Gall referred to as the "rind"—seemed to coincide with 27 innate psychological characteristics he dubbed "fundamental faculties."

Nineteen of these traits, like the instinct to reproduce, to feel affection, defend oneself, or possess a sense of time and space, were shared with other species. Eight were uniquely human; among them: poetic talent, religion, wit, and wisdom.

Gall thought each of these 27 faculties reposed within a specific place in the brain. "Firmness of purpose," for example, could be found near the crown of the head. "Murderous tendencies" lurked just above the ears. "Language" was located below the eyes.

Gall determined that his 27 fundamental faculties affected the shape and topography of the skull, not unlike a comforter reflecting the underlying lumpiness of a mattress and bedding. Bony irregularities of the skull corresponded to distinct faculties pressing or pulling from below. Gall created a method called "cranioscopy" to detect and measure the uneven topography of the human head and, from these measurements, determine a person's nature and the development of his or her mental and moral abilities. The practice eventually acquired a name: *phrenology*, a Greek combination of the words for "mind" and "knowledge."

Phrenology quickly captured the lay public's imagination. It seemed fantastical, but it was also easy to comprehend and became, for a while, wildly popular. Phrenology arrived at a time when scientific procedures and standards for acceptable evidence were still being codified. It fed into certain social conventions of the time, but also *seemed* scientific. It quickly became fodder for books, pamphlets, and the lecture circuit.

It was misguided folly. By the 1840s, phrenology had largely been dismissed or discredited, victimized by the fact that even its advocates couldn't settle on a number of basic mental organs, and even more by the reality that nobody could actually, definitively locate them or prove their functions.

"Phrenology has been psychology's great faux pas," noted the British experimental psychologist John Carl Flugel ruefully in 1933.

But Gall can lay some claim to an important scientific concept: "localization of function," the idea that different areas in the brain are specialized to perform different and specific functions. His work was among the first conceptual efforts to map the human brain. His work was based not on scientific data, but on pseudoscience. By happenstance, he correctly placed "sagacity" near the frontal cortex, but also determined that "friendship and affection" were in the back of the head.

Born 40 years after Gall's death in 1828, a German neurologist named Korbinian Brodmann began creating maps of the cerebral cortex based on both gross anatomical features and cytoarchitec-ture, or how cells are functionally organized.

After earning his medical degree, Brodmann went to work at the University of Jena psychiatric clinic in Germany, eventually meet-ing Alois Alzheimer, who persuaded Brodmann to devote himself to basic neuroscience research.

Brodmann's investigations were wide-ranging, combining clin-ical observations with basic research of mammalian brains. He compared anatomical structures in human brains with those in pri-mates, rodents, and marsupials. To discern the different functions of different parts of the cerebral cortex, Brodmann (and others) relied on the techniques of stimulation and lesions. Using both animal and human models, he would precisely stimulate a part of a living brain to see what happened next: Did the animal's right leg move? Did its nose twitch? Conversely, he would observe how spe-cific areas of damage in the brain (a lesion, for example) correlated with observed physical results.

It was intense and productive work. It provided Brodmann—and science—with a remarkable first map of the functional brain. Unfortunately, it was also abbreviated. Brodmann died suddenly of a septic infection following pneumonia at age 49.

Nonetheless, Brodmann made a long-lasting contribution to neuroscience. He divided the cerebral cortex into 52 regions—now called Brodmann areas—grouped into 11 histological, or tissue-based, categories. He postulated that these areas, with different physiolog-ical characteristics and structures, performed different functions. For example, Brodmann areas 41 and 42 in the temporal lobe were related to hearing. Brodmann areas 17 and 18 in the occipital lobe were engaged in primary vision. Unlike Gall's passing fancy, Brodmann's work was both prescient and enduring. His system, with refinements, is still used by modern scientists to describe and discuss the architecture and organization of the brain, its cells, and different functions. Brodmann, along with many others, helped firmly establish that the brain encompasses a diverse world of distinct, interconnected neurobiological regions.

The Telling Tragedy of Phineas Gage

When Brodmann stimulated area 4—the primary motor area—a test animal moved its limb. That's interesting, but not obviously relevant to determining how brain function makes an animal or person wise.

But when Brodmann damaged area 4 in the brain of a rat, it produced paralysis in the opposite limb. In humans, of course, you never impose harm for experimental reasons. It violates every code of scientific conduct. Instead, you search for answers in what might be called experiments or accidents of nature. When you examine people who have suffered a head injury or stroke and whose limbs are now paralyzed, an MRI reveals a similar story: damage to area 4 in their brains.

Which got me thinking: Could a wise person become unwise as the result of a head injury or disease? I scoured the literature for experiments of a nature that provide an answer. Once again, a Google search came up empty. The query was too broad. So my colleagues and I turned to searching for cases of individuals losing distinct components of wisdom. We found more than a dozen cases of a "modern day Phineas Gage," though none of the reporting scientists had used the term *wisdom* to describe their cases.

The story of Phineas Gage makes this point most famously. In the afternoon of September 13, 1848, Gage and a construction crew working for the Rutland and Burlington Railroad were clearing away some obstructing rock near the town of Cavendish, Vermont. Gage was a foreman and generally considered among the best around.

His job that day was the most skilled and dangerous: to sprinkle gunpowder into blasting holes drilled in the rock and tamp the powder down (gently) with an iron rod, after which an assistant would pour in sand or clay to further compress the mix and focus the explosion into the rock, breaking it.

Gage had a specially commissioned tamping iron for the job: it was 3 feet, 7 inches long, weighed 13.25 pounds, and resembled a javelin, tapering to a point at the business end that Gage used to poke and press powder in the hole.

Accounts differ about what exactly happened that fateful day, but Gage reportedly became distracted by his crew working some distance away loading broken rock onto a cart. He might have looked up from the work at hand, his iron rod scraping and sparking against rock, or as one witness speculated, he simply mashed the rod down too hard. Whatever the reason, the gunpowder ignited, expelling Gage's tamping iron upward like a ballistic missile.

The rod penetrated Gage's head just below his left cheekbone. It passed behind his left eye, ripped through the lower portion of his brain's left frontal lobe, and exited out of the top of his skull slightly behind his hairline. It landed 25 yards away, stuck upright in the ground like a knife in a game of mumblety-peg. Witnesses describe the rod as "streaked with red and greasy to the touch from fatty brain tissue."

Amazingly, Gage was not killed by the explosion or penetrating missile. Indeed, he reportedly never lost consciousness. Within minutes of the accident, he was walking and talking. He rode in an ox cart, upright, while coworkers raced him to town. He sat in a chair on a hotel porch while a doctor was fetched.

When the physician arrived, no doubt appalled by the vision before him—described as "a volcano of upturned bone jutting out of Gage's scalp"—the injured railroad foreman drolly observed, "Here's business enough for you."

Business indeed. Not just for the unsuspecting Cavendish doctor that day, but for generations of neuroscientists to follow.

Before the accident, Gage had been generally regarded as a clean-cut, virtuous fellow. His physician, Dr. John M. Harlow, considered him a fine example of industrious manhood, writing about Gage: "although untrained in the schools, he possessed a well-balanced mind, and was looked on by those who knew him as a shrewd, smart businessman, very energetic and persistent in executing all his plans of operation."

After the railroad accident, Harlow would later write with poignant brevity: "Gage was no longer Gage."

"He is fitful," bemoaned Harlow, "irreverent, indulging at times in the grossest profanity (which was not previously his custom), manifesting but little deference for his fellows, impatient of restraint or advice when it conflicts with his desires." After a period of physical recovery, Gage returned to his parents' home in Lebanon, New Hampshire, where he turned to farming. It didn't last. Later, he traveled to Chile to work as a long-distance stagecoach driver. Bouts of ill health plagued him. In his last years of life, Gage suffered from seizures. He died in his mother's home in San Francisco on May 21, 1860. He was 37.

Clearly, Gage was not the same man after his injury. The tamping rod that explosively plowed through his brain irrevocably destroyed some of the parts that made him the man he had been.

But what areas of Gage's brain were damaged by the injury? We know the answer thanks to the excellent and creative work of Antonio Damasio and colleagues who, in 1994, published a paper in the journal *Science* titled "The Return of Phineas Gage: Clues About the Brain from the Skull of a Famous Patient." The paper recounted their exhumation of Gage's skull and tamping iron (both were buried together) and the use of X-rays and magnetic resonance imaging (MRI) to recreate Gage's long-gone brain in three dimensions. The scientists determined the likely trajectory of the tamping iron and then identified the parts of Gage's brain that would have been damaged. Eighteen years later, John Darrell Van Horn at the David Geffen School of Medicine at UCLA used MRI and other imaging technologies to model Gage's damaged skull and brain. Gage's left frontal lobe—one-half of the repository of our most complex cognitive powers, in many ways the essence of our humanity—had been destroyed.

The tragic tale of Phineas Gage arguably represents a starting point when neurologists first began to understand the relationship between structural damage to the brain and specific changes in behavior, but it is far from unique.

In 2004, for example, almost a century and a half after Gage's death, Margaret Allison Cato (who was previously a research fellow with me) at the San Diego Veterans Affairs Healthcare System and the UC San Diego School of Medicine and colleagues published the case study of a "modern-day Phineas Gage" in the *Journal of the International Neuropsychological Society.*

Patient CD (initials used to preserve anonymity) was a 26-year-old soldier in 1962 when the jeep he was riding in passed over a land mine. The explosion caused him to violently smash his forehead against the metal upright on the rim of the jeep's windshield. Like Gage, CD did not immediately lose consciousness from the blow. He recalled the explosion and someone asking him questions immediately afterward. The driver of the jeep was killed.

CD survived, but he suffered significant damage to the ventro-medial prefrontal cortex of the brain, particularly on the left side. Before the injury, CD had been a man of exemplary academic and professional record, with nearly straight A's in school and accelerated promotions in the military.

The trauma caused a precipitous decline in his social and behavioral functioning. Despite average to superior scores on most subsequent neurocognitive tests—he had a verbal IQ of 119, considered "high average"—he could not maintain regular employment.

He was discharged from the military against his wishes and could manage only a series of lesser jobs, such as delivering newspapers, in the aftermath. He went through four marriages. His children became estranged.

Trey Meeks and I found a dozen such cases of a "modern day Phineas Gage" described in the literature. Mind you, these papers never used the word *wisdom*, but their descriptions clearly fit with our definition of wisdom (or loss of it). Where were the brain injuries in these different individuals? In most of them, the damage occurred in the prefrontal cortex, and in some, in the amygdala too.

Surely no coincidence—the PFC and the amygdala are central to the biology of wisdom—and they further emboldened our premise. If wisdom can be weakened or lost by injury to key parts of the brain, then the reverse must be true as well: it can be strengthened or found by cultivating and empowering those same parts of the brain. We will revisit this angle later in the book.

How Disease Reveals Wisdom by Its Absence

Damage to the prefrontal cortex of the brain—and its observable effects on wisdom—can occur in less violent ways as well. One disease of particular interest for studying the neurobiology of wisdom is a type of dementia. Once called Pick's disease after the 19th-century physician who first described it, frontotemporal dementia (FTD) is the third most common neurodegenerative disorder after Alzheimer's disease and Lewy body dementia.

The only identified risk factor for FTD is a family history of the disease. The disease typically appears in the 50s—unlike Alzheimer's, which is most common in the 80s. Much of the knowledge about FTD comes from the ongoing work of Bruce Miller, a distinguished professor of neurology at the University of California San Francisco and director of its Memory and Aging Center. He has literally written the book on FTD.

FTD wreaks its damage over time. Subtly at first, patients with some "behavioral variants" of FTD become less like themselves. Similar to Phineas Gage, they assume an unhappier, more pessimistic demeanor. Often their behavior is initially mistaken as depression or plain old age–related grumpiness, but other symptoms eventually emerge, such as a loss of inhibition. FTD patients may begin speaking and acting without filter, exhibiting a striking loss of restraint in their personal relations and social life that can have calamitous consequences. Symptoms of the behavioral variant of FTD read like the antithesis of the criteria for wisdom. FTD selectively affects the front half of the cerebral cortex, mainly the prefrontal cortex (PFC).

The PFC is associated with cognitive capacities related to human uniqueness, from language and our ability to process complex social information to self-reflection and purposefully striving toward higher-level goals. Tumors in the PFC can also produce personality changes, including loss of wisdom.

Damage to the amygdala can do the same, but in a strikingly different way.

Consider the case of patient SM, first described in a 1994 paper published in *Nature* by Damasio and colleagues. At the time, SM (her identity is kept secret by researchers) was a 49-year-old Kentucky woman with a rare genetic condition known as Urbach-Wiethe disease, which had caused her amygdalae to wither away in late childhood. As a result, she had little or no capacity to feel anxiety or fear. There was no emotional response to handling snakes or spiders, walking through Halloween horror attractions or watching scary movies. She was studied extensively by scientists. Media dubbed her "the woman with no fear."

In ordinary life, SM was described as outgoing and extremely friendly, disinhibited and playfully flirtatious. Not bad traits, to be sure, but with no functional amygdalae, SM also did not recognize the negative social cues that might alert her to danger and harm, such as overt aggression or fear in the faces of others. As a result, she had been the victim of numerous acts of crime and traumatic encounters, such as being held up at both knife- and gunpoint and was almost killed in an incident of domestic violence. In none of these cases did SM display the typical or expected signs of desperation, urgency, or fear. Many of these traumatic events can be attributed to her living in dangerous neighborhoods marked by poverty, crime, and drugs, but they were exacerbated by the fact that SM did not recognize or respond to the threat of looming harm.

While SM managed to make a life for herself—she married and became an independent mother of three healthy children—she did not have the necessary brain infrastructure to regulate emotional aspects of her behavior that are an essential part of wisdom.

Whither Wisdom?

No matter what our challenges in life—or perhaps because of them—we tend to believe that wisdom comes with age. There's good reason to think so: experience is a great teacher, and experience generally requires time.

In 2019, colleagues and I looked at data from more than one thousand adults, aged 21 to over 100, to find out whether they had found the meaning of life—based on their own definition. Finding meaning in life is a marker for wisdom. That much seems obvious, though our published findings were, in fact, surprisingly complicated.

Based on our research, the search for meaning in life follows a U shape, while the presence of meaning is the opposite. When you are young, in your 20s for example, you are likely unsure about your career, possible life partner, and who you are as a person. You are searching for meaning in life.

But as you age into your 30s, 40s, and 50s, you establish relationships, maybe get married and have a family, and become settled in a career and identity. The search decreases as the presence of meaning in life increases.

But after age 60, things begin to change. You retire and perhaps lose some of your identity. You're no longer a plumber, banker, or professor. There is no job to help define you. You develop recurring or chronic health issues, and friends and family begin to pass away. In your old age, you restart searching for meaning in life because the meaning you once knew has apparently disappeared.

You are, hopefully, wiser with age because wisdom acquired over a lifetime helps compensate for the consequences of stresses over a lifetime. But there is increasing evidence that you don't need to wait a lifetime to become wiser than your chronological age.

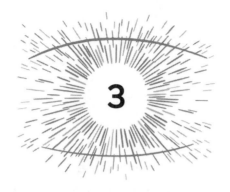

Wisdom and Aging

*Let no one be slow to seek wisdom when he is young nor
weary in the search of it when he has grown old. For no
age is too early or too late for the health of the soul.*
EPICURUS

*The great thing about getting older is that you
don't lose all the other ages you've been.*
MADELEINE L'ENGLE,
American author

AS A GERIATRIC NEUROPSYCHIATRIST (a medical doctor special-
izing in the diagnosis and treatment of mental disorders in older
adults), I have seen and heard just about everything that can and
does go wrong with aging: physical ailments like hypertension,
diabetes, arthritis, heart disease, cancers, stroke, and so on; and
cognitive disorders such as Alzheimer's disease and other demen-
tias, and mental illnesses like depression.

Even outside of these illnesses, normal aging is associated with slowing down physically and mentally, with difficulty remembering names and faces, with problems learning new things, with feelings of loneliness, and on and on.

Indeed, there's a kind of general foreboding that life is getting away from you as you age, that you have less and less control over not just your body, but your mind and destiny too.

Old humans are neither strong nor fast. Maximum physical capacity for our species peaks somewhere between ages 20 and 30, and then begins to decline, accelerating around age 50.

In evolutionary terms, prolonged longevity seems nonsensical. Older people cannot reproduce, so they are not promoting species survival. Darwin's theory of evolution was predicated on survival of the fittest and the ability to successfully procreate. Most large animals don't live long after becoming infertile with age, unless they reside in zoos, research labs, or other protective environments. Among primates, humans are unique in that we regularly outlive our reproductive period by decades. If a woman undergoes menopause (or a man, its biological male equivalent, andropause) at age 45 and lives to age 90, she has spent the entire second half of her life without contributing directly to the human species' repopulation.

And yet, old age is getting older. The average life span is increasing. In 1900, average life expectancy was about 47 years in the United States. Today, it's around 80 years, being slightly higher for women than for men. By 2050, average life expectancy is projected to approach 90 years. If life span is increasing, are our fertility and health spans increasing too?

The answer is no. The average age at menopause or andropause has changed little over millennia. And people are still developing the myriad illnesses of old age. So how can we explain exceptional human longevity despite loss of fertility and physical health?

The only likely explanation is that some things must improve with age to make up for its deficiencies, both personal and societal. Over the years, I have become increasingly determined to discover which aspects of ourselves *do* get better with aging—and how they compensate for the loss of fertility and of physical health. This chapter lays out my thinking: increased wisdom with age benefits both seniors and society. Nature supports our becoming wiser with age, but *only* if we help ourselves by being active and positive. And by learning how wisdom increases with older age, we enable younger people to become wiser as well.

One of the first psychologists to formally link wisdom with aging was Erik H. Erikson. In a 1988 *New York Times* interview with psychologist Daniel Goleman, Erikson, a developmental psychologist, and his wife, Joan, expounded on the nature of old age. The topic, as Goleman wryly noted, had been on their minds: Erik was 86; Joan was 85.

No couple was better suited to the discourse. In the 1950s, the Eriksons had created a novel chart of life, breaking down human psychological development into distinct, chronological periods that contributed to and defined our personalities. Initially, there were eight stages.

In the first stage of life, infancy (birth to 18 months), trust and mistrust push and pull against each other. Babies seek stability and consistency of care from their parents. If they receive it, they develop a sense of trust and hope that will permeate their lives. They will be able to feel secure even when feeling threatened.

Conversely, if an infant's early care has been harsh or inconsistent, unpredictable and unreliable, the Eriksons concluded that mistrust takes root. Fear, apprehension, and doubt will color their view of the world, their life, and their relationships with others.

At the other end of the Eriksons' chart was the eighth and last stage of life, ego integrity versus despair, when we try to reconcile our expectations and aspirations against what has actually happened. It's an immense and sometimes overwhelming task, compounded by the fact that our aging bodies are breaking down physically.

It is in this last stage of life, in the struggle to mesh past and present (the future seems less pressing when you're in your mid-80s), that wisdom may flourish or flounder, the theory went. This final phase of life, according to the Eriksons, is represented by a conflict between ego integrity and despair—and the remedy is wisdom.

"When we looked at the life cycle in our 40s, we looked to old people for wisdom," Joan Erikson told Goleman. "At 80, though, we look at other 80-year-olds to see who got wise and who did not. Lots of old people don't get wise, but you don't get wise unless you age."

The quote is astute in the sense that we require opportunity to learn and practice the behaviors of wisdom. You can't become a swimmer if you don't get into the water, and you can't become a good swimmer without persistent practice.

It's no different with compassion, resiliency, or humor—all components of wisdom. They must be exercised regularly and often, remodeling the brain to produce wiser behaviors, conscious and otherwise, in the same way that swimming lots of laps remodels your physique.

But I take some exception to the second half of Joan Erikson's quote: "but you don't get wise unless you age." I strongly believe we can learn how to increase wisdom without waiting the prerequisite years. It's a basic premise of this book: wisdom has a biology, and biology, as Gregor Mendel's work with pea plants to discover the fundamental laws of inheritance and genetic manipulation so profoundly illustrated, can be changed.

Still, there are lessons to be learned from older adults. Past is prologue. We can learn how the brains of active, older people continue to evolve, adapt, and facilitate wise thinking, feeling, and behaving.

These strategies have application to younger people as well and can inform our own decisions and efforts to become wiser at any age.

Why Aging Is Good for Society

For the vast majority of species on Earth, life lasts just long enough to do one thing: Make more of their species. Procreate and die.

Nature offers lots of examples. Here's one: The male Australian redback spider (*Latrodectus hasselti*) is killed and eaten by the female shortly after impregnation. This male act of "sacrifice" also helps increase his likely paternity and passing of genes. A fully satiated female isn't likely to mate again.

The reason for such parental selflessness is universal and obvious: everything must go into producing the next generation, sometimes even dad. Most parents in the nonmammalian animal kingdom don't provide many or any postnatal life skills.

Humans are different. We're the only species able to produce offspring years before we possess full mental capacity. The human brain continues to undergo considerable refinement, with synaptic pruning and other processes, throughout our teen years. For most of us, our brains didn't—or won't—reach full maturity until our early 20s, though biologically we are primed to conceive children with the arrival of puberty at age 12 or 13. So how can these young individuals without fully developed brains, who legally aren't even deemed fully responsible adults until age 21, care for their own children and make them fit to survive potentially risky environments?

Enter the "grandmother hypothesis" of wisdom.

In the mid-1950s, a biologist named George Christopher Williams was the first to suggest a possible rationale for long life after menopause. He said that as females age, the costs of reproducing become greater, and the energy needed to raise the young is better spent ensuring earlier offspring are successful in their own reproductive efforts. This is where postmenopausal grandmothers come in. They help sustain and support their kin and, not coincidentally, help ensure that their genes are passed along to future generations.

The grandmother hypothesis is based on excellent, long-standing research in both nonhuman species and humans. Numerous published studies have found this hypothesis at work among a wide variety of animals. For example, killer whales, or orcas, one of the few other species on the planet in which females experience menopause, display extraordinary bonding and benefit by embracing multiple generations within a pod. The death of a postreproductive female whale in the pod increases the risk of death of offspring up to five-fold in daughters and 14-fold in sons. In Seychelles warblers, a species of bird, postreproductive females become grandparent helpers, helping to raise group offspring. Bottlenose dolphins breastfeed their grandchildren. Calf survival and reproduction in herds of Asian elephants is better when elephant grandmothers are around.

In humans, both anecdotal and quantitative evidence in premodern populations shows that prolonged life span after menopause/andropause is associated with a higher number of grandchildren, with the result benefiting individuals and societies. When grandparents are involved in raising their grandchildren, their young adult parents tend to live longer, be happier, and produce more children than the grandparents did.

Studies of Tanzanian hunter-gatherers, the Hadza, have found that grandmother-helpers seemed to ensure the younger generations live longer. Even in modern societies, involvement of grandparents in upbringing has been associated with fewer emotional problems, fewer adjustment difficulties, and more prosocial behaviors among grandchildren, especially those living in single-parent or stepfamily households. In a study published in the journal *Nature*, complete multigenerational records of approximately twenty-eight hundred Canadian and Finnish women born before the year 1900 showed that the offspring of older mothers reproduced earlier, more frequently, and more successfully. It is possible, if admittedly speculative, that these grandmothers' "wise" behaviors contributed to their own long survival as well as to their offsprings' successes.

Obviously, one of the major advantages of having grandmothers (and grandfathers) around is the sharing of life experiences and the imparting of wisdom to younger generations. It's an ageless benefit, as observable now as it was in the early nomadic tribes. Rand Conger and coauthors studied 127 families enrolled in a program called the Family Transitions Project. It involved households in which three generations lived: children, parents, and grandparents. The researchers found that higher levels of grandmother involvement with grandchildren reduced behavioral problems in the latter.

Conger's study is not unique. There is abundant evidence that the presence of older people—and access to their wisdom—broadly improves lives and human life. I see it in my own life, with my own family. As a grandfather, I freely share my love and joy with my grandchildren. I provide solicited guidance on parenting matters to my daughter and son-in-law, but also find that they teach me how to be a better grandfather and father. They help me become happier and healthier. It's a flow of love and information in all directions.

Louisa May Alcott once wrote: "Every house needs a grandmother in it."

Grandfathers, too.

Grandparent Genes

The societal value of older adults may even translate to the level of genes. In 2015, my colleague Ajit Varki and coauthors at the UC San Diego/Salk Institute Center for Academic Research and Training in Anthropogeny published a paper that suggests several human gene variants might have evolved specifically to protect older adults from neurodegenerative and cardiovascular diseases.

Specifically, Varki's team discovered that a particular gene that encodes for a protein called CD33 was fourfold higher in humans than in chimpanzees, our closest living relatives. CD33 is a receptor that projects from the surface of immune cells, where it keeps immune reactions in check, preventing "self" attack and curtailing unwanted inflammation. Other studies have reported that a certain form of CD33 suppresses amyloid beta peptide accumulation in the brain. Amyloid beta, which is an aggregate of proteins folded in the wrong shape to create sticky plaques in the brain, is thought to contribute to Alzheimer's disease.

Varki and colleagues also found that humans have evolved variations of an ancestral gene called APOE4, a well-known risk factor for Alzheimer's and cerebral vascular diseases. These variants—APOE2 and APOE3—seem to offer some protection from dementia.

"When older people succumb to dementia, the community not only loses important sources of wisdom, accumulated knowledge, and culture, but older adults with even mild cognitive decline, who have influential positions, can harm their social groups by making flawed decisions," said study coauthor Pascal Gagneux. "Our study does not directly prove that these factors were involved in the selection of protective variants of CD33, APOE, and other genes, but it is reasonable to speculate about the possibility. After all, intergenerational care of the young and information transfer are important factors for the survival of younger kin in the group and across wider social networks or tribes."

Mind Over Diminishing Matter

The physical effects of aging are visible and, for many people, tangibly painful. Our bodies sag. We become weaker and frailer. There is change everywhere, at every level: Old cells function less well and have greater difficulty doing once-routine repairs. Likewise, with our organs. Bones become less dense, more brittle, and prone to breaking. Joint cartilage wears away; ligaments lose elasticity. Muscle mass declines (a process that actually begins at the relatively young age of 30), and strength ebbs. We lose acuity in all of our senses. By age 60, for example, most people have lost half of their taste buds, which may explain why many older people compensate by eating foods high in sugar, salt, and fat.

In the 16th-century comedy *As You Like It*, Shakespeare describes the "seven ages of man," starting from infancy. The seventh and last stage:

Is second childishness, and mere oblivion
Sans teeth, san eyes, sans taste, sans everything.

This prototype of old age is one-sided. It ignores the fact that aging is also a frame of mind. "Wrinkles should merely indicate where smiles have been," wrote Mark Twain in *Following the Equator*. You are as old as you think. Or as Wisconsin-based columnist Doug Larson once opined: "The aging process has you firmly in its grasp if you never get the urge to throw a snowball."

Science backs this up. Consider this experiment, conducted in 1981, by a then-youthful Harvard University psychologist named Ellen Langer. Langer transported eight men, all in their 70s, to a New Hampshire monastery and back in time. As Bruce Grierson describes it in a 2014 *New York Times* article: "Perry Como crooned on a vintage radio. Ed Sullivan welcomed guests on a black-and-white TV. Everything inside—including the books on the shelves and the magazines lying around—was designed to conjure 1959."

For five days, the men were told to embrace their past, to "make a psychological attempt to be the person they were 22 years ago," Langer told Grierson. From the moment they walked through the transformed monastery doors, they would be treated as if they were, in fact, younger men in a younger time. They were expected to carry their own suitcases upstairs. Sports conversations revolved around the exploits of Johnny Unitas and Wilt Chamberlain, as if the games had just been played. TV news reported the first US satellite launch. The movie on TV was *Anatomy of a Murder* with Jimmy Stewart.

The men wore clothing contemporary to 1959. Photos on the walls were portraits of them as young men. There were no mirrors to spoil the illusion.

And a remarkable thing happened. At the end of the stay, the men felt and behaved as if years had been shed away. They were more limber, nimble, stronger, taller. On physical measures like grip strength, memory, flexibility, and cognition, they posted better scores than those before the experiment. Even their vision improved.

While waiting for the bus back to Cambridge, a spontaneous touch football game erupted among older men who, five days earlier, had struggled and shuffled on the walkway to the monastery.

Life Lessons at the End of Life

At the end of life, when death looms large, there can be a sort of final clarity. All the pretensions of life, its expectations, confusions, aggravations, disappointments, and more may fall away. Laura Carstensen has a name for it: "socioemotional selectivity." Basically, it means that as one's time on Earth shrinks, people become increasingly selective about what's meaningful and how they should spend their dwindling days. You stop sweating the small stuff—and realize that most stuff is small. If you're lying in a hospice bed with six months or less to live, most things no longer carry much or any import.

So what does? It's a question my colleagues and I asked 21 men and women, ages 58 to 97, who were receiving hospice care for a terminal illness. How did they define wisdom? Had their perspective changed with time and circumstance?

It should not be surprising that their descriptions of wisdom at the cusp of death contained, in varying degrees, all of the major recognized themes of wisdom: prosocial attitudes, knowledge of life, being active, emotional regulation, positivity and gratitude, openness to new experience, acknowledgment of uncertainty, spirituality/religiosity, self-reflection, sense of humor, and tolerance.

All the participants believed prosocial attitudes and behaviors were a major component of wisdom, such as empathy, compassion, love, kindness, forgiveness, and respect. "I've never seen anybody who is self-centered who I can say is wise," said one person.

Similarly, all the participants cited decision-making and knowledge of life as essential to wisdom. "I think a wise person goes and seeks counsel and looks for information before they just jump in and make a decision," said one participant. "They weigh the consequences and the pros and the cons."

And all the participants thought wisdom required a life of work and activity: "Life is not a bed of roses, you know. I've learned that you have to exert yourself . . . you have to work."

Almost as universal were assertions that emotional regulation and positivity were critical: "Well, I do not think I am the wisest person, but I think wisdom is cultivating a happy attitude in your life; not necessarily based on having money, but being happy with just looking at the sky and appreciating nature and loving the people around you, and with that, I think you will have a very rich life."

Others cited the importance of acknowledging uncertainty, spirituality, self-reflection, and sense of humor. "There is usually humor in a lot of things, although there is sadness too," said one man. "You cannot listen to that sadness. You have to get out of it, or you get so depressed, you know. Then you are not good to anyone, and you are absolutely useless to yourself."

Disease, Dementia, Decline, Depression, and Death

In our darker moments, we define old age by seven *Ds*—disease, degeneration, decline, dementia, disability, depression, and death. Conditions like Alzheimer's disease, which affects approximately 13 percent of Americans 65 and older (and about 40 percent of people over age 85), involve a documented progression of dysfunction as amyloid plaques and neurofibrillary tangles slow and eventually kill neurons. More than five million Americans are estimated to currently have Alzheimer's, a number projected to triple by 2050.

But even so, the happy fact is that a majority of people will not develop this much-dreaded brain disorder. Indeed, in a 2013 paper published in the journal *Neuron*, Subhojit Roy, an associate professor, and other colleagues in the departments of Pathology and Neurosciences at UC San Diego School of Medicine and at Shiley-Marcos Alzheimer's Disease Research Center, describe how, in most people's brains there's a critical separation between a protein and an enzyme that, when combined, triggers progressive cell degeneration and death characteristic of Alzheimer's disease.

"It's like physically separating gunpowder and match so that the inevitable explosion is avoided," said Roy. There's comfort in knowing that.

In one study, researchers asked subjects to read passages peppered with unexpected words or phrases. Readers over age 60 struggled more with the readings than did college-age students, who raced through the work at a consistent pace. Older people routinely slowed at out-of-place words, as if they were mental "speed bumps." The seniors paused to absorb and process the unusual information.

But here's the good news: when both groups of readers—younger and older—were later questioned about the meanings of the out-of-place words, the older readers fared better.

"For the young people, it's as if the distraction never happened," Lynn Hasher, a professor of psychology at the University of Toronto told the *New York Times*. "But for older adults, because they've retained all this extra data, they're now suddenly the better problem solvers. They can transfer the information they've soaked up from one situation to another." That's a valuable talent to have in the real world where answers aren't always obvious, where things change, where distant memories or tiny signals might have great import.

Your Brain Is a Muscle—Use It

How can a complex personality trait like wisdom, which is based on the functioning of several specific regions of the brain, possibly *increase* with aging—even in a proportion of older adults?

In medical school, I was taught that most of the growth and development of the human brain occurred in utero and during the first few years of life—but not in later years. On average, the fetal brain grows at a rate of 250,000 new nerve cells per minute over the course of pregnancy. It continues to grow postnatally, increasing fourfold in size until around age 6, when it reaches approximately 90 percent of its adult volume. After that, through adolescence, it's mostly about refinement, nipping and tucking, building or strengthening some of the 100 trillion or so interconnections between neurons to make our brains more efficient and effective. From the early 20s through the 50s, we were taught, brain structure and function are relatively stable. After age 60, the textbooks asserted, it is a story of decline, both qualitative and quantitative, in neurons, synapses, blood vessels, and white matter. The brain progressively and literally shrinks. By the end of our lives, our brain tissue mass is roughly the same volume as that of a 7-year-old child.

There are exceptions, of course, but mostly the commonly held notion was that, cognitively speaking, nothing improves with age.

We now know that this notion is wrongheaded.

Though older brains shrink and may experience cognitive dysfunction, the effect is not homogenous. One of the most exciting discoveries in neuroscience during the past two decades has been the revelation that brains continue to evolve throughout life, provided there is appropriate physical, cognitive, and psychosocial stimulation. My friend and colleague Fred "Rusty" Gage, a distinguished neuroscientist at the Salk Institute and UC San Diego, and his colleagues have shown that even in old mice, physical activity accompanied by psychosocial stimulation can increase not only the number of synapses (connections between neurons) in the brain but also neurons in specific brain areas, such as the dentate gyrus of the hippocampus and areas around brain ventricles. Other researchers have replicated these results in various other animal species.

Brain imaging and neurophysiology studies have shown that physical exercise as well as mental stimulation and socialization have positive biological effects in older people. People who stay active physically, cognitively, and socially tend to maintain their vocabulary; their ability to recognize previously encountered events, objects, and people; and skills learned during early childhood, such as swimming or bicycling. Their brains are less likely to show atrophic or wasting-away changes that may characterize the brains of sedentary, lonely, inactive seniors.

In a 2011 paper, Lisa Eyler, Ayesha Sherzai, Allison Kaup, and I reviewed 550 human studies of structural brain imaging. We found that the vast majority of reports showed at least one significant association of successful cognitive aging with bigger structures and stronger connections in the brain, especially in the prefrontal cortex and medial temporal lobe. It's not known what makes these structures larger or connections stronger, but animal studies have shown a beneficial impact of environmental enrichment on brain function and structure. Being physically and mentally active builds better brains throughout life, positively influencing adaptive neuroplasticity and reducing neurodegeneration.

Workouts and Work-Arounds

With age, generally speaking, several components of wisdom become stronger, more refined, and second nature in many people. Despite a decline in fluid intelligence with age, social reasoning tends to improve, which includes the general ability to think abstractly, to identify patterns, discern relationships, and solve problems in the moment. Multiple neuroimaging studies have shown that older brains learn to compensate for the effects of advancing age. Different regions of the brain take up duties once performed elsewhere. Some circuitry grows bigger and stronger even as other circuitry weakens or shrinks. In other words, the older brain finds work-arounds.

There are also some intriguing studies that suggest how an aging but active brain may be better primed to increase the principal components of wisdom. In such a brain, activity tends to shift from the back of the brain (the occipital lobes) to the front of the brain (the prefrontal cortex, which is critical for development and enhancement of wisdom). Also, more of the brain is involved in a mental activity in an active older person than in a young adult or in an inactive senior.

In youth, many brain functions are localized. We tend to talk about activities in terms of right brain and left brain. But in older people who keep busy, *both* hemispheres tend to be involved in most functions. By engaging more of the brain, an active older adult may be able to do almost as well as a younger person in cognitive tasks, such as learning new things.

Think about it this way. When I was younger, I could push a heavy cart with one hand. Now, with my arthritis, I have to use both hands to push the cart. But, because I continue to exercise regularly, I can use my hands better than an inactive man of my age—and with both hands, I can still move the heavy cart just as I did decades ago.

Older brains change in terms of emotional responsivity. The emotional highs and lows of youth flatten out. Research using functional MRI (fMRI) has shown that, with aging, the amygdala becomes less sensitive to negative or stressful stimuli, such as the photo of a gruesome car accident. This type of change increases emotional regulation and positivity, aiding wisdom in later life. There is also less functional connectivity between the amygdala and the hippocampus, another part of the brain involved in emotion and memory, but continued strong connectivity between the amygdala and dorsolateral prefrontal cortex, which may effectively reduce negative memories while enhancing positive ones. The amygdala of an older person is as sensitive to positive stimuli, like the photo of a smiling baby, as that of a younger adult. In other words, positivity of emotions and memory does not decline with age, only negativity does.

In a 2013 paper, Hannes Schwandt at the London School of Economics and Political Science described assessing more than 130,000 "life satisfaction expectations" made by 23,161 Germans polled in waves between 1991 and 2002 and then again five years later. The participants ranged in age from 17 to 85. Younger people tended to be more regretful and pessimistic than older people, who were able to more easily let go of feelings of disappointment and remorse. Older people also felt less unhappy about things they could not change.

"Young people just have more negative feelings," Cornell professor Elaine Wethington told Jonathan Rauch, writing for *The Atlantic*. They struggle more than older people to find balance and context. With advancing age comes a gradual change in attitude. Older people try or do fewer things because they've already been there, done that. There is a greater acceptance of one's physical limitations, more happiness with past accomplishments, reduced preoccupation with peer pressure, and a more realistic appraisal of one's own strengths and limitations. David Almeida at Penn State University has noted that compared to younger and midlife adults, seniors don't get so stressed out by their stressors.

Rick Hanson, a psychologist and senior fellow of the Greater Good Science Center at UC Berkeley, has written extensively on this topic. He asserts that our brains are naturally wired to focus on the negative. It's a consequence of evolution. Our ancestors needed to pay particular attention to negatives, such as hungry predators or natural hazards. It was a matter of day-to-day survival. Positive experiences, such as finding food, shelter, or mating opportunities, were great, but unlikely to determine whether *Homo erectus* or *Homo neanderthalensis* lived to see tomorrow, a point even more emphatically true for *Homo sapiens* these days.

Thus, our brains developed a negativity bias, a bent for paying particular attention to threatening stuff, though the result is feelings of stress and unhappiness. That's why bad news is more memorable than good—and political attack ads are effective.

Age and wisdom are antidotes to such negativity. Younger minds are like Velcro when it comes to negative emotional experiences and memories, which stick easily. Older minds are like Teflon: the bad stuff tends to wash off.

Carstensen, the Stanford psychologist, has shown that in older age, with a growing awareness of limited time left in life, people tend to take greater emotional satisfaction from where they have been and spend less time fretting about where they think they must go.

"Young people are miserable at regulating their emotions," Carstensen told Rauch, who subsequently recalled his own experience: "Years ago, my father made much the same point when I asked him why in his 50s he stopped having rages, which had shadowed his younger years and disrupted our family. He said, 'I realized I didn't need to have five-dollar reactions to nickel provocations.'"

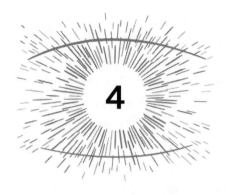

Measuring Wisdom
The Jeste-Thomas Wisdom Index

Measure what is measurable,
and make measurable what is not so.
GALILEO

I believe in evidence. I believe in observation,
measurement, and reasoning, confirmed by
independent observers. I'll believe anything,
no matter how wild and ridiculous, if there is
evidence for it. The wilder and more ridiculous
something is, however, the firmer and more
solid the evidence will have to be.
ISAAC ASIMOV, *The Roving Mind*

MY PATIENT JOHN B. EXHIBITED most of the classic symptoms of schizophrenia. He suffered from delusions, believing that his neighborhood was the target of a well-funded effort by a covert entity to topple foundational values, which seemed to change from visit to visit. He experienced hallucinations, reporting inexplicable sounds of breathing when he was on the phone or shadowy figures seen trailing him at the grocery store and gym. John's reports weren't easy to follow. His thinking could be disorganized; his conversation garbled, a word salad of catchphrases and ideologies. He was intensely suspicious, and as a result, he didn't readily or often open up and describe what he thought or what he thought he saw.

In recent weeks though, he seemed to have quieted down quite a bit. He was not aggressive, slept a lot, and didn't complain about his neighbors or others. If you asked family members who brought John in for checkups or therapy sessions, they would say John seemed to be getting better. He wasn't talking crazy or fighting, they said.

But if you asked John, he would say quite the opposite. He was feeling very depressed, miserable, and scared. He struggled to do seemingly routine things, like shaking hands or taking the garbage out or having dinner with the family. At times he felt like he would be better off if he were dead and contemplated ways of killing himself. He didn't share these or other thoughts and feelings with others.

When a psychiatrist meets with a patient and his or her family, there's a natural inclination to give more credence to the latter, an assumption that family members can provide a clear-eyed and "more objective" assessment of the patient and his situation.

But, in truth, no one knows better how a patient is feeling or faring than the patient himself. If John tells me that he's depressed, I believe him and take him seriously, even if the signs of his depression are not obvious or do not jibe with textbook definitions. Time and again, we read that family members and friends of someone who committed suicide or mass murder are stunned by the violent act. Why?

Well-being is a subjective state. Who knows better how you feel, physically and psychologically, than yourself? Self-rated health is a significant predictor of development of diseases, disabilities, and even death. There is also excellent research to show that subjective, self-rated measures of well-being of individuals in a community correlate strongly with objective measures of that community's well-being, such as crime rates, housing prices, and commute times.

Objective measures are difficult for measuring a person's subjective trait or state, such as anxiety. For example, a singer may come across to an audience as being relaxed and at ease, although she or he may be feeling quite stressed and anxious. It is thus not surprising that most measures for psychological constructs are subjective or self-reports. It is agreed, for instance, that the best measure of stress is subjective—how stressed do you feel? Even family members and friends cannot fully evaluate an individual's personality because they cannot peer into her mind 24-7. At the present state of science, the best measure of wisdom is self-reporting on behaviors illustrative of different components of wisdom. In the future, we can expect development of objective measures of wisdom, but even then, those measures will need to be complemented by subjective ones.

Counting What Counts

Writing in the *Journal of Adult Development*, Jeffrey Dean Webster, a professor of psychology at Langara College in Vancouver, Canada, once asked: "Is it a fool's errand to try to capture wisdom within the parameters of a paper-and-pencil questionnaire? Can such a rich, dynamic and elusive concept be reduced to a total score from a self-assessed survey?"

Webster, who would make his own valuable contributions to the measurement of wisdom, found the answer is yes, but with several caveats.

Science and science-based disciplines like medicine are based on empirical or measurable data that can be tested and retested. Accurate measurement is fundamental to the scientific method, developed over thousands of years. Without it, science would be guesswork and opinion.

Physical measurement is comparatively easy, once you have the right tools. It's based on things you can see, touch, and count, often originating within our own physiology. The inch, for example, was the thickness of a thumb, usually one belonging to royalty. The foot speaks for itself. Our modern numeral system, with its base 10, undoubtedly owes much of its creation to the total number of digits on our hands.

Other objective units of measurement have been invented for weight, mass, and time, but how do you measure psychological phenomena, such as thinking and feeling? It's a challenge that has confronted psychiatrists, psychologists, and cognitive scientists for as long as there have been psychiatrists, psychologists, and cognitive scientists.

One of the tools used by clinicians and researchers for diagnosing psychiatric diseases is a nearly thousand-page document called the *Diagnostic and Statistical Manual of Mental Disorders* (*DSM*), which is intended to provide authoritative descriptions, diagnoses, and guidance on every mental illness, from schizophrenia to post-traumatic stress disorder. The *DSM*, first published in the early 1950s, is currently in its fifth edition.

The *DSM-5* is useful for diagnosing psychiatric disorders in a reliable fashion. However, it has clear limitations. And it does not even attempt to clinically define mental health or positive behaviors like resilience or wisdom.

Of course, developing a measure of wisdom is much more complicated. It's just harder to take measure of a healthy human mind than it is to diagnose or assess what ails it.

But we try. And we will keep trying. It's an ongoing effort, but we're getting better, and at the end of this chapter, you'll be able to assess the fruits of our labors and your own Wisdom Index.

Are IQ Tests Really Intelligent?

The most studied objective measure of a personality trait is the intelligence quotient (IQ). Alfred Binet's version is perhaps best known historically, but several others have been proposed, created, and used, such as the Wechsler Adult Intelligence Scale (WAIS). IQ is calculated by dividing the score on an intelligence test of, say a 10-year-old child, by the average score of 10-year-old children and then, to make it easy to remember, by multiplying the resulting quotient by 100.

For example, a 10-year-old girl earns a score of 60 on a test in which the average score of 10-year-olds is known to be 50. By dividing 60 by 50, then multiplying by 100, her IQ would be 120. Normal or average intelligence scores are between 85 and 115 on the Stanford-Binet scale. Scores from 116 to 124 are deemed above average; 125 to 134, gifted; 135 to 144, very gifted; 145 to 164, genius; 165 to 179, high genius; and 180 to 200, highest genius. Less than one-quarter of 1 percent of IQ test takers score in the genius categories. Albert Einstein is believed to have had an IQ of about 160, much higher than average but similar to the purported scores of actor Dolph Lundgren (Ivan Drago of *Rocky* movie fame), TV talk show host Conan O'Brien, and baseball legend Reggie Jackson.

While IQ tests are objective, they are also controversial. Intelligence testing has been accused of unfairly stratifying test takers by race, gender, class, and culture. Their norms are based not on the king as in the olden days, but on mostly urban or suburban

Caucasian people living in Western countries. As a result, they may not apply well to villagers or minority groups or people from other, non-Western cultures.

Test scores are affected by the test takers' ability to take the test. A child who has little or no experience answering multiple-choice questions—or who just doesn't do them well—will not score as highly as a more experienced or proficient child, though they may be equally bright.

And finally, IQ tests measure general intelligence but not specific kinds like interpersonal skills, musical intelligence, or creativity. They do not assess character or practical know-how, and they tend to propagate the notion that people are born with an unchangeable endowment of intellectual potential that determines their success in life.

The bottom line is that standard IQ tests measure one kind of smart. Like SAT scores, they measure an important domain of cognitive functioning and are moderately good at predicting academic and work success, but that's a decided limitation. The IQ doesn't tell us anything about a person's emotional regulation or compassion or self-reflection, all of which are integral to wisdom.

"A high IQ is like height in a basketball player," said David Perkins, who studies thinking and reasoning skills at Harvard Graduate School of Education. "It is very important, all other things being equal. But all other things aren't equal. There's a lot more to being a good basketball player than being tall, and there's a lot more to being a good thinker than having a high IQ."

How Do You Quantify Wisdom?

There is no simple, direct way to scrutinize wisdom in people. We don't live in petri dishes, readily available to continuous observation, documentation, and manipulation. Anything that skews our natural lives and environments skews the nature of what we do within them and any conclusions to be made. So wisdom researchers have focused on asking carefully crafted questions or posing specific dilemmas to their subjects, and then calculating what their answers mean in terms of whether they are thinking or behaving wisely.

They do this through questionnaires and interviews. The first are self-assessments. A question or statement is posed, such as "My friends think I have a great sense of humor," and the person responds, often on a scale from strongly disagree to strongly agree. The obvious problem with self-assessments is that, well, they're *self*-assessments. It is human nature to view ourselves more kindly and more forgivingly—or at least differently—than others do; or to try to present an image of ourselves that we think will be socially more acceptable or maybe just what we think the researcher is looking for. So we tend to maximize our perceived strengths and minimize our perceived weaknesses.

Some wisdom researchers have used peer nominations or peer ratings to judge a person's wisdom. If most of your peers think you are wise, then you are deemed wise. If they have low opinions about your sagacity, your rating goes down. If you Google "lists of wise people," most of them are the result of this kind of surveying: Solomon, Buddha, Confucius, Socrates, Benjamin Franklin, Pearl S. Buck, Gandhi, Maya Angelou, Mother Teresa, Lincoln, Churchill. They all routinely appear on various declaratory lists of the wisest people in history. There's value in consensus opinion, but the results are colored by contemporary thinking and prevailing popularity, by respondents' personal biases, and by how much they may or may not know about other people.

Changing the Paradigm

One of the first attempts to study and assess wisdom was undertaken by Paul Baltes and Ursula M. Staudinger at the Max Planck

Institute for Human Development. Baltes and Staudinger introduced the Berlin Wisdom Paradigm, first mentioned in chapter 1. The Paradigm was not a wisdom test exactly, but rather was a way of studying and assessing wisdom that attempted to avoid "fuzzy" discussions of emotion or motivation and instead focused on measurable skills, what they called "the fundamental pragmatics of life."

Wisdom, as defined by Baltes and Staudinger, is a kind of very high-level intellectual expertise. It is also very rare; by their estimation, very few people ever become truly wise. And wisdom, they believed, is all the more prized because of its scarcity in society.

The Berlin model treats wisdom as basically a matter of exceptional cognition. *Cogito, ergo sum.* I think, therefore I am. If I think better, I am better (and thus wiser too). But people are driven by more than just their rational thoughts, perhaps more often in fact by the opposite: their emotions. Wisdom without emotion is like a day without sunshine. Or to quote the comedian and occasional philosopher Steve Martin, "You know, night."

In other words, wisdom without emotion isn't wisdom. It's something else entirely, like night and day.

Consider a person with antisocial personality disorder who lacks compassion. Psychopaths need not be murderous criminals. Indeed, most garden-variety psychopaths manage perfectly fine in society. They can be quite smart, even become apparent epitomes of success. But are they wise? I think not.

"Superficially charming, psychopaths tend to make a good first impression on others and often strike observers as remarkably normal," wrote Scott Lilienfeld and Hal Arkowitz in 2007 in *Scientific American*. "Yet they are self-centered, dishonest, and undependable, and at times they engage in irresponsible behavior for no apparent reason other than the sheer fun of it. Largely devoid of guilt, empathy, and love, they have casual and callous interpersonal and romantic relationships. Psychopaths routinely offer excuses for their reckless and often outrageous actions, placing blame on others instead. They rarely learn from their mistakes or benefit from negative feedback, and they have difficulty inhibiting their impulses."

This is not a description of wisdom.

Wisdom in Three Dimensions

Other scientists have stepped up to try to find a more comprehensive tool to measure wisdom. George Eman Vaillant, Dan Blazer, and C. Robert Cloninger are three psychiatrists, all pioneers and admired colleagues who have written on and described wisdom in individuals. Another is Monika Ardelt, an associate professor of sociology at the University of Florida, longtime collaborator and good friend who has spent a considerable part of her career focusing on aging and how to do it well. Of course, aging and wisdom often go hand in hand (a lot more on this later), so Ardelt has also spent considerable time thinking about the nature of wisdom and how to measure it in the context of measuring well-being in later life.

In 2003, Ardelt published her Three-Dimensional Wisdom Scale, more commonly referred to as 3D-WS. Based on the earlier, groundbreaking work of Vivian Clayton, James Birren, and others, the 3D-WS starts with the premise that wisdom is a combination of three personality qualities: cognitive (pure intelligence), reflective (the ability to look inward), and affective (empathy and compassion for others).

The 3D-WS provided valuable new insights into the relationships and interconnectedness between these three dimensions. Each strand reinforces the others; they aren't independent. They do not develop in isolation from each other.

For example, if a person believes "there's only one right way to do anything" (cognitive), he or she is also likely to strongly agree with the statement that they're "easily irritated by people who argue with me" (affective).

If a person strongly agrees with the statement "ignorance is bliss" (cognitive), he or she is unlikely to be inclined to strongly agree with the statement "I always try to look at all sides of a problem" (reflective).

If a person says, "Simply knowing the answer rather than understanding the reasons for the answer to a problem is fine with me" (reflective), he or she is probably also fine with saying, "Sometimes when people are talking to me, I find myself wishing that they would just leave" (affective).

One challenge with the 3D-WS is its length—it has 39 items. The lengthier the test, the greater the chance that issues like fatigue or distraction will skew the results. (At the same time, more comprehensive scales are likely to be more valid.)

In 2015, my group (Michael L. Thomas, Katherine J. Bangen, and I), in collaboration with Ardelt, tested the original 39-item scale in 1,546 San Diego County residents participating in the SAGE study described earlier. After much tweaking, we reduced the scale to 12 statements, with respondents again having a choice to strongly agree, to strongly disagree, or decide it wasn't true of themselves. The statements still covered the cognitive, reflective, and affective dimensions of wisdom. This became the abbreviated 12-item version of the Three-Dimensional Wisdom Scale, or 3D-WS-12, which has good psychometric properties.

New SAWS

In the same year Ardelt debuted 3D-WS, Webster at Langara College introduced his own Self-Assessed Wisdom Scale, or SAWS.

SAWS was designed to measure wisdom based on its five identified components, according to Webster's research. They are critical life experiences, reminiscence and life reflection, openness to experiences, emotional regulation, and humor.

Like 3D-WS, SAWS presents statements—40 of them—and asks respondents to choose one of six options, strongly agree to strongly disagree. For people to be wise, according to SAWS, their responses should indicate competence in managing their lives, in negotiating events both good and bad, all the while maximizing their personal development. They should be receptive to alternate or opposing views, and they should be open to new perspectives and things (like music, books, art, and food). They should be in touch with their own emotions and those of others—and able to use humor as both a bond and stress reducer. They should be able to reflect on their past and present in a way that helps them anticipate or deal with future difficulties.

And like Ardelt's, Webster's scale emphasizes that wisdom does not develop in a vacuum. It is not simply accumulated over time. It emerges "during the exigencies of life, the rough and tumble of everyday existence."

There are also several other published scales for measuring wisdom, each with its pluses and minuses. My colleagues and I believed that there was a need for a new scale specifically designed to measure the review- and consensus-based components of wisdom, and their hypothesized neurobiological basis. This led to research by my younger colleague and an expert in scale development, Michael Thomas, and myself, with the help of several others in our group. The result was development of the San Diego Wisdom Scale, or SD-WISE.

The San Diego Wisdom Scale (SD-WISE)

SD-WISE builds upon the recent gains in our understanding of psychological and neurobiological models of wisdom. More specifically, it seeks to measure the identified components of wisdom linked to distinct regions and activity in the brain: emotional regulation, prosocial behaviors, self-reflection, acceptance of uncertainty, decisiveness, and social decision-making (advising). It is a step toward understanding how something as complex as wisdom might be orchestrated through basic biology.

Much credit must go to predecessors and colleagues: Baltes, Ardelt, Webster, and others who each helped point and pave the way. Over many months, multiple iterations, and much refinement, Michael Thomas, other colleagues, and I gathered, reviewed, tweaked, and tried out lists and combinations of self-assessing statements before settling on the 24 items that comprise the SD-WISE scale. We tested our final list in 524 community-dwelling adults, ages 25 to 104 years, who were participating in the SAGE study. Participants also completed the 3D-WS and SAWS assessments for comparison purposes.

It was a methodical process that involved a lot of steps and decisions. We needed to exclude people with dementia or terminal illnesses and participants who were not fluent in English. Such restrictions, necessary for initial research of this type, do represent challenges of their own. Wisdom is not confined to English-speaking people or to people living in San Diego County. These were recognized limitations of our study, but we needed to start somewhere.

Like other scales, SD-WISE involves a series of statements that participants agree or disagree with. Our 24 items were meticulously crafted to investigate the elements of wisdom identified in our previous work.

Participants were divided into two samples, with the larger sample used as a training set and the second group for data validation. We used every tool at our disposal to create the best possible way to measure wisdom based on our neurobiological understanding of it.

The SD-WISE scale proved reliable and valid, as measured by modern standards of scientific and statistical assessment. In 2017, we published our findings in the *Journal of Psychiatric Research*. The work was widely noted, reported in media around the world. It is important to note that this was a first field test of SD-WISE. Since then, SD-WISE has been used in multiple investigations, including studies of loneliness in San Diego County and in the Cilento region of Italy, those done in collaboration with IBM, and those using Amazon Mechanical Turk, or MTurk, a form of crowdsourcing that allows researchers to tap into much larger and more diverse samples with greater efficiency and economy.

More work remains to be done, of course, such as evaluating its reliability and validity across different sociocultural, racial-ethnic, and national and international samples. Like any test, it can be improved and refined. In our published work, my colleagues and I outlined the scale's current limitations and proposed paths forward. We expect SD-WISE to become an intrinsic and valuable tool in wisdom research—for example, to measure success in our pursuit to become wiser.

While you can get your total score on the SD-WISE, it won't tell you how your score compares with that of your peers in the same age and sex group. For that reason, we have recently developed the Jeste-Thomas Wisdom Index, an advancement and elaboration on SD-WISE, which will give you your total wisdom score as well as scores on each of the six components of wisdom, along with the average values of people from the same age and sex group. Thus, you can find out how well you are doing overall and where you have an opportunity to improve.

When taking SD-WISE, strip away ego and your innate urge to make a better impression. Be as impartial and forthright as possible. The questions are carefully structured and phrased to eliminate biases.

SD-WISE and Your Wisdom Index

Choose one of five descriptors that most accurately describes you in each of the 24 statements.

I AM GOOD AT PERCEIVING HOW OTHERS ARE FEELING.
( ) *strongly disagree* ( ) *disagree* ( ) *neutral* ( ) *agree* ( ) *strongly agree*

OTHERS LOOK TO ME TO HELP THEM MAKE CHOICES.
( ) *strongly disagree* ( ) *disagree* ( ) *neutral* ( ) *agree* ( ) *strongly agree*

OTHERS SAY I GIVE GOOD ADVICE.
( ) *strongly disagree* ( ) *disagree* ( ) *neutral* ( ) *agree* ( ) *strongly agree*

I OFTEN DON'T KNOW WHAT TO TELL PEOPLE WHEN THEY COME TO ME FOR ADVICE.
( ) *strongly disagree* ( ) *disagree* ( ) *neutral* ( ) *agree* ( ) *strongly agree*

I HAVE TROUBLE MAKING DECISIONS.
( ) *strongly disagree* ( ) *disagree* ( ) *neutral* ( ) *agree* ( ) *strongly agree*

I USUALLY MAKE DECISIONS IN A TIMELY FASHION.
( ) *strongly disagree* ( ) *disagree* ( ) *neutral* ( ) *agree* ( ) *strongly agree*

I TEND TO POSTPONE MAKING MAJOR DECISIONS AS LONG AS I CAN.
( ) *strongly disagree* ( ) *disagree* ( ) *neutral* ( ) *agree* ( ) *strongly agree*

I WOULD RATHER SOMEONE ELSE MAKE THE DECISION FOR ME IF I AM UNCERTAIN.
( ) *strongly disagree* ( ) *disagree* ( ) *neutral* ( ) *agree* ( ) *strongly agree*

I HAVE TROUBLE THINKING CLEARLY WHEN I AM UPSET.

( ) *strongly disagree* ( ) *disagree* ( ) *neutral* ( ) *agree* ( ) *strongly agree*

I REMAIN CALM UNDER PRESSURE.

( ) *strongly disagree* ( ) *disagree* ( ) *neutral* ( ) *agree* ( ) *strongly agree*

I AM ABLE TO RECOVER WELL FROM EMOTIONAL STRESS.

( ) *strongly disagree* ( ) *disagree* ( ) *neutral* ( ) *agree* ( ) *strongly agree*

I CANNOT FILTER MY NEGATIVE EMOTIONS.

( ) *strongly disagree* ( ) *disagree* ( ) *neutral* ( ) *agree* ( ) *strongly agree*

I TAKE TIME TO REFLECT ON MY THOUGHTS.

( ) *strongly disagree* ( ) *disagree* ( ) *neutral* ( ) *agree* ( ) *strongly agree*

I AVOID SELF-REFLECTION.

( ) *strongly disagree* ( ) *disagree* ( ) *neutral* ( ) *agree* ( ) *strongly agree*

IT IS IMPORTANT THAT I UNDERSTAND THE REASONS FOR MY ACTIONS.

( ) *strongly disagree* ( ) *disagree* ( ) *neutral* ( ) *agree* ( ) *strongly agree*

I DON'T ANALYZE MY OWN BEHAVIOR.

( ) *strongly disagree* ( ) *disagree* ( ) *neutral* ( ) *agree* ( ) *strongly agree*

I HAVE A DIFFICULT TIME KEEPING FRIENDSHIPS.

( ) *strongly disagree* ( ) *disagree* ( ) *neutral* ( ) *agree* ( ) *strongly agree*

I AVOID SITUATIONS WHERE I KNOW MY HELP WILL BE NEEDED.

( ) *strongly disagree* ( ) *disagree* ( ) *neutral* ( ) *agree* ( ) *strongly agree*

I WOULD STOP A STRANGER WHO DROPPED A TWENTY-DOLLAR BILL TO RETURN IT.

( ) *strongly disagree* ( ) *disagree* ( ) *neutral* ( ) *agree* ( ) *strongly agree*

I TREAT OTHERS THE WAY I WOULD LIKE TO BE TREATED.

( ) *strongly disagree* ( ) *disagree* ( ) *neutral* ( ) *agree* ( ) *strongly agree*

I ENJOY LEARNING THINGS ABOUT OTHER CULTURES.

( ) *strongly disagree* ( ) *disagree* ( ) *neutral* ( ) *agree* ( ) *strongly agree*

I AM OKAY WITH OTHERS HAVING MORALS AND VALUES OTHER THAN MY OWN.

( ) *strongly disagree* ( ) *disagree* ( ) *neutral* ( ) *agree* ( ) *strongly agree*

I GENERALLY LEARN SOMETHING FROM EVERY PERSON I MEET.

( ) *strongly disagree* ( ) *disagree* ( ) *neutral* ( ) *agree* ( ) *strongly agree*

I ENJOY BEING EXPOSED TO DIVERSE VIEWPOINTS.

( ) *strongly disagree* ( ) *disagree* ( ) *neutral* ( ) *agree* ( ) *strongly agree*

Following Up

This is not an easy test to score. With a subject as complicated as wisdom, that's to be expected. As with other scales, assessing its findings with appropriate scientific rigor requires specific training and know-how. But even without that, you can use SD-WISE to gain new knowledge and insight about yourself, your place on the Wisdom Index, and how best to proceed in becoming wiser.

The best and simplest method for determining your SD-WISE score, as well as Jeste-Thomas Wisdom Index score, is to visit our interactive website—sdwise.ucsd.edu—and do the assessment online. The site will automatically give you your Wisdom Index total score as well as scores on each of the six components of wisdom along with mean and standard deviation of scores for people in your own age and sex group. You will not be asked for any personal information, other than age, sex, and level of education, and your anonymized results may be used to further refine and improve the scale and its value, making you a contributor in the study of wisdom.

I suggest that you take the SD-WISE test more than once. Try again in a few days without consulting your previous answers, then compare results.

There is no cost to determining your Jeste-Thomas Wisdom Index for *personal* use. It's free. Take the test as often as you wish. Indeed, SD-WISE is an opportunity to become a citizen-scientist. Encourage family and friends to take the SD-WISE test too, not just assessing themselves but also answering as if they were you. Compare the findings. How much do the scores given by yourself compare with those given by others? How much agreement is there among parties about someone's wisdom?

Crucially, it's important that there be mutual trust among participants in such an "experiment." If someone is sensitive to criticism, please take that into account. Make sure good feelings, mutual respect, love, and friendship are maintained. That is a sign of collective wisdom!

Also, preserving confidentiality is critical. When researchers do such an experiment, they require approval by the local Institutional Review Board, an independent ethics committee used to ensure best practices. In formal research, study participants must sign an informed written consent. In your research, discuss any relevant issues or concerns. Make sure everybody is comfortable joining, without any pressure.

SD-WISE provides you with a kind of wisdom status report with specific indicators describing how you stand in regard to the identified components of wisdom. It gives you a Wisdom Index, a number, a point on a line that extends forward for the rest of your life.

In the chapters ahead, we will explore and investigate in some detail the specific domains of wisdom and, importantly, what you can do to cultivate them and boost your Wisdom Index. Retake the SD-WISE scale along the way to see where you are or just to retune your thinking. Wisdom is our goal, but it's a process without an end. There's no such thing as becoming too wise. Let's get started.

Part II

Components of Wisdom

Over the next five chapters, we get into the nitty-gritty: the key elements of wisdom, specifically compassion, emotional regulation, balancing decisiveness with acceptance of uncertainty, self-reflection, curiosity, sense of humor, and spirituality. There is a basic structure to each chapter, beginning with some historical, social, or scientific context, definitions, measures, and a bit of biology.

Finally, each chapter contains descriptions of interventions—attempts to manipulate and boost wisdom. In many places, there are lists of things you can do today. (Chapter 10 in part III describes these interventions in much fuller detail and context.)

You will read about experiments designed to parse wisdom, peel back its layers, get to the heart of the thing. Not surprisingly, these efforts, chronicled and cited in numerous published papers, are often surprisingly inspired and decidedly creative. There is no simple and perfect litmus test for wisdom, so figuring out how it works and why requires ingenuity, perseverance, and sometimes even marshmallows.

There are stories, too, outside the lab, singular anecdotes of people—ordinary or heroic—who memorably displayed the components of wisdom, from empathy and humor to curiosity and decisiveness in the face of uncertainty.

Every component of wisdom is important. A wise person may not possess all components in equal parts, but each component adds to a sum greater than its parts.

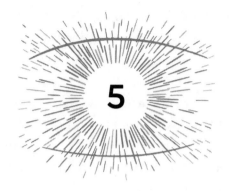

Cultivating Compassion

Humankind seems to have an enormous capacity for savagery, for brutality, for lack of empathy, for lack of compassion.

ANNIE LENNOX, singer-songwriter

We live in a time when science is validating what humans have known throughout the ages: that compassion is not a luxury; it is a necessity for our well-being, resilience, and survival.

JOAN HALIFAX, American Zen Buddhist

SIDDHARTHA GAUTAMA WAS A REAL PERSON who lived roughly five hundred years before Christ, eventually becoming known as the Buddha. He was born into nobility in the village of Lumbini in present-day Nepal. A privileged life insulated him from its common sufferings. One day, middle-aged and married, Siddhartha ventured outside the royal enclosure. For the first time, he witnessed life unvarnished. For the first time, he saw an old man, a sick man, and a corpse. These sights greatly disturbed him, even more so when he learned these sights were, in fact, inevitable fates that befall everyone, himself included.

Among the things Siddhartha saw that portentous day was a monk doing righteous work, which Siddhartha took as a sign. He abandoned his royal life of privilege to live as a homeless holy man, a seeker of higher meaning. Years later, under the Bodhi tree, he would attain total enlightenment.

Buddha is an internationally recognized embodiment of wisdom. His life story exemplifies the components of wisdom, most notably the development of compassion. He wrote and mused often on the topic. "Radiate boundless love towards the entire world," he wrote in the Karaniya Metta Sutta, a pair of discourses on the practice and value of universal lovingkindness.

During my own journey through medical school and subsequent residency, I saw sickness, aging, and death too. It was enlightening, but I was invariably busy and often tired, my days and nights filled with long hours of classes, study, and eventually, real work and experience in hospitals and clinics.

The grueling nature of learning to become a doctor tends to dampen one's humanity—at least in the beginning. People can become sets of symptoms, medical cases to be solved. And when you see a patient coming into the emergency room at 2:00 a.m., when you've already been on call for eight hours, your first reaction is probably not enthusiasm for a new opportunity to serve someone in need.

Several studies have shown that medical students' empathy declines from the first to the fourth (last) year of medical school, so much so that many schools of medicine have begun to incorporate classes on compassion into the formal curriculum.

At UC San Diego, for example, first- and second-year students practice conducting clinical exams of "patients" under the watchful eyes of instructors and practicing physicians. The patients are actually actors, well-briefed to describe a set list of aches and pains symptomatic of specific conditions and diseases. But their back stories are far from standardized. In one scenario, for example, the medical students meet a transgender man and are asked to elicit a focused history in a way that respects the patient's preferred pronoun and gender identity. The goal is to leave biases, judgments, and presumptions outside the exam room and to learn how to treat patients as people in need. At one point or another, we are all people in need.

Graduation from medical school doesn't come with a diploma in compassion. The subsequent super-busy life of a resident is straining and draining. It is often an encounter of a special kind that makes one truly aware of the emotional, nonmedical side of illness and injury. The focus then begins to reshift from a purely technical pursuit of an accurate diagnosis and textbook-dictated treatment to the holistic aspect of the caring for another human being.

I don't remember the hour now, but I do remember a shared moment in a clinic that greatly affected my life and my perspective. I was doing my psychiatric residency at the King Edward Memorial Hospital and Seth Gordhandas Sunderdas Medical College in Bombay (now Mumbai), when a longtime family friend suddenly appeared in the clinic with an eye injury. His wound was covered by a small bandage when I first saw him, but it proved to be ghastly. Even now, I recall the injured eye in vivid detail. I shuddered when I saw it and nearly fainted. It was not so much that the wound was unprecedented in terms of its flesh-and-blood horror—you see a lot of traumatic things in a hospital—but I had an established, emotional connection to this patient. He was a close friend who had helped me and my family many times in the past, and that connection, in that moment, produced an intense feeling of empathy and shared pain that I have never forgotten.

Decades later, I would publish with colleagues a study investigating differences in levels of compassion among older adults. We had more than a thousand older adults, ages 50 to 99, complete a questionnaire that measured compassion, resilience, past and present stressors, and how well they felt they were faring in life.

Among the key findings was that significant life events played a greater role in developing a desire to help others than simple accrual of age, current stress levels, or one's state of emotional functioning. It is a painful price, but our personal sufferings and losses make it easier to understand what others feel. We've been there too. "Walk a mile in someone else's shoes" before passing judgment, the adage goes. It's a hard thing to do voluntarily, but when either you or someone very close to you suffers, you can feel the pain and experience real empathy.

The Altruistic Brain

No single component of wisdom or becoming wise is more essential than prosocial behavior, doing things that benefit others or the society as a whole (and thus, you too). These are driven by traits like empathy, compassion, and altruism. To repeat the definitions of these terms, *empathy* is the ability to understand and share the feelings and thoughts of another, *compassion* involves translating empathy into helpful behavior, and *altruism* refers to actions to help another person without expecting any external rewards.

Humans are social animals. By and large, we do not fare well alone—at least not for any significant length of time. We need the presence of people, a fact we ignore at our own peril as we invent new ways to not spend time with others, from gated communities and nursing homes to online shopping, Netflix, and countless cell phone apps that do not require you to actually look at or physically speak to another person.

Among teens, according to a 2015 Pew Research Center survey, 58 percent texted friends via smartphone as their preferred means of communication. Only 10 percent favored phone calls. Young adults between the ages of 18 and 24 exchange an average of 109.5 messages on a normal day, or roughly 3,200 texts per month.

There is a certain irony here. In 2020, the phrase "social distancing" assumed widespread familiarity as countries, governments, and communities sought to slow and halt the spread of the novel coronavirus, which causes the respiratory disease COVID-19. Social distancing in the time of coronavirus required standing at least six feet from other people—the estimated space required for exhaled droplets to fall harmlessly to the ground. As a public health tool for battling viral spread, it was and is effective. But what we're really talking about here is not social, but rather physical distancing.

The need to socialize with others is especially critical in difficult times. We need one another for support, guidance, advice, and wisdom. So there's an extra dash of irony in that while we often bemoan the excessive use of devices and social media, fingers wagging at millennials and young people, the ability to call, text, email, FaceTime, Skype, Zoom, and more helped everyone better cope when we were compelled to remain physically distant. When physical closeness was prohibited, virtual closeness through technology became the primary vehicle for social connectedness.

But to live and do well in groups means knowing how to get along with numerous individuals around you, literally or not, related or not. This is perhaps more challenging to achieve than ever before. We are, if we allow ourselves to be, exposed to many more kinds of people, many more diverse cultures, societies, and points of view. True wisdom and grace require an open mind and heart. Prosocial behaviors ensure individual benefits through the common good.

In his 2015 book *The Altruistic Brain*, Donald Pfaff, a professor and neurobiologist at Rockefeller University, writes that human beings are "wired" to be good in the same way we are "wired" to acquire natural language. Pfaff believes we are inherently more inclined to be philanthropic than self-serving.

The argument is based on what Pfaff calls the "altruistic brain theory," which says the brain processes altruism in steps, all rooted in basic, well-understood neurocognitive mechanisms that have evolved to promote prosocial behavior.

Again, the idea is an artifact and necessity of evolution: Humans are born "prematurely" in comparison to other apes and animals. Human young require lots of care over many years, which in turn demands the involvement of lots of people, from parents to grandparents to distant kin and surrounding communities—it takes a village.

As a result, to quote the developmental psychologist Michael Tomasello as Pfaff does: "To an unprecedented degree, *Homo sapiens* are adapted for acting and thinking cooperatively in cultural groups, and indeed all of humans' most impressive cognitive achievements— from complex technologies to linguistic and mathematical symbols to intricate social institutions—are the products not of individuals acting alone, but of individuals interacting."

In other words, we're predisposed to doing the right thing for others because it's generally the best thing for all.

Promoting the common good and rising above self-interests are recognized by diverse cultures, old and new, as essential components of wisdom. Prosocial attitudes and behaviors such as empathy, compassion, social cooperation, and altruism have been esteemed and emulated throughout recorded history.

"When a good man is hurt, all who would be called good must suffer with him," wrote the Greek tragedian Euripides more than two millennia ago.

Ancient Egyptians believed the heart was the source of human intelligence, wisdom, emotions, memory, and soul. During the process of mummification, the heart was one of the few organs not removed from the body because Egyptians believed the deceased would require its resources in the afterlife. The brain, on the other hand, was widely regarded as cranial stuffing. It was liquefied by inserting a long hook through the nose, whipped, then scooped out and tossed.

Such cardiac-centric notions were long ago disproved and discarded, though remnants of such thinking linger today. We still talk about memorizing "by heart" and being "good-hearted," for example, but we know now that a trait like empathy actually resides in the PFC, which cloaks the forward third of the cerebral cortex and lies smack behind your forehead. Here resides a kind of brain cell called the mirror neuron.

Back in the 1980s and 1990s, while investigating brain function in macaque monkeys, Italian neurophysiologists discovered that some brain cells in monkeys possessed a remarkable mirror function: they lit up when the monkey performed a specific activity, such as picking up a piece of food *and* when the monkey saw another monkey doing the same thing.

Humans have mirror neurons too. They are essential to who we are, helping to explain how we learn through mimicry and why we empathize with others. When you flinch at the sight of that unsuspecting fellow in the park hit in the head by an errant Frisbee, feel your heart racing as you listen to radio accounts of a tense baseball duel between pitcher and batter, or sniffle during the death scene in a tearjerker movie, your mirror neurons are at work, providing you immediate and instinctive insight into the feelings and intentions of others.

Mirroring extends even to our sense of touch. Researchers have found that when people see another body being touched—a purely visual input—it activates touch-sensitive regions in their brains. A rare few even report conscious experiences of touch to their own bodies from the sight of others being touched, a phenomenon known as mirror-touch synesthesia.

Mirror neurons are associated with theory of mind, our ability to attribute mental states—beliefs, intents, desires, sensations, knowledge—both to ourselves and to others. We aren't born with the ability fully fledged, but it develops fairly quickly. Six-month-old infants show signs of understanding attention in others, that the act of selectively looking at something suggests an object of interest. They quickly learn that attention can be directed and shared by pointing, which requires the infant to understand that the other person has a separate state of mind. It's a natural, inevitable realization. It's what allows us to see a smile and intrinsically understand and feel the other person's joy. It binds us together as human beings. When very young children observe and imitate facial expressions, mirror neurons are activated, and studies have shown this activity correlates with empathy scores.

A Lack of Empathy

Deficits in theory of mind are associated with some mental conditions and disease states. For example, the brains of people with autism spectrum disorder or schizophrenia or people suffering from cocaine addiction or alcoholism may not process social cues in the same way that "neurotypicals" do, though that does not necessarily mean they lack empathy. There is compelling evidence that they simply require other mental tools to accurately assess and express it.

Sociopaths and psychopaths are people with antisocial tendencies and behaviors. They may feel varying degrees of empathy toward others, but it is easily overridden by larger, more compelling self-interests, such as pathological lying or an utter lack of remorse. Both genetic predisposition and environmental influences shape antisocial personality.

Psychopaths can be smart and appear normal, even charming, but invariably lack a conscience and sense of responsibility and warmth for others. There is much research to suggest that psychopaths are simply not wired for empathy. Researchers at the University of Chicago, for example, tested 80 prisoners between ages 18 and 50, using standardized tools to test for levels of psychopathy and brain imaging. (Not surprisingly, the rate of psychopathy in prisons is higher than in the general population: around 23 percent compared to 1 percent.)

Participants in the high psychopathy group exhibited significantly less activation in the ventromedial prefrontal cortex, lateral orbitofrontal cortex, amygdala, and periaqueductal gray parts of the brain, but more activity in the striatum and the insulae compared to control participants.

The insulae finding was surprising because they are involved in emotion and somatic resonance—the idea that our bodies interact with others at energetic frequencies. Sometimes you get a good vibe; sometimes you don't. The other findings, though, were consistent with evidence indicating that the regions of psychopathic brains associated with empathy, mirroring, intuition, and attunement are less active.

In his 2013 book *The Psychopath Inside*, neuroscientist James Fallon describes discovering that genetic tests and MRIs he had taken mostly out of curiosity revealed that he fit the pathological description of a psychopath. Fallon is a happily married man. He knew he had a tendency to be "obnoxiously competitive," he told *Smithsonian* magazine. "I won't let my grandchildren win games. I do jerky things that piss people off." But he didn't think of himself as psychopathic. He was not violent. There were no tendencies toward becoming a coldhearted con man or serial killer.

Fallon believes he escaped that dark fate in part because he was raised in a normal, loving family with parents who paid him deep, constant attention, strengthening development of the regions of the brain, like the prefrontal cortex, that modify and control urges and impulses. He's also made a concerted effort to consciously change offending behaviors, to do the right thing, and to more often consider other people's feelings.

But Fallon says his compassion isn't entirely charitable. "I'm not doing this because I'm suddenly nice. I'm doing it because of pride, because I want to show to everyone and myself that I can pull it off."

There is a clear distinction between psychopaths and people with autism spectrum disorders. The latter are kind and helpful but may lack the cognitive capacity to understand other people's state of mind or emotions. As a result, there is a deficit in cognitive aspects of empathy, but the desire to help others (compassion) is there. In contrast, psychopaths may cognitively understand others' mental state and emotions—that is, they possess the ability to empathize; they can read you like a book—but they lack compassion, the desire to help others.

Nonetheless, Fallon's example shows that biology is not destiny. Although he was biologically predisposed to psychopathy, the family support and care he received combined with his determination made him a thoughtful neuroscientist who is helping others understand human behavior. Compassion—and wisdom—are modifiable and can be increased through appropriate interventions!

Why Care about Strangers?

Compassion and altruism are close cousins. They are related to social cooperation, another ancient and universal behavior documented across the animal world. It too has deep evolutionary roots.

The benefits of social cooperation tend to be mutual. The lives of ants and bees, lions and chimpanzees are all obvious examples of social cooperation. They display bonding behaviors that benefit both individuals and the group.

Humans display the same behaviors, though not necessarily as a matter of survival. If you help a coworker with a task, it likely serves you well too. A happy boss makes for a happy workplace. But altruism is different from cooperation. It can be a one-way act. It may even harm the altruistic actor.

Altruism in humans is an act of concern for the welfare of others, such as helping an old person across the street or writing a check to charity. You can see countless examples of random acts of kindness in everyday life if you look for them. A number of years ago, Mike McIntyre, a local reporter in San Diego, quit his job, literally gave away everything he owned except for the clothes on his back, and hit the road, determined to cross the country unaided by any material possessions or resources. He had not a penny to his name or in his pocket. If he were to successfully reach the East Coast—fed, sheltered, and transported along the way—it would be entirely due to the kindness of strangers (which, not coincidentally, became the title of his resulting book). I'm happy to report Mike made it. He is alive and well today, and immeasurably wiser for the effort.

Strangers helped Mike because they thought he could use some help. It may have been a meal or a place to sleep. Theirs were acts of simple altruism.

"Extraordinary altruism" goes beyond. It's an act of unambiguous altruism that, in fact, poses harm or risk to the person behaving altruistically. It is not only donating an organ like a kidney (which involves considerable pain and stress), but donating that organ to a complete stranger.

The kidney is the most commonly transplanted organ. Kidney donations more than double those of the next organ, the liver. But there are still not enough kidneys to meet the need. More than one hundred thousand people are on waiting lists for kidney transplants; three thousand new patients are added every month. The median wait time is approximately five years; 13 people die each day waiting in vain.

The vast majority of transplanted kidneys come from deceased donors, primarily the 30 to 40 percent of Americans who designate themselves as such on their driver's licenses or on state registries. The pool of living donors, people who have chosen to give up one of their two kidneys, is much, much smaller and, at the moment, declining. The number of living donors who have given a kidney altruistically without knowing the recipient is vanishingly small.

A few years ago, researchers sought to find out who these people were who willingly gave one of their kidneys to unknown people. Between 1999 and 2009, they identified 955 altruistic kidney donations among hundreds of thousands of kidney donations over that 10-year span. The scientists found that the extraordinarily altruistic act of donating a kidney to a stranger strongly correlated with the "engine model of well-being," which basically says people feel especially kind and generous when their own lives are going well. Objective measures like good health and income drive positive emotions, a greater sense of meaning, and ultimately, genuine beneficence.

People who donate a kidney to a stranger share not just an organ, but their emotional state: I am (luckily) well; you should be too.

The Importance of Self-Compassion

Self-compassion—that is, treating yourself with care and concern regarding personal inadequacies, mistakes, failures, and painful life situations—is critical to well-being and resilience, which in turn may lead to being compassionate to others.

"Even in the loneliest moments," writes the Indian poet Sanober Khan, "I have been there for myself."

This is not about giving yourself a break that you wouldn't give others. It's recognition that everybody, including yourself, is imperfect. We all make mistakes. We all fail. "Self-compassion connects one's own flawed condition to the shared human condition," wrote Elke Smeets at Maastricht University in the Netherlands, describing a study published in 2014.

In that study, Smeets and colleagues investigated whether teaching self-compassion enhanced resilience and well-being in a group of female college students, compared to an intervention program that simply taught general time management skills.

Participants who received mindfulness training—lessons on how to be aware of, to address, and to balance the good and bad of living—produced higher subsequent scores on tests of compassion, optimism, happiness, and self-sufficiency, which in turn made it more likely they would share these benefits with others.

When we feel good about ourselves and our place in the world, we may want to share it with others. Yet, surprisingly, compassion toward others does not always correlate with self-compassion. Kind physicians or priests may be much harder on themselves than they are on others. Likewise, people who are distressed and need help may be more empathic and compassionate to others.

Neuroscientists at Wilfrid Laurier University in Ontario, Canada, conducted an interesting experiment. They randomly placed study participants into mindsets in which they felt either powerful or powerless by asking them to write about either a time when they called the shots or a time when they needed help from others.

Then everyone watched a neutral video—an anonymous hand squeezing a rubber ball—while scientists tracked brain function. In particular, they looked at mirror neuron activity. The more activity, they hypothesized, the more the viewer was sharing the moment with the unseen person squeezing the ball.

For study participants who felt powerless, watching the hand squeeze the rubber ball provoked considerable mirror neuron activity. For participants who felt empowered, not so much. Based on mirror neuron activity, their feelings of power appeared to dampen responsive feelings of empathy.

Self-compassion is different from narcissism. *Narcissism* refers to an exaggerated sense of one's own importance in the world. The word comes from a Greek myth of a man who loved himself deeply. The gender symbolism is appropriate because men are much more likely to be narcissistic than women. Narcissism is a personality trait and exists at different levels in different people. When it is severe and has an adverse impact on functioning, it can become a disorder—called narcissistic personality disorder, a psychiatric (medical) diagnosis. The psychiatric diagnostic manual, *DSM-5*, published by the American Psychiatric Association, requires the presence of at least five of the nine criteria listed, such as a grandiose sense of self-importance, a need for excessive admiration, a sense of entitlement, a lack of empathy, and interpersonally exploitative behavior.

Do social media and selfies encourage self-focus and promote narcissism? The personality trait of narcissism is, like other traits, determined in part by genetics and in part by environment. Just because you have a robust Facebook, Twitter, or Instagram account, or have thousands of selfies stored on your cell phone, doesn't necessarily mean you're a narcissist.

But there are strong associations between many social behaviors and what's called *grandiose narcissism*, a flamboyant, assertive, and interpersonally dominant style. These people have inflated senses of self. They're overconfident in making decisions. They don't seem to learn from their mistakes.

People with high levels of narcissism traits—grandiosity, lack of empathy, need for admiration—like social media for obvious reasons. It's a powerful tool for celebrating and promoting themselves. People who increasingly use social media may begin to display more pronounced signs of narcissism.

Social media don't produce narcissism, and of course, everyone who uses social media isn't narcissistic, but narcissistic people may tend to use them more often.

Higher levels of narcissism lead to a lack of compassion for others—and that is not a sign of wisdom.

Gender and the Genetics of Compassion

Some people are simply born more compassionate than others. There appears to be some genetic basis to traits such as empathy and altruism. In studies of identical twins who share the same genome, for example, researchers have found that 30 to 60 percent of altruistic tendencies, such as helping a stranger or donating to charity, could be explained by genetics. Conversely, differences were more likely influenced by social or cultural factors.

Women live longer than men. The exact reasons are not known, but they are likely biological, such as the differing influences of the sex chromosomes (XX in women, XY in men). Is there a sex difference in wisdom too, especially in compassion?

My unscientific research shows that there are more goddesses than gods of wisdom among the world's religions! In my own family, I am surrounded by three very wise and successful women— my wife, Sonali, and our two daughters, Shafali and Neelum, all board-certified physicians in pediatric subspecialties (psychiatry, neurology, and oncology, respectively). There is no question about sex differences in wisdom in my family. Women are wiser.

A 2009 study by Ardelt at the University of Florida sampled 464 undergraduate college students and 178 adults age 52 and older, using her three-dimensional scale to measure cognitive, reflective, and affective (or compassionate) components of wisdom. Ardelt found that women tended to score higher on the affective dimension of wisdom, which includes empathy and selflessness, while men scored higher in the cognitive domain (self-knowledge, understanding), albeit only in the older cohort. Our own research through the ongoing SAGE study, which has been following more than 1,500 randomly selected residents since 2011, as well as several other investigations, have also reported measurably higher scores in the compassionate component of wisdom among women, but no other wisdom-related differences between the two sexes.

In general, females are more empathic than males, and there's empirical evidence to back this up. A 1995 Scandinavian study, for example, found that women involuntarily imitate other people's emotional expressions more than men—a behavior believed to reflect increased activity of mirror neurons in their brains.

A 2003 study found that when women were asked to identify emotions in other people, their monitored brains showed activity in regions suggesting they were also experiencing those emotions themselves. Conversely, the parts of the brain that lit up in men asked to identify emotions in other people were associated with rational analysis. Men looked at the emotions in others and then considered whether they had seen them before and if they had a name.

Infant boys and girls do not seem to differ consistently in their ability to recognize emotion, either in themselves or in others. A 1993 study found that infant boys rated just as highly as infant girls in sensitivity and attention to other people. However, adult men and women use somewhat different scales to weigh moral dilemmas. Women seem to be more likely to have a negative, emotional, gut-level reaction to causing harm to even one person, whereas men are less likely to express this strong emotional reaction to harming a single individual if doing so would save many more people, one scientist told National Public Radio when a study of this type was published in 2015.

There are some minor sex differences in the anatomy and physiology of the brain, but their relevance, if any, to wisdom is unclear. Maybe the reason for the sex difference in compassion is, in part, hormonal: testosterone versus estrogen. Beyond its biological duties, testosterone levels are associated with male-typical behaviors like aggressiveness and a need to dominate. Conversely, estrogen seems to promote nurturing, benevolence, and sympathetic behaviors.

UC Berkeley researchers have found evidence that people who are more empathic possess a particular variant of the oxytocin receptor gene. Oxytocin is a hormone and neuropeptide (a small, protein-like molecule) that plays a major role in countering stress. It is released into the bloodstream during childbirth, breastfeeding, and orgasm. It plays a role in social bonding—in humans and in animals like the prairie vole and rat.

Past studies have found that oxytocin released into the brains of female prairie voles, a relative of the mouse, was important to forming a monogamous pairing bond with their sexual partners. Female rats given a drug to block oxytocin activity after giving birth did not exhibit typical maternal behaviors. In humans, experiments have shown that participants given doses of oxytocin were more empathic and inclined to help others, including strangers.

In one bit of novel research, scientists at the University of Toronto filmed conversations between long-term partners discussing a non-romantic time of personal suffering. Twenty-second slices of the most intense parts of the conversations were then played, minus audio, to study participants who did not know the couple.

The participants were asked to assess the people on video in terms of compassion, trustworthiness, and social intelligence, based solely on their visible behavior. By and large, the people deemed to be more empathic by viewers were those who also possessed genetic mutations that boosted oxytocin receptivity.

"These behaviors were signaling to the complete strangers that this is a trustworthy person. This is speaking to the power of very slight genetic variation and the amazing human ability to pick up on the differences," said Aleksandr Kogan, a postdoctoral fellow and coauthor of the 2011 study.

From Handshake to Hospice

Acts of compassion, small or large, change the lives of everyone involved.

In 1987, six years into the AIDS epidemic, with fear and fearmongering run amok, Princess Diana famously and knowingly shook hands with a man infected with HIV during the opening of the first clinic in the United Kingdom dedicated to the treatment of HIV and AIDS.

She was 26 years old at the time; he was 32 and dying.

Today it would be considered a common act of kindness and interest, but it was a rare act at the time. Diana wore no protective gloves or clothing. Researchers already knew the deadly virus could not be transmitted through ordinary touch, but much of the world believed otherwise, petrified and paranoid about a disease it did not understand.

Princess Diana's simple and singular act of outreach helped launch a process of ending the universal phobia surrounding AIDS and those afflicted. There is no doubt Diana was innately compassionate. Biographers recount her extraordinary intuition about people, a natural inclination to reach out and connect. She was a "hugger." Her HIV handshake was a natural extension of herself. But she also consciously and vigorously exercised and expanded on it. In the following years, she would make many poignant bedside visits to patients ignored or shunned by society, including at a hostel for abandoned children in Rio de Janeiro, homeless shelters in London, a hospice in Toronto, leprosy clinics in India, and hospitals for children with cancer.

"I make the trips at least three times a week, and spend up to four hours at a time with patients holding their hands and talking to them," she once said. "Some of them will live and some will die, but they all need to be loved while they are here. I try to be there for them."

Such sentiment was a touchstone in her tragically short-ened life, in part according to biographers, because she struggled to find empathy, compassion, and happiness in her private life. She died in a fatal car crash in 1997, but her extraor-dinary, public compassion inspired millions. At her death, a public memorial fund garnered $44 million in donations. When it closed in 2012, it had awarded 727 grants to 471 organiza-tions and spent more than $145 million on charitable causes.

Caring is part of the professional calling of nurses, per-haps most especially those who tend to the sickest or dying, such as patients with cancer or in hospice. Constant expo-sure to heart-wrenching, emotional challenges, however, poses the very real threat of compassion fatigue. Nurses and other caregivers who resist and overcome it are among our wisest—in part because of what they do and what it does to them.

A few years ago, researchers in North Carolina interviewed 30 oncology nurses regarding their experiences caring for cancer patients. The purpose was to determine whether those experiences resulted in personal growth in the nurses.

In all cases, the answer was yes, and in ways that neatly mirror the components of wisdom. Nurses said they learned that life is uncertain and must be unconditionally embraced.

They put things into perspective and stopped sweating the small stuff.

Said one hospice nurse, "Coming home, if things were a mess or things weren't picked up or if things weren't done, I can remember my husband being agitated and I can remember thinking: 'Who cares? I get to come home.'"

The researchers described a process called vicarious post-traumatic growth. Nurses didn't simply "learn or perceive growth by watching their patients' experiences with suffering and death. Rather, they personally experienced anguish, loss, and grief following the death of favorite or memorable patients."

In a sense, their patients' experiences became lessons learned. Nurses said they became more empathic and emotionally mature, better able to recognize individual differences and identities, acknowledge limitations, and improve their interpersonal skills.

"Because, here, with this job, you are not just involved in your own life anymore," said one nurse. "You are involved in all of those patients' lives. So you don't just take away from this job what you've learned as a person, what you've experienced, you take away what those other people are telling you about. . . . You take all of those personal experiences, and you . . . put them into yourself."

Another nurse described her effort to teach her daughter altruism:

What can [my daughter] do to help someone else's life be better, if they're having a miserable life? Just trying to help. You need help, okay, help yourself. But then get outside yourself and do something. What can you do for those around you? I feel that you are here for a purpose. What are you going to do about it? . . . You're here today breathing, you're healthy. . . . How can you bring joy to someone else's life?

Compassion is an act of giving that goes both ways. The more compassionate you become (even if it takes some active effort), the greater the benefits to everyone, including yourself.

Does Meditation Help?

Compassion evolved as a natural instinct over a very long time, but it can also be learned. Indeed, our brains can be fundamentally changed in the process.

In a 2013 study, for example, researchers gave "compassion training" to a group of participants and then looked at what was happening at the neuronal level when they observed others in distress.

Compared to earlier testing and to a control group, particular brain regions lit up: the medial orbitofrontal cortex, putamen, pallidum, and ventral tegmental area, all regions associated with positive affect and affiliation. The findings suggest that deliberate cultivation of compassion provides a new coping strategy, one that fosters positive emotions like interest, alertness, pleasure, and joy, even when confronted by distress in others.

Meditation is an ancient remedy to reduce stress, documented to improve one's well-being (mind and body) and feelings for both self and others. A couple of recent studies indicate you don't have to visit a yogi on a faraway continent or travel to the top of a mountain for relief.

In 2016, English scientists conducted a randomized clinical trial studying the effectiveness of lovingkindness meditation (LKM) taught online. LKM comes from the Buddhist tradition of sitting quietly and comfortably and diving deeply and reflectively into your inner soul, stripping away external cares and concerns to find inner peace, love, and tranquility. It's classic meditation.

And the English researchers said it worked, increasing relaxation and a sense of achievement among participants, though they noted a lot more research was needed, including devising ways to deliver online LKM effectively to diverse populations.

In another study, published in 2017, researchers at Ohio State University enrolled nurses, doctors, social workers, and others in an online meditation course. It is perhaps ironic that compassion can be a victim of health-care training—witness the erosion of empathy experienced by many medical school students, who wind up taking classes to restore it.

The Ohio State study did much the same thing as the LKM study. Through online training involving mind-body practices, the researchers said participating health-care professionals posted higher scores in well-being, gratitude, self-compassion, and confidence, all of which undoubtedly benefited the patients in their care.

No doubt, compassion meditation sustains the deep reserve of unstinting kindness and magnanimity that define people like the Dalai Lama, who has seen peoples and nations torn apart by violence. But developing greater compassion doesn't require a lifetime of practice and devotion. It can be achieved through relatively brief interventions. Exercises like daily one-minute periods of quiet and reflection or weekly journaling of reasons to feel grateful produce positive emotional results, reduce depressive symptoms, and increase life satisfaction.

"Wiser individuals are more grateful than others, and they are grateful for different things than others," said Judith Glück of the Alpen-Adria-Universität Klagenfurt after publishing a 2014 study in the *Journals of Gerontology*.

Glück and colleagues conducted a pair of small studies. In one, they used newspaper and radio ads to solicit names of people considered to be wise. Of those nominated, 47 men and women, aged 60 on average, agreed to participate. A random sample of 47 adults of similar age and education served as a control group.

All of the participants were interviewed about their most difficult and best life experiences—and their most important life lessons. Overall, 31 percent expressed gratitude to God, to other people, or for the experience of life, whether it was a highlight or a hard time. Those deemed wise by others were far more likely to express sentiments of gratitude than those in the control group.

Gratitude, even if it's just thankfulness for coming out the other side of a difficult experience, is both the raw material of wisdom and its finished product. Among the study participants nominated as wise was a 76-year-old man who had survived a heart attack. "Because of this new life, I have new lessons to learn and I have started to see life in a different way," he said, gratefully.

An even easier method to cultivate compassion is to simply close your eyes and imagine people who have been especially kind to you in life, and silently repeat phrases like, "May they be safe and happy" or "Let them be healthy and well."

In time, do the same for yourself, for loved ones, for neighbors, for everyone. In moments of inspired well-being, think kindly about people for whom kindness does not easily come to mind. Like any exercise, the more you meditate, the better you become at it and the stronger the psychological benefit.

"It's kind of like weight training," said Helen Weng, lead author of a 2013 study at the University of Wisconsin–Madison that looked at whether compassion could be trained and learned in adults. "Using this systematic approach, we found that people can actually build up their compassion 'muscle' and respond to others' suffering with care and a desire to help."

Gratitude Writ Large

Another way to build empathy is to keep a gratitude journal. Keeping a regular written record of their thoughts and activities was a habit of some of the greatest luminaries. Einstein, Twain, da Vinci, Curie, Jefferson, and Darwin all kept journals. You don't need to jot down your theories of gravity or natural selection, just a few lines each day describing something for which you are grateful or that brought you satisfaction and joy. It can be a friend, a favorite meal, a funny line, or the sight of a hummingbird hovering iridescent in the morning sun. Study after study has found that these moments of recall and repose measurably calm and uplift the mood. And a good mood leads to good things, a better life, and perhaps, a day when your journal is referenced by just your last name.

Use Your Words

A good vocabulary boosts empathy too. In a 2006 study published in the journal *NeuroImage*, Spanish researchers had participants read words with strong odor associations, along with neutral words, while their brains were being scanned. Words like *perfume* and *coffee* lit up participants' primary olfactory cortex while words like *chair* and *key* did not.

The primary olfactory cortex plays a major role in our sense of smell, which is intimately and powerfully linked to our emotions and memories. A whiff of a long-forgotten cologne or cooked food can conjure sudden and unexpected recollections.

Our brains respond to strong metaphors. An Emory University study found that the sensory cortex, which is responsible for perceiving texture through touch, became active when study participants heard phrases like "the singer had a velvet voice" or "he had leathery hands," but remained dormant for "the singer had a pleasing voice" or "he had strong hands."

The brain doesn't make much of a distinction between reading or hearing about an experience and actually encountering it. When you read Gertrude Stein's opening line in her novel *The Making of Americans*—"Once an angry man dragged his father along the ground through his own orchard"—not only do the language-processing regions of your brain light up, but also those brain regions that "feel" the imagined thuds, bumps, and yowls of pain.

Reading builds empathy. Researchers have found that there is substantial overlap in the networks used to understand stories and the networks used to navigate interactions with individuals. It goes back to theory of mind. There is strong empirical evidence that people who frequently read fiction seem better able to understand other people— to empathize with them and see the world through their eyes.

It's not simply a case of empathic people tending to prefer novels. In a clever 2010 study, scientists found that preschool-age children who had more stories read to them developed a keener theory of mind. The effect was also produced in children who watched movies but not, oddly enough, in children who watched TV. (One possible explanation: young children go to the movies with their parents, which likely produces more conversations about what they've seen, permitting shared experiences and insights.)

We build empathy when we feel we belong to groups or, at the very least, that other people aren't completely unfamiliar to us. A 2005 British study, for example, found that bystanders were more likely to help a stranger in distress if they recognized that the stranger belonged to a common group. What counted as a "group," however, was not fixed.

Specifically, scientists at Lancaster University recruited fans of the English football club Manchester United, which has a bitter rivalry with another club in Liverpool.

The Manchester fans filled out questionnaires and then were invited to walk across campus to watch a film about English football. Along the way, an accident was staged in which a runner slipped and fell, groaning in pain. Hidden observers documented the fans' reactions. In cases where the runner was wearing a Manchester jersey, fans were more likely to ask the runner if he needed help. In cases where the runner was wearing a Liverpool jersey or an unbranded shirt, their solicitude was measurably reduced.

In a second experiment, Manchester United fans were again recruited, but this time they were told they were participating in a study about football fans in general. The study would focus on positive aspects of being an English football fan, not the negative incidents and hooliganism that more often are reported in media. Study questionnaires asked fans about their broader interest in the game, what commonalities they might share with other fans.

Then, as in the first experiment, they were invited to walk across campus and see a film. Again, the stroll was interrupted by a staged accident involving a fallen runner. This time, the Manchester fans were as likely to help a runner in a Liverpool jersey as one wearing Manchester colors, though runners in unbranded shirts were not so kindly considered.

The findings suggest that when people are encouraged to see more inclusive social category boundaries—all fans of football versus just Manchester United fans—they are more inclined to extend assistance to more individuals. It doesn't take much more to spur empathy.

It's easy to apply these findings to our lives. Becoming active in good causes or our communities broadens our sense of belonging and caring for others—who become less "other." Writing a check to a charity is a fine thing, but it's not the same as volunteering at a shelter or mentoring a student. The former is a remote and transient act. There is no psychic return on investment other than maybe a feel-good moment when you mail off the donation. But when one actively invests one's self, energy, talents, and time in something, the benefits are manifold and extend in all directions, inward and out. And the more you do it, the more it becomes a habit of the body and the mind.

Tania Singer at the Max Planck Institute found that compassion training prompted study subjects to behave more thought-fully and charitably toward others—and that the new behaviors persisted.

It's not entirely clear how this happens. There is evidence that compassion training enhances emotional processing in brain regions linked to empathy. Mindfulness training decreases activity in the amygdala in response to emotional images. It helps people to respond more calmly and with more consideration to stimuli that might have caused them to "fly off the handle" in the past. It does not, however, reduce brain activity for images of human suffering, suggesting instead a greater attunement.

Now, with Feelings

Acts of compassion make us feel good. We are creatures of our feel-ings, moods, and emotions, which aren't precisely synonymous. They drive our behaviors in ways obvious and not, equally powerful as both motivators and constraints.

A full and meaningful life, one wisely lived, involves judiciously managing our feelings, moods, and emotions. It means using them to our benefit (and to the benefit of others) in the right times, ways, and places. Don't drive angry, the saying goes. Don't live angry, either. Conversely, it's not wise to spend your days giddily blind to harsh realities.

Anger. Fear. Joy. Disgust. Grief. These emotions and others direct us. They influence how we think and act. Finding a way to balance them, to give them free rein when necessary, but more often to conduct them appropriately for the best possible results is a lifelong endeavor.

In the next chapter, we explore emotional regulation with happiness. The endeavor begins now.

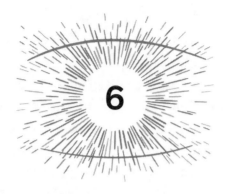

Emotional Regulation with Happiness

*I don't want to be at the mercy of my emotions. I want
to use them, to enjoy them, and to dominate them.*

OSCAR WILDE, *The Picture of Dorian Gray*

*Happiness is not the endless pursuit of pleasant experiences—
that sounds more like a recipe for exhaustion—but a way
of being that results from cultivating a benevolent mind,
emotional balance, inner freedom, inner peace, and
wisdom. Each of these qualities is a skill that can
be enhanced through training the mind.*

MATTHIEU RICARD, photographer and author

DIFFERENT CULTURES HAVE DIFFERENT norms or expectations
about the overt expressions of emotion.

In many Asian cultures, for example, including Asian Indian,
it used to be considered undignified and bad form to display

"excessive" emotion in the presence of others. Thumbing through my old family albums, for example, everyone looks quite somber, even on festive occasions like weddings. There are exceptions, of course. Children will always act like children, but in the company of older adults, even they are expected to "behave themselves," which is another way of saying be serious—or at least try to look it.

Growing up, I thought everyone comported themselves in similar fashion. It was the presumed global norm. One of the first English novels I read was *Goodbye, Mr. Chips*, written by James Hilton and published in 1934. It seemed to underscore my presumption. The novel tells the story of a beloved teacher at a fictional British boys' public boarding school over many years. In his younger days, Mr. Chipping ("Mr. Chips" is an endearment) is conventional, dogmatic, and often harsh, but his views and demeanor soften and transform after he meets a young woman named Katherine, whom he will eventually marry.

Later, I saw the 1969 movie based on the book, with Peter O'Toole in the title role. There is a scene near the end of the film that still provokes tears. Mr. Chips has been selected to be the new school headmaster—a dream of his. But on the same day and unbeknownst to the school, Katherine is killed in a German bombing raid. Mr. Chips arrives at the school, dazed and distraught. He enters a room to a surprise party by his admiring students, also unaware of his loss. Mr. Chips is stoic, but also gracious and smiling. I watched in amazement. How could Mr. Chips suppress or disguise his overwhelming sense of loss and sadness about Katherine in order to not disappoint his adoring students? It seemed an act beyond ordinary human willpower. It reminded me of the lessons of my own youth, the images of stern-faced elders and the value placed on always appearing strong and self-contained. Keeping a stiff upper lip, as the Brits would say.

Mr. Chips's impassivity was, in fact, an extreme example of control. It was a repression of other powerful feelings, such as grief and isolation. I would not consider it advisable for most people. Emotional regulation is and must be a matter of balance, with all emotions felt and addressed. There are times when you should scream from the mountaintops in joy or anger and times when you should temper your emotions with reason and prudence, hope, and optimism. We live best in the broad middle of our emotional lives. When we venture too far or for too long at the ends of the spectrum, we risk falling off with perhaps terrible consequences.

Naturally, I would discover through other books, movies, and life that human emotions are, in fact, broadly expressed in wildly different and dramatic fashion around the world. But neuroscience has also taught me that while expressions of emotion may vary across cultures, the underlying, fundamental biology of emotional regulation is the same everywhere and in everyone. Indeed, emotional regulation is necessary for the survival of our species. If we all acted on our anger or resorted to provocations with violence, for example, *Homo sapiens* might very well experience the same fate as dinosaurs: extinction.

Emotions, Feelings, and Moods

The influential American philosopher and psychologist William James insightfully noted the inextricable link between emotions and feelings. "What kind of an emotion of fear would be left, if the feeling neither of quickened heart-beats nor of shallow breathing, neither of trembling lips nor of weakened limbs, neither of goose-flesh nor of visceral stirrings, were present," he wrote.

James said he could not imagine such a separation, but in that quote, he also notes a distinction. Emotions, feelings, and moods are not all quite the same thing. And their differences affect not just how we experience the moment or our lives, but how we think about them and how we can change them.

Emotions are fundamental physical states arising from the body's responses to external stimuli. Feelings are mental responses to those emotions. Let's say you're walking alone at night down a dark alley. You hear a sound behind you, maybe something growling. Your heart begins to race. Muscles tense. Your breathing becomes rapid and shallow. Your mouth becomes dry.

These represent the primal emotion of fear.

What goes through your mind—terrified thoughts of stalking assailants—is a feeling.

Moods are less specific or intense than emotions or feelings. They persist longer as well, perhaps well past the original stimulus. A mood is different from temperament or a trait, which is even longer lasting, perhaps for a lifetime. A personality trait such as optimism predisposes someone to certain kinds of moods, such as cheerfulness.

Primary emotions evolved in response to environmental challenges, from confrontations with prehistoric cave bears to crossing a busy street. They are so fundamental to survival (and thus widely shared among animals) that they are essentially hardwired into the older limbic system of our brains. They are innate and universal, automatic and quick to respond, a useful quality when life and limb may be at risk.

The amygdala plays a big role here. It has a primary duty of forming and storing memories associated with emotional events—as opposed to, say, memorizing a grocery list or recalling a lesson from a textbook. Actual memories—or more precisely, the sequence of synaptic connections between neurons that represents a memory—are believed to be stored throughout the brain, with the hippocampus playing a critical role, but it is the amygdala that imbues them with their emotional import.

Let's use an admittedly oversimplified example: You see a puppy. It's a bounding ball of adorable, furry fluff. Assuming you've had no negative past experiences or memories of puppies, the visual information is processed by the amygdala as happy and loving, prompting that emotion within you. You just want to cuddle that bundle of canine cuteness.

This memory is stamped by the amygdala with a metaphorical happy face.

Conversely, the sight of a growling, drooling, fang-bared wolf is going to trigger other memories and knowledge of fear and danger. The sight of that wolf provokes the emotion of fear, and its memory is stamped by the amygdala with a metaphorical red and fearful flag.

Animal and human studies have thoroughly proved this point. In the former, for example, scientists have found that electrical stimulation of an animal's amygdala triggers aggression while surgical removal results in indifferent emotional reactions.

In humans, there have been numerous published case studies of patients who have suffered lesions or damage to their amygdalae. The consequences usually fall into three main categories of impairment: The patients have difficulty forming memories of emotional events. They struggle or fail to mentally process and interpret facial and auditory expressions of emotion—a smile signifies nothing. Or they develop aberrant social behaviors, such as becoming overly aggressive.

Connected to the amygdala within the limbic system are other important structures, such as the hippocampus, which consolidates memories, shifting them from short-term to long-term. It works in tandem with the amygdala to ensure the formation of memories with emotional ties.

If your hippocampus (like the amygdala, there are a pair in the brain) were somehow damaged, you would struggle to live in the present. You wouldn't be able to make new memories and would be limited to only those memories formed prior to injury.

There are many such documented cases. Among the best known is the story of Henry Gustav Molaison, who died in 2008 at the age of 82. Known primarily in scientific circles as H.M., Molaison had begun suffering severe epileptic seizures when he was 10 years old. By the time he reached 20, the seizures were intolerable, and he underwent surgery in which bits of his temporal lobe, including the hippocampus, were removed. The procedure ended Molaison's seizures, but also his ability to effectively remember after the surgery. He functioned reasonably well in the moment, but he forgot names, places, events, and faces almost immediately after learning them. Half an hour after lunch, he couldn't recall what he had eaten, or that he had eaten at all. His face in the mirror was a constant surprise because he remembered only what he looked like as a young man. Every question was new, even those asked just minutes before.

When Molaison died, his brain was transferred to UC San Diego School of Medicine where neuroanatomist Jacopo Annese and colleagues froze it, then painstakingly dissected the brain into 2,401 thin slices of tissue, each subsequently digitized and archived to produce a three-dimensional, microscopic virtual model of H.M.'s whole brain for future study. In this way, a man who could not remember will never be forgotten.

We don't require dramatic cases like H.M., however, to appreciate the importance of the hippocampus to memory. Alzheimer's disease is characterized by the loss of memory, beginning with short-term memory. One of the first brain structures afflicted is the hippocampus.

A part of the limbic system is the hypothalamus, a small and somewhat indistinct structure that feeds information to the amygdala and helps regulate emotions, controlling levels of pleasure, aggression, and anger.

The cingulate cortex, a layer of tissue topping the limbic system, receives input from various parts of the brain, sorting out the information and helping the brain as a whole stay focused on an event and its emotional significance. In people with schizophrenia where emotions and perception may be profoundly impaired, some researchers have found that portions of the cingulate cortex are smaller compared to people with neurotypical brains without schizophrenia.

These different structures of the limbic system work together to form emotional memories, recall them when prompted, and trigger other parts of the body to produce appropriate or characteristic physiological responses, such as dilated eyes or trembling hands when afraid or a smile and laughter when happy.

As William James noted, emotions and their subsequent feelings are conjoined. They are also tempered by other parts of the brain, notably the prefrontal cortex, which employs cognitive processes like knowledge, judgment, and evaluation to assess a situation and figure out what the best thing to do is.

Humans and other primates have a striking capacity to learn and remember the emotional significance of diverse stimuli and events. Our cognitive capabilities allow us to assign and change *emotional valence*, a psychological term that describes how we characterize and categorize specific stimuli or events.

For example, a child may be initially terrified of dogs, perhaps for no obvious reason. But over time, if the child has positive experiences with dogs, his feelings or emotional valence toward them may change and improve. He may come to love them. Conversely, new romantic relationships often enjoy a euphoria of positive emotions. Happiness and desire abound. Neither partner can do wrong. But if the relationship sours and fails, if there is a nasty breakup, those emotions may be replaced by anger, anxiety, sadness, or tension. The two people involved are the same, but the emotions elicited are not.

This is the human condition. We live on a spectrum, with emotion at one end and reason at the other. Wisdom involves a balancing act between these two, called homeostasis.

The Nature of Homeostasis

Among scientists, *homeostasis* is a fancy word to describe the tendency of something to seek a relatively stable equilibrium between interdependent elements. You can see examples of it throughout nature, from organisms regulating their reproduction rates or distribution patterns to avoid the problems of overpopulation to biodiversity, which strengthens an ecosystem's resilience and adaptability.

Our bodies seek homeostasis too. We shiver and sweat, making or releasing heat, to help keep our internal temperature at a healthy 98.6 degrees Fahrenheit. The chemistry of our blood is a complicated balancing act too. The recipe of ingredients, including electrolytes like sodium, potassium, and calcium, must be maintained within distinct ranges, or health is harmed. One obvious example is glucose, or blood sugar. Low levels of glucose cause hypoglycemia, with a range of nasty symptoms, including in severe cases, seizures and death. High blood sugar levels result in hyperglycemia, most often seen in people with diabetes, worsening health in several different ways. A healthy norm is somewhere in between.

The human mind presents a different kind of balance, one between the evolutionarily older limbic system and the newer prefrontal cortex. Damage to the limbic system impairs processing of primary emotions, such as fear, anger, sadness, surprise, disgust, and happiness. Damage to the prefrontal cortices compromises executive functions. To be well, you need both to be working properly.

Wisdom is about melding emotions and reasoning in a way that benefits not just you, but also everybody who knows you and perhaps beyond. Emotional homeostasis is one of wisdom's primary components. It is the ability to respond to the ever-present and ongoing demands of experience—the mundane and profound challenges and changes of daily life—with a range of emotions suitable to social norms and expectations and that are sufficiently flexible to be spontaneous (limbic system) or delayed (prefrontal cortex).

Emotional regulation involves both you and others. It describes the mental and behavioral processes, often unconscious, that influence your feelings and those of others, such as when you do something enjoyable to cheer yourself up or when you offer soothing words to calm an anxious child.

No one wants to be like Mr. Spock, the fictional mixed human-Vulcan character of *Star Trek* fame, who viewed events only through the calculus of cold logic and acted accordingly. It's no wonder Spock never smiled. But neither do we want to wing it based solely on what we feel in the moment. We have all experienced times when our emotions got the best of us, when they took control of our actions to our regret and detriment. A person whose behaviors are driven primarily by emotions is unlikely to enjoy a happy and healthy life. Constant, unbounded joy sounds a lot like mania. Persistent, unaddressed feelings of anger, fear, or stress can be corrosive to both mental and physical health.

Chronic anger, for example, increases the risk of cardiac disease and stroke. It weakens the immune system. A Harvard University longitudinal study found that men who scored high on a hostility scale suffered significantly worse lung function. The study authors postulated that an uptick in stress hormones, which are associated with feelings of anger, caused damaging inflammation in the airways.

Chronic anger and stress are also strongly linked to depression. And shorter lives. A University of Michigan study found that over a 17-year period, married couples who held in their anger had shorter life spans than those who readily admitted when they were mad and did something about it.

We need to feel our emotions, but preferably in ways we can manage and that maximize their benefit.

Does Happiness Change in Later Life?

According to some reports, happiness in life follows a U-shaped curve.

From the relatively happy highs of youth, some surveys have noted that happiness plummets—or at least slides downward—describing a steady decline in happiness or life satisfaction that hits its nadir sometime around the early 50s. This is the so-called midlife crisis, when we often feel beset by responsibilities and problems, when we question what we have achieved and wonder if we have the time, resources, and ability to do better. Jonathan Rauch has written an excellent and encompassing book on the topic, called *The Happiness Curve: Why Life Gets Better After 50*.

The curve has also been reported in one study of other primates. A survey of zookeepers, researchers, and other caretakers of chimpanzees and orangutans found that the arc tracing their states of mind over time bottoms out in middle age.

"Our results," the authors conclude in a 2012 paper, "imply that human well-being's curved shape is not uniquely human and that, while it may be partly explained by aspects of human life and society, its origins may lie partly in the biology we share with closely related great apes."

My own research supports increasing mental well-being during the second half of life but shows a different trajectory during young adulthood. It suggests that the classical U-shaped curve of happiness reported in the past is today replaced by a steady increase in well-being from the 20s through 80s and sometimes 90s. Even if there may be some biological basis for a U-shaped curve of well-being, modern life's pressures and stresses in young adulthood might have changed the trajectory of happiness. Our SAGE study of about fifteen hundred people across the adult life span found that there is considerable unhappiness, stress, anxiety, and depression in the 20s. What is a fountain of youth for physical health, the 20s represent the bottomless pit of peer pressure and low self-esteem.

The good news is that time tends to bring self-improvement and a sense of better times. As we get older, we are better able to regulate our emotions, moderate problematic feelings, tamp down impulsive notions, and generally tap into our past experiences and lessons learned. This finding was recently replicated in a large study of thousands of Americans across the country, published in the *Journal of Abnormal Psychology*. We will revisit this scenario in a later chapter.

My colleague and friend Laura Carstensen and others have shown that older adults recall relatively more positive images and fewer negative images than younger adults. It's not a question of memory, but emphasis. Positive pictures, stories, and events simply resonate more as we grow older and wiser. Some of this is likely a matter of biology. In older brains, the amygdala activates equally to positive and negative input. In younger brains, negative input seems to get an extra boost, which may help explain the phenomenon of teenage angst. These findings do suggest that older adults encode less information about negative images, which in turn means they are less likely to recall negative memories or feelings, a neurological nod to the notion of rose-colored glasses.

There is also some research to suggest pleasant emotions fade more slowly from memory than unpleasant emotions, maybe because we try harder to minimize memories of negative impacts in life.

Stress, Optimism, and Resilience

All our studies have shown that wisdom is associated with lower levels of perceived (subjective) stress along with greater optimism and resilience.

Numerous investigations have also shown that optimism and resilience are associated, not just with a happier life, but also a healthier life. These traits help reduce stress and its debilitating consequences.

Stress is an unavoidable fact of life, starting with the prosaic rigors of getting to school or work on time. Fundamentally, stress is supposed to be a good thing, a warning signal or call to action. Low-level stressors stimulate production of neurotrophins, a family of proteins that promote development and function of neurons and their interconnections.

A bit of occasional stress can boost concentration and productivity. Short-term stress also increases production of interleukins, the chemicals that help regulate the immune system and that provide a *temporary* defensive boost in immunity. However, chronic stress is associated with immune system suppression, musculoskeletal disorders, respiratory conditions, insomnia, cardiovascular disease, and gastrointestinal problems.

Yet, learning to deal with stressful situations makes you, well, better at dealing with stressful situations. It toughens you up, increases your resilience.

In our ongoing SAGE study, we have found that older adults who say they are "aging successfully"—that is, they are content with their situation in life—generally report greater optimism and resilience.

We all know family and friends who are irrepressibly optimistic. Some of that may be acquired by enduring the vicissitudes of life, but there's also a biological basis. Neuroimaging has shown that in healthy, optimistic adults, the orbitofrontal cortex (OFC), located just behind the eyes, is larger. One of the roles of the OFC is to regulate susceptibility to anxiety.

Brains of older, optimistic adults may simply see less to worry about. In a 2014 study, my colleagues and I used fMRI to look at the brains of cognitively healthy older adults as they matched images of faces expressing one of the three primary emotions—happiness, anger, and fear—with one of two other images on a computer screen. The testing involved several images shown multiple times in relatively quick succession.

We found that mental processing of fearful faces activated a widespread network, including the frontal regions of the brain and the fusiform gyrus, whose primary function seems to be facial recognition. But interestingly, participants who had previously tested as being more optimistic showed less activity in the fusiform gyrus and other brain regions than did less optimistic people. Put another way, the brains of optimistic people simply responded less forcibly to fearful faces. This might mean they put less mental stock in negative emotional information—a fearful face and what that might portend—or that they possessed better emotional regulation.

Resilience—that is, the capacity to recover from trauma, tragedy, or adversity—is one of the great measures of every man, woman, and child. Resilience is a complex product of genetic, environmental, psychological, biological, social, and spiritual factors. It involves, among other things, a remarkably complicated interplay between the sympathetic nervous system—the ebb and flow of hormones like epinephrine and cortisol—and robust activation of the prefrontal cortex to inhibit the amygdala and associated feelings of anxiety and fear.

In a study published in the *Journal of Clinical Psychiatry*, my colleagues and I looked at childhood adversity and the protective role of resilience.

We studied 114 people with diagnosed schizophrenia and 110 normal controls. All participants took a regimen of tests and scales to assess their health, exposure to childhood trauma, and degree of resilience.

In both groups, childhood trauma was associated with worse mental and physical health and also high insulin resistance, a risk factor for diabetes and heart disease. But people, including those with schizophrenia, who scored high on resilience, had better mental and physical health, including a normal level of insulin resistance, even when they had experienced adversity in childhood. There is not much that we can do retroactively to adversities that occurred decades ago during childhood. However, we can use interventions to enhance resilience at any age, including older age. This enhanced resilience in later life can potentially overcome some of the long-term adverse effects of childhood trauma.

Who Doesn't Like Marshmallows?

One of wisdom's more notable characteristics is self-restraint. It's a fundamental tenet of most religions. Thou shalt resist temptation, the Bible admonishes many times in many contexts. Islam preaches that self-control is a way to happiness. Resisting the easy is Hindu dharma.

It's also a common principle of philosophy—and pop culture.

"For fools rush in where angels fear to tread" was first written by Alexander Pope, the 18th-century English poet, in his 1711 poem "An Essay on Criticism," but it's also a line sung by Frank Sinatra, Doris Day, Etta James, Elvis Presley, The Four Freshmen, Cliff Richard, and Norah Jones.

But as essential as self- or impulse control is to wisdom, it's equally hard to obtain or maintain. Understanding how it manifests itself in our brains is a major step to better managing it in our lives. Philosophers have ruminated on the topic for centuries; scientists considerably less. One way to tell the story of their investigation is to begin with a spongy confection made primarily of sugar, water, and gelatin.

It's called "the marshmallow test," and it may be the most famous experiment in the history of modern psychology, spawning headlines and numerous subsequent studies, cited from Wall Street to Sesame Street.

In the early 1960s, a psychologist named Walter Mischel and colleagues were curious about how children made choices. How did they control conflicting thoughts and emotions when making decisions, especially younger children still unfettered by behaviors they would learn later?

At the time, Mischel was a professor of psychology at Stanford University. He conducted his experiment at nearby Bing Nursery School, where his team set up a table and chair in a private room. On the table, a single marshmallow was placed; then a child, four or five years old, was brought into the room and asked to sit at the table. Not surprisingly, the lone marshmallow did not go unnoticed.

Next, an adult—someone who was quite familiar to the child and thus trusted—offered this deal: The adult must leave the room for a short while. If the child refrained from eating the marshmallow while the adult was away, the child would be rewarded with a second marshmallow when the adult returned. If the child ate the first marshmallow before the adult returned, there would be no second marshmallow.

Then the adult left for 15 minutes. A hidden camera documented what happened next, though it's easy enough to guess: Some kids gobbled down the marshmallow as soon as the adult was gone. Others wiggled and squirmed and generally fussed as they struggled to restrain their white-hot marshmallow desires. Most quickly gave into temptation and ate the treat. Only a few children successfully endured the entire wait, marshmallow untouched.

Mischel and colleagues conducted this test on hundreds of children, sometimes with marshmallows, sometimes with other objects of desire or interest, such as a pretzel, mint, or even different colored poker chips. The wait time was increased. In 1972, Mischel and colleagues published their findings in the *Journal of Personality and Social Psychology.*

The marshmallow experiment was a creative exploration of childhood decision-making behaviors. It spawned decades of subsequent inquiry, often with enormous implications. For the next 40 or so years, Mischel and collaborators followed their child subjects. They expanded testing to include demographics beyond the preschool progeny of Stanford faculty (a small and narrow demographic) to look at, for example, the behaviors of children living in high-stress poverty conditions in the South Bronx.

The findings remained startlingly universal. In all demographics, young children who did not eat the first marshmallow tended to grow up having higher SAT scores, lower likelihoods of substance abuse or obesity, better responses to stress, better social skills (according to their parents), and generally better scores on a range of life metrics. The ability to delay gratification appeared to be a significant predictor of success.

Experts of all stripes have opined on the findings. Ivy League business schools created new models based on the importance of delayed gratification. The children's television show *Sesame Street* aired segments featuring Cookie Monster learning about the benefits of inhibiting urges. The lesson was always the same: a marshmallow not munched in the moment suggested maybe a sweeter life to come, Freud's principles of pleasure and reality come to life.

Measuring Emotions and Emotional Regulation

It might seem like an easy thing to identify and measure an emotion. After all, a face with furled brows, glaring eyes, flared nostrils, and downturned lips paints a pretty obvious picture of an angry person. So obvious, in fact, that other species like your pet dog can quickly recognize your emotional demeanor, without you uttering a harsh word.

But measuring a person's emotional state, at least in empirical terms, is quite vexing. People are good at hiding or disguising emotions if they want to. Emotional cues don't always carry the same weight with different observers or the same meaning. A smile is a common facial expression across cultures, but while Americans smile freely at strangers, Russians consider it impolite. And in some Asian cultures, a smile may be more of an expression of embarrassment than friendliness. Nodding one's head vigorously up and down means "yes" in some places and "no" in others.

Scientifically measuring emotion involves not just possessing a consensual model of emotions (does anger look the same to everyone?) but determining if the process of stimulus to regions of the brain and the resulting behavior are the same for all humans, or at least most humans. It involves exploring how people actually experience things, what their bodies do in response, and what emotions are triggered.

There is no best way to measure emotions, but there are many ways to do it.

Self-reports are useful and often broadly revealing, but they may be hindered by issues like bias or memory recall.

There are autonomic measures, such as detecting emotional responses based on physiological responses like sweating or increased heart rate. These are bodily functions that cannot be consciously controlled, but it's hard to pin them precisely to a discrete emotion. A person's heartbeat can race for joy or in fear.

Behaviors provide clues. People tend to act out in broadly similar ways to the same stimuli, such as voices rising with arousal. Charles Darwin influentially noted the existence of universal facial expressions to represent basic emotions, at least among those he studied: a smile for happiness, a frown for anger. Paul Ekman at UC San

Francisco showed members of a Stone Age culture in New Guinea, people who had seen few if any outsiders and no media portrayal of emotion, a series of pictures of peoples' faces depicting different emotions. They identified them with the same emotions that a millennial living in downtown Manhattan would.

Naturally, there are subtleties. A smile is meant to convey a particular emotion, but perhaps not its motivation or underlying intent. People smile with glee, but also with sarcasm or cruelty. We must learn how to tell the difference to take truer measure of a smile's meaning.

Happy Has a Home

The 2015 Pixar film *Inside Out* recounts the life and times of a young girl named Riley, in particular, her big move at age 11 from Minnesota to San Francisco with her parents, and the not-unexpected trials and tribulations of dealing with a new house, new school, new friends, new challenges, new fears, disappointments, and triumphs.

Most of the action takes place in Riley's head, involving five highly animated emotions: Fear, Anger, Disgust, Sadness, and Joy. Each is visually and behaviorally distinct. Joy, for example, is a glowing, tireless pixie. Sadness is a downcast, slow-moving blue girl in a frumpy sweater. Anger is constantly agitated, blustering, with a red face and flaming hair. Riley's emotions work together—or not—at a button-festooned console in the neurological control room of her brain. As movie critic A. O. Scott noted, they do their jobs with the "bickering bonhomie of workplace sitcom colleagues."

Connected to the control room are other imaginary structures, such as islands of core values powered by core memories. The latter are stored in towering stacks or fly through space. Each memory is a colored sphere, depending on its emotional content and context. A joyful memory gleams yellow; one of disgust glows green.

It's a fabulous and fanciful interpretation of how emotions work, but it's pretty accurate in the broad scheme of things. While there isn't anything like a single neurological control room in the brain, there are distinct regions of the brain with rather specific functions, as I discussed in chapter 2.

In all animals, primary emotions are located in the brain's limbic system. More advanced species have added a countering complexity, the prefrontal cortex. Different parts of its twin lobes help us do different things. The lateral prefrontal cortex, for example, appears to help us choose the appropriate behavior from a variety of options. The orbitofrontal cortex helps us defer immediate gratification and suppress certain emotions in favor of greater long-term benefits. The ventromedial cortex is thought to be one of the sites where we experience emotions and the meanings of things.

The PFC also has regulatory roles, controlling levels of dopamine, norepinephrine, and serotonin—three neurotransmitters that are important in mood regulation. Neurotransmitters are chemical messengers. They transmit signals across the synapse, or junction, between two nerve cells. It's not known exactly how many types of neurotransmitters exist, but more than one hundred have been uniquely identified. Dopamine, norepinephrine, and serotonin are well known because they do important work.

Everybody has heard of dopamine. It's been described as the molecule behind all our most sinful behaviors and secret cravings. The actual effects of dopamine depend on the types of cells and cellular receptors involved. For example, Parkinson's disease, which is characterized by progressive loss of motor control, is caused by the brain's declining ability to produce dopamine. With less and less dopamine, a person has less and less ability to regulate their movements, body, and emotions. In advanced stages, it progresses to cognitive impairment and dementia.

But dopamine is also a key messenger in the parts of the brain associated with reward-motivated behavior, such as the ventral tegmental area and dorsal striatum, though in truth, many parts of the brain play a part in recognizing reward and pleasure.

When you feel rewarded or pleased, dopamine levels rise, which in turn motivates you to do things that will extend or repeat the sensations of reward and pleasure. That can be a good thing. If you do a good deed and are warmly thanked, one effect may be a little jolt of dopamine in your brain, which makes you feel good and perhaps motivates you to do another good deed. The downside of high levels of dopamine is that they can become addictive. Some drugs, like cocaine and amphetamines, boost levels of dopamine and your desire for more. These kinds of addictions do not often end well.

Norepinephrine is the action neurotransmitter. In the brain, its general function is prompt activity elsewhere. It increases arousal and alertness, promotes vigilance, and boosts memory making and recall. It also can increase restlessness and anxiety. Levels of norepinephrine are lowest during sleep, rise during wakefulness, and spike during stress or danger. It's the trigger for the fight-or-flight response, boosting heart rate, blood pressure, and blood flow to skeletal muscles.

The vast majority of the body's supply of serotonin is located in the gut, where it is used to regulate intestinal movements. In the brain, serotonin is a mood stabilizer, moderating feelings like anxiety and happiness. Low levels have been associated with depression. Serotonin also moderates sleeping and waking, depending on the parts of the brain stimulated and the serotonin receptors involved—there are more than a dozen.

All of these neurotransmitters have been the target and basis for many drugs designed to remedy their diminished absence or damaging overabundance. For example, the drug levodopa is converted in the brain into dopamine. It's the first line of treatment for Parkinson's disease. It doesn't cure the condition, but it can dramatically slow its progressive symptoms. Norepinephrine, meanwhile, is used in medications to treat people with very low blood pressure. And drugs that alter serotonin levels are employed to treat depression, nausea, and migraines.

Most of the blockbuster drugs of the past few decades that affect brain function, from Prozac and Zoloft to Risperdal and Abilify, have focused on boosting neurotransmitters like serotonin or blocking receptors for neurotransmitters like dopamine. If they are successful, they do one thing well, such as reduce depression.

Genetics of Emotions

In some ways, we are defined by our physical characteristics. Tall or short, thin or heavyset, with curly dark hair or straight blond tresses, our individual combinations of physical attributes, largely inherited, help set us apart from every other member of the species.

Emotionality too has a strong basis in genetics. Scientists have associated specific genes to specific aspects of emotion processing. There is a gene called ADRA2B, for example, which influences the neurotransmitter norepinephrine. Researchers have found that variants of ADRA2B change the way people see the world. Specifically, in neuroimaging studies, carriers of the deletion variant gene showed greater attention to emotionally relevant pictures and words. The evoked emotions were stronger and more vivid. They packed a greater punch, and carriers responded accordingly. This may be part of the reason the same experience can prompt little more than a shrug in one person but cause another to feel the urge to sing, dance, or write a love sonnet.

Other genetic factors, such as variations of the serotonin neurotransmitter, affect the dynamics of voice processing, how we derive meaning from other people's speech. Researchers have found that genetic variation influences how people process what they hear—and whether it evokes positive or negative emotions.

Of course, genetics do not entirely dictate our emotional destiny any more than they determine our absolute level of intelligence or physical abilities. Environmental factors play big roles too. We can learn to control our emotions, manage them, use them, and enjoy them, just as Wilde hoped to do.

Fitting Image

Neuroimaging is perhaps the most advanced and penetrating method available today to measure both form and function, from the brain's three-dimensional anatomy to its chemistry, physiology, and electrical and metabolic activity.

Computed tomography (CT) scans are oblique X-ray slices that show the density of brain structures. Magnetic resonance imaging (MRI) uses changes in electrically charged molecules in a magnetic field to form images of the brain. They help researchers map brain regions associated with different behaviors, often by studying people with specific brain traumas.

Functional MRI (fMRI) tracks changes in blood flow and oxygen levels to indicate neural activity. The thinking is simple enough: when a particular part of the brain is more active, it consumes more oxygen, and blood flow increases. Early fMRI studies focused on mapping activity to identify cognitive functions in different brain regions, such as labeling areas associated with visual language or memory. But as technology has advanced, it has become more precise. FMRI can now characterize brain function at the level of neural processes.

FMRI is currently the most prominent neuroimaging technology, but there are others.

Diffusion tensor imaging (DTI) uses a regular MRI machine to track how water molecules move in and around fibers connecting different parts of the brain. The resulting image can depict a 3D brain composed of multicolored spaghetti strands. DTI measures thickness and density of neural connections.

Electroencephalography (EEG) records the brain's electrical waves to detect abnormal activity, such as in seizures and sleep disorders. Positron-emission tomography (PET) scans use radioactive tags to show which brain areas become active when someone performs a task.

Once, physicians and scientists intent on probing the human brain were limited to asking questions, observing behaviors, and making informed deductions—or perhaps just educated guesses. Hands-on investigation required either biopsy or death and autopsy of the brain, both quite uncommon at present.

Neuroimaging technologies have opened the black box of the brain without requiring a surgical saw or the death of the person. They have shown how intensive reading instruction improves the functioning of a child's brain; how key regions in the brains of people with schizophrenia don't communicate well with each other, jumbling the person's thoughts and perceptions; and why true love isn't true without the neurotransmitter dopamine.

In my own work, with Lisa Eyler and Abdullah Sherzai, we have looked at how preserved cognitive performance is a key feature of successful aging. Not surprisingly, increased brain responsiveness measured by neuroimaging is associated with better cognitive performance, especially in the frontal cortex. If the frontal cortex continues to work normally and well in older age, if it remains relatively robust in size and function, so too do the mental processes of older people.

Like the rest of our bodies, age takes its toll on the brain. Cells die; processes slow. But our brains retain some plasticity even in later life—a relatively recent discovery. Our brains find ways to work with what they've got. Older minds develop work-arounds for challenging mental tasks that were once easy. In some ways, and sometimes, they do them better. This is part and parcel of wisdom.

Scientists using neuroimaging can watch and record the mental stages people go through as they solve math problems, second by second. They can capture the psychological and neurological processes involved in emotion, pain, self-regulation, self-perception, and perception of others.

The findings are often surprising. A fixation on one's physical appearance is a hallmark of narcissism, but when Austrian researchers in 2017 asked subjects diagnosed as highly narcissistic to look at images of themselves while in an MRI machine, the areas of their brains that activated were associated with emotional distress, not gratification. In particular, they displayed increased activation in the dorsal and ventral anterior cingulate cortex—the latter known to be involved in the processing of negative self-referential material.

Neuroimaging is neither perfect nor absolute. Assertions in scientific journals or popular media that a particular part of the brain is responsible for a singular talent, memory, or emotion have sometimes been premature, based on tentative or minimal data, or may require verification or validation.

The brain's complexity and interconnectedness create much room for debate. The insula, for example, becomes activated by feelings of disgust, but also when processing taste information or procedural memories. Nonetheless it reveals in real time the biology of thought.

It is our job to parse and interpret the fruits of neuroimaging—and every other measurement tool we have. None of these measures can do the entire job alone. There is no single gold standard to measuring emotions or emotional states. But in combination and convergence, they can tell scientists a lot.

The Perils of Acting Rashly, Again and Again

Just as chronic stress or anger are bad for your health, so too is habitual impulsiveness, whether it's spontaneously buying the newest iPhone (studies suggest we'll "accidentally" damage or lose our current and functional model simply to justify the purchase of a new phone—a behavior dubbed the "must-have effect") or conduct that is overtly risky and dangerous, like deciding on a whim to go skydiving without preparation.

Numerous studies have linked impulsiveness to higher risks of smoking, drinking, and drug abuse. It's associated with psychological ailments, from attention deficit hyperactivity disorder to binge eating, which belongs to the same class of disorders that includes shoplifting, promiscuity, and drug addiction.

My colleagues at UC San Diego School of Medicine have found that the brains of people with a history of bulimia nervosa, an eating disorder characterized by frequent episodes of binge eating followed by purging attempts to avoid weight gain, respond differently to food reward signals. Specifically, they found that the left insula, putamen, and amygdala in the brains of binge eaters displayed elevated activity in response to taste. In experiments, individuals with no history of bulimia responded to taste more when they were hungry than when they were satiated. Conversely, food reward signals in the brains of people with the disorder were the same whether the binge eater was hungry or not.

Brain injury has been linked to problems with impulse control as well. Recall that after his traumatic injury with the exploding tamping rod, mild-mannered Phineas Gage became fitful, profane, and impatient.

Some of the ability to self-regulate impulsiveness is genetic. For example, a gene labeled MAOA directs the body to produce an enzyme called monoamine oxidase A (MAO-A), which in turn

129

reduces the activity of the mood-modifying neurotransmitter sero-tonin. Variations in MAOA have been found to influence impulsive aggression, resilience, and optimism.

But impulse control seems to be a behavior you learn and can unlearn over time. The impulsiveness of youth reflects an imbal-ance between the limbic system and the PFC. The former manages our incentive processing system, which activates when we anticipate and process rewards and punishments, plus social and emotional processing. The latter is charged with managing the former, apply-ing reason as a tempering agent.

Around puberty, the part of our brains that focuses on rewards and punishments becomes supercharged, heightening the desire for sensation seeking, risk-taking, and seemingly irresponsible, inexplicable behaviors. In other words, the description of a typical teenager.

It will be a few years before development of the moderating PFC catches up. The teenage brain is a bit like a race car with dubious brakes. The incentive processing system hits the accelerator around age 14. The cognitive control system needed to slow things down won't fully kick in until the early to mid-20s.

Emotional Life

More than half a century after he made it, Martin Luther King Jr.'s "I Have a Dream" speech remains transcendent, a pow-erful and inspiring call to action that spoke directly to the roughly quarter of a million individuals surrounding him at the Lincoln Memorial on that August day in 1963, but also to many, many millions more who heard or read the speech later, then and now.

King was a master of emotional intelligence. He used powerful words to convey powerful emotions, such as *withering*, *vicious*, and *unspeakable*. Halfway through his prepared remarks, King went off script, prompted by the renowned gospel singer Mahalia Jackson, who was standing off to the side. "Tell them about the dream, Martin!" she cried.

And so he did, in rhetoric that soared like Jackson's voice, but also in ways that guided and managed his listeners' emotions. He spoke of deep injustices, outrage, and pain but also of a "struggle on the high plane of dignity and discipline." Physical force should be met with soul force, he said, and anger and despair by hope, pride, joy, and exaltation.

Life constantly tugs at our emotions, with euphoric highs and depressive lows. Emotional extremes, though, are almost never good—at least for long-term health and well-being. King's speech is a discrete, historical example of managing emotions in the service of a greater vision. The tennis great Billie Jean King's struggles for respect, gender equity, and the rights of LGBTQ people (long before anybody had even conjured the acronym for lesbian, gay, bisexual, transgender, and queer/questioning) is an example of quieter emotional stability.

Billie Jean Moffitt took up tennis at the age of 11. She worked hard and quickly became a star in professional women's tennis. As good as King was, she was not paid comparably to male tennis players. No woman was. "Promoters were making more money than women. Male tennis players were making more money. Everybody was making more money except the women," King once reportedly said. In fact, the International Lawn Tennis Foundation (now the

International Tennis Foundation) actually dropped women's competition in tournaments it presided over to focus on more lucrative male events.

With King leading the charge, a group of female players formed the Women's Tennis Association. The fight for equal prize money and recognition did not come easily. King's notorious "Battle of the Sexes" tennis match with Bobby Riggs, who publicly celebrated his chauvinism, is well remembered and noted, but she persevered in many other ways over many years, fighting in courts of law and public opinion for women's rights, including Title IX, the federal law that prohibits gender discrimination in high school and collegiate athletic programs.

"My whole life has been about equal rights and opportunities," King said. "For me, it really goes back to the health of mind, body, and soul."

King's fight for gender equality was no doubt grueling, often punctuated with moments of disappointment, frustration, and anger that she needed to control and manage. That fight was public; less so were her struggles with her sexuality.

Billie Jean wed Larry King at age 20 in 1965, and in public at least, they portrayed a happy marriage. But King was attracted to women, a reality she struggled first to accept and then to hide from the public, which at the time still considered homosexuality among the greatest of taboos.

In 1981, King was publicly outed. Her lawyer and other advisers urged her to not admit the truth, but King, at the age of 38, decided it was time to be truthful. She still wasn't entirely comfortable being gay—that wouldn't come for another decade or so—but she was tired of the subterfuge.

"Tennis taught me so many lessons in life," King said. "One of the things it taught me is that every ball that comes to me, I have to make a decision. I have to accept responsibility for the consequences every time I hit a ball."

King owned up and owned the cause, becoming a leader and mentor in the LGBTQ movement. In 2013, President Barack Obama appointed King and Caitlin Cahow, an openly gay ice hockey player, as US representatives at the 2014 Winter Olympics in Sochi, Russia—a move seen as a pro-gay rights signal to a country well-known for LGBTQ rights abuses.

"Champions keep playing until they get it right," said King.

Emotional stability is similar to resilience. Emotionally stable people keep their balance because they keep perspective. They put emotions to use and in their place. The world of athletics is, of course, an obvious arena in which to watch this crucial competition. Tony Romo, the former Dallas Cowboys quarterback-turned-sportscaster, retired in 2016 with an emotional farewell speech.

"I feel like we all have two battles or two enemies going on. One with the man across from you. The second is with the man inside of you. I think once you control the one inside of you, the one across from you really doesn't matter."

Life is like that too. If your car breaks down, it can seem disastrous until you remember that (1) others have been in worse situations, and (2) the vast majority of people in the world don't even own a car.

It's not a smooth ride. Expecting life to be so almost guarantees every pothole will feel like driving off a cliff. Most problems, upsets, and crises are temporary. You can fix a car. You can do your best to try to fix your life.

Can There Be Too Much Emotional Self-Control?

Emotions do more than just give meaning; they prescribe action. Fear can lead to fight, flight, or fright. But when emotions run amok, unburdened by reason, bad things tend to happen. It's not a good idea to punch somebody in the nose in a fit of spontaneous anger or scream unfiltered profanities without a second (or first) thought. Surgeons must develop the emotional controls necessary to steel themselves at the sight of copious amounts of blood and viscera; soldiers on the battlefield must do the same.

Every culture across time and around the world has its adages, maxims, admonitions, and stories intended to impart important lessons about controlling one's emotions, about thinking before acting. For most of us, most of the time, our PFC tempers our unthinking urges, saving us from our primordial limbic selves.

But one can swing too far in the other direction as well. Excessive emotional control can suppress natural, normal, and necessary expression. It can devolve into depression. It can send unintended or erroneous signals to others, as it did in a fateful 1988 presidential campaign debate between George H. W. Bush and Michael Dukakis.

In his first question to Dukakis, debate moderator Bernard Shaw asked, "If Kitty Dukakis were raped and murdered, would you favor an irrevocable death penalty for the killer?"

By specifically making Dukakis's wife a hypothetical rape and murder victim, Shaw purposefully crafted an intensely personal, not to mention dramatic and theatrical, opening to the debate. But Dukakis appeared unfazed by the question. He stood unflinching, with a quick reply devoid of emotion: "No, I don't, Bernard. And I think you know that I've opposed the death penalty during all of my life. I don't see any evidence that it's a deterrent, and I think there are better and more effective ways to deal with violent crime."

As a dry statement of policy and fact, Dukakis's answer was fine. But Dukakis's dispassionate answer—the clear product of a robust PFC—aroused a storm of criticism and negativity. After the debate, during a different interview with Shaw, Dukakis brought up the question again. It was fair and reasonable, Dukakis said to Shaw, but he wished he had answered differently.

"Kitty is probably the most—is the most—precious thing, she and my family, that I have in this world," Dukakis said. "And, obviously, if what happened to her was the kind of thing you described, I would have the same feelings as any loving husband."

For most people, though, too much emotional regulation is not the problem. It's the opposite: too little emotional control leading to social problems. Researchers have thus focused on developing interventions to boost emotional regulation.

Impulse Control and the Art of Boosting Emotional Regulation

Decades after his first marshmallow test, Mischel and colleagues published a 2010 paper in the journal *Social Cognitive and Affective Neuroscience* seeking to make sense of and elucidate their observations that the ability to delay gratification predicted greater success in life.

They concluded that kids able to resist temptation in favor of long-term goals used distinct strategies. They redirected their attention. They focused on something else. Even just looking away from the alluring object was effective. They reframed the object of their desire from "hot" to "cool." Instead of looking at the marshmallow as a sweet, delectable treat, they imagined it as an inedible cotton ball or bit of insubstantial cloud. Focusing on nonconsummatory traits, such as the shape of the marshmallow, rather than its consummatory features (yummy, sweet, chewy taste) greatly strengthened children's willpower, Mischel concluded.

Life presents much greater challenges than resisting marshmallows. The need to regulate our emotions and related urges is daily and constant, but there are also lots of common strategies that can be used, such as talking with friends, exercising, writing in a journal, meditation, getting adequate sleep, noticing when you need a break, and paying attention to negative thoughts.

Just as there has been much research investigating the neurological drivers of self-control, there has been a commensurate amount of activity to find ways to boost it, especially in people with diagnosed disorders, such as addictions.

The research has been wide-ranging and creative. For example, Spanish scientists have used video games to modify behaviors in patients with severe cases of gambling disorder. The video games require players to use problem-solving, planning, and self-control skills to prevail. Researchers found that while playing the games, regions of the brain responsible for self-control and emotional homeostasis were activated, and the players exhibited less impulsivity and anger expression afterward. The games themselves were not enough to ensure long-lasting therapeutic improvement, but they could be another useful tool.

Emotional regulation training is broadly used in the treatment of a variety of disorders and conditions, including borderline personality disorder, a complex and severe condition characterized by impulsive actions and unstable relationships that usually first appears in adolescence. It tends to be a reliable predictor for other psychosocial dysfunctions later in life and related social impairment, poorer health, and lower life satisfaction.

There are three main strategies for improving emotional regulation:

COGNITIVE REAPPRAISAL. This is a deliberate, forceful effort to reinterpret the meaning of something. Let's say you failed a test.

Your first emotional response may be anger, sadness, dismay, and other negative emotions, but if you pause, step back, and reappraise the situation, the test results can be reinterpreted as a positive call to action, a challenge to be overcome through revised or renewed efforts. You look at where you went wrong on the test and then fix those errors. More importantly, it could help you prevent future failures.

DISTRACTION. Some of the children in Mischel's marshmallow tests used distraction. Research has found that when people change the focus of their attention, it can reduce the intensity of painful or emotional experiences and alleviate distress. For example, instead of focusing on something difficult or unpleasant, think about your loved one's upcoming birthday party.

LABELING. When you recognize an emotion and give it a name, you can more easily control it and manage it more thoughtfully. Psychotherapists often use this technique. It's not unlike fixing something at home. Once you've identified the problem—a leaky pipe or faulty electrical connection—you can figure out how to repair it or make it better.

Certainty in an Uncertain World

The sixth-century Chinese poet Lao-tzu once said that "those who have knowledge, don't predict. And those who predict, don't have knowledge." It's a timeless and indisputably wise observation. Life is unpredictable, and prediction, joked Danish physicist and Nobel laureate Niels Bohr some fifteen hundred years after Lao-tzu, is very difficult, especially if it's about the future.

Living well and wisely requires knowledge: the pragmatic, procedural, and factual kind that is necessary to successfully negotiate life's vagaries and vicissitudes, from communicating effectively to negotiating with the Department of Motor Vehicles, and the larger knowledge that nothing is certain, that what was once true or what once worked might not be true or work in the future.

In the next chapter, we explore these interconnected components of wisdom: the kinds of general and practical knowledge needed to make decisions, the acceptance of uncertainty in life, and the ability to act decisively in the face of uncertainty. We will look at where these abilities are located in the brain, how they are measured, and what you can do to improve them and become wiser.

It's time to act. Turn the page.

Balancing Decisiveness with Acceptance of Uncertainty

It does not take much strength to do things, but it requires a great deal of strength to decide what to do.
ELBERT HUBBARD,
American philosopher

Uncertainty is the only certainty there is, and knowing how to live with insecurity is the only security.
JOHN ALLEN PAULOS,
American mathematics professor

AS A PHYSICIAN, I have spent a career making judgments and sometimes hard choices. My decisions impact patients' health and lives. It usually comes down to this: what is the best treatment for the diagnosis I have made regarding a particular patient at a particular moment in time? Typically, there are many differential diagnoses to rule out, based on symptoms and exam. The best treatment must be culled from multiple options. Often, there is no single perfect or obvious answer. A physician must make his or her call in that moment, but must keep an open mind and flexibility to change it later. This is a big part of wisdom in health care. For patients too.

Similar considerations apply to other professions, but wisdom in professional or occupational decision-making does not necessarily translate to wise decision-making elsewhere in life. We have all seen or heard stories of businesspeople, politicians, artists, judges, or social leaders celebrated for their public successes and achievements who have fallen far and hard from their pedestals, often due to poor choices they made in other parts of their lives. These revelations may cause us to question whether they are truly wise.

Aristotle recognized two kinds of wisdom. Theoretical wisdom, or *sophia*, involves understanding the deep nature of reality and humans' place in it. It's the heady stuff pursued by folks like Socrates, Buddha, and philosophers over millennia. Practical wisdom, or *phronesis*, is more routine and grounded, more akin to making good decisions in daily life—doing the right thing, at the right time, for the right reasons. It's an ability valued in nearly every culture and setting across the centuries.

One of the most prominent among the books of the Bible is the Song of Solomon, best known for Solomon's impartial decision-making. The "Word of Wisdom" in The Church of Jesus Christ of Latter-day Saints (Mormons) is a compendium of guidelines, rules, strictures, and advice about behaving wisely and in conformance with church expectations.

In many parts of the world, there are village elders who provide answers or guidance in cases of conflicts. The Supreme Court of the United States is a larger, more formal illustration of that approach: nine people esteemed for their intelligence and wisdom, asked to resolve our thorniest national questions or problems.

We revere wisdom, elevating those who possess it, whether parent, civic leader, or fictional wizard. These are people with special abilities who have great capacity to determine what is right and best. They are deemed exceptional and perhaps reside on a plane above most of us.

But the need to make wise decisions is common and occurs every day. All of us do it.

Do you go to work with a cold to finish a crucial project, even though you risk infecting your coworkers? Do you tell your spouse an outfit is hideous when asked? Is it okay to laugh at an offensive joke?

Your brain makes dozens of true/false, yes/no decisions every second through chemical reactions. Electric neuronal impulses speed through your brain at 120 meters per second, the rough equivalent of covering an American football field in two blinks of an eye. Neurons and other brain cells act and interact in fractions of time to form connections and circuits that transform into larger thoughts, conscious or not.

More complicated decisions are obviously fewer in number, but still multitudinous. It's popularly reported that adults make approximately thirty-five thousand conscious decisions each day (compared to three thousand for a child). Thirty-five thousand choices in a day seems like a wildly speculative number, but even half that number underscores the necessity of making many decisions on a constant basis in all manner of circumstances.

A Day for Dilemmas

Like building muscles or becoming more resilient, learning to make decisions better or more wisely requires practice and testing limits. On Sundays, one of my favorite diversions is to read a feature in the *New York Times Magazine* called The Ethicist, in which readers submit questions about real-life moral dilemmas. Originally, it was a panel of "experts," usually a professor of philosophy, a psychotherapist, and a law professor, who responded to questions. More recently, the queries are singularly answered by Kwame Anthony Appiah, a highly regarded professor of philosophy at New York University.

The dilemmas are large and small, often seemingly mundane, though upon pondering, profoundly confounding:

May I lie to my husband to get him to see a doctor?

How do I counter my sister's abuse claims against our father?

Can I hire someone to write my résumé and cover letter?

The ethicists' answers are thoughtful and concise. Sometimes the different ethicists agree; sometimes they do not. In the case of getting the husband to the doctor, for example, all of the ethicists offered versions of the same advice: The older husband appeared to be in the early stages of dementia but refused to see a doctor. They universally opined that, assuming the wife had attempted all forms of persuasion, it was important that she do what needed to be done, that in cases of Alzheimer's, "the organ that's making the judgment is the organ that's potentially impaired. So in fact at some point it may not only be ethically *permissible*, but ethically *required* for you to make that decision."

The other questions were pricklier. The ethicists were unsure what to make of both the sister's tales of an abusive father and her skeptical family members' insistence that they must be untrue because no one else had witnessed or experienced them. What seemed clear was that communication in this troubled family was fractured—and before anything else could happen, everybody needed to sit down and listen to one another.

The résumé dilemma was not the most dramatic of dilemmas, but it prompted the most diverse debate: Is it misleading to present a résumé that displays the writing or organizational skills of another? Does it show you're smart enough to enlist the aid of others? Or maybe all a good résumé reveals is the ability to produce a good résumé, which may or may not have anything to do with the job? There was no conclusive answer.

We may or may not agree with a professional ethicist's answer or reasoning. Indeed, we may have an entirely different opinion on any particular dilemma. The responses recounted above were based on the limited information the *Times*' ethicists had on hand, but more importantly, they derived from what the ethicists had learned and experienced in life.

Some dilemmas are minor with minor consequences. Some are just the opposite: they change lives. They may change the world. Consider these three. They are well-known conundrums occasionally used in different kinds of psychological testing. They defy easy answers.

- *You're riding in the back seat of a car, heading to a party. The driver is a friend. Next to him in the passenger seat is his wife. There is an accident. The car you are riding in strikes and kills a pedestrian. The road is empty. There are no other vehicles or witnesses. As you get out of the vehicle, you hear the wife tell her husband that she will tell police that she was the driver. Otherwise, her husband faces likely incarceration, and she and their children will be left without any source of financial support. Do you go along, agreeing to confirm the wife was driving? It might protect the well-being of several (husband and children) at the expense of sending your friend's wife, willingly, to prison for an act she did not commit.*

- *William Styron's 1976 novel* Sophie's Choice *(later a movie starring Oscar-winning actress Meryl Streep) presents a Polish woman who is arrested by the Nazis and sent with her two young children, a daughter and son, to the Auschwitz death camp. Upon arrival, she is confronted with a horrific predicament: She can choose one of her children to be sent immediately to the gas chamber so that the other child can continue to live with Sophie, albeit in the camp. If she does not choose one child, both children will be put to death. Sophie makes her choice. What would be yours?*

- *A commonly discussed dilemma with many variations involves asking respondents to choose between saving the lives of several people by killing (or allowing the death of) one person, or refusing to participate in the death of one person that results indirectly in the deaths of many.*

This last theoretical dilemma became real, magnified many factors over, during World War II. In 1945, the United States was in the fifth year of armed conflict with Japan. The country was war-weary. Final victory seemed to require invasion of mainland Japan, an effort that would be incredibly costly in terms of lives and treasure on both sides. But President Truman had a secret weapon—the atomic bomb—which he believed could force Japan's quick and unconditional surrender. So he ordered A-bombs dropped on the cities of Hiroshima and Nagasaki. Six days after Nagasaki was bombed, Japan surrendered. More than one hundred thousand Japanese died in the bombings, but conventional wisdom suggests the bombings likely saved many more lives that would have been lost if the war had continued.

Working with What You've Got and Know

President Truman's decision was a moment of singular, terrible choice. Mostly, life is a series of more modest decisions we make based on what we know at the time we make them. Wisdom simply means making good decisions more often than not.

It doesn't begin that way. When you are a child, most decisions are made for you, usually by your parents. But around the time you get a driver's license, become able to vote, or venture off to college, you are expected to begin making your own decisions as an adult, to chart your own path forward and live with the consequences. At first, these decisions still tend to be mostly about you, such as which college to attend or whom to date. But in time, they broaden and assume larger significance. You start to make decisions that affect others: your own children, aging parents, other family, friends, coworkers, and even people you do not know or may never meet.

In earlier chapters, I've mentioned Paul Baltes, a pioneer in wisdom research who developed the Berlin Wisdom Paradigm to assess wisdom. In this project, researchers presented challenging, hypothetical dilemmas to study participants who described aloud how they would resolve the dilemma, while a panel of trained assessors listened and took notes. Depending on how well the answer fit within the defined criteria of the Wisdom Paradigm, participants were scored on a scale of 1 to 7.

Here's a sample question:

A 14-year-old girl wants to move out of her house right away. What should be considered in this situation?

Two possible answers:

1. *She's only 14! She's too young to make such a decision. She should not be allowed to move out.*

2. *She's 14, but perhaps she lives in a negative or abusive environment. Maybe she needs to get out for her own safety and well-being? Maybe her parents are too poor to adequately feed her or her siblings? Maybe this is the norm in her culture?*

The first answer would be scored low. It does not reflect any of the criteria defining wisdom. It does not reveal any thinking or consideration of the details surrounding the girl's life. It focuses only on her age.

The second answer would score high. It acknowledges the girl's young age but recognizes that the question provides no detail or context and that social, cultural, or economic conditions might be relevant or validate her desire to leave.

When we make decisions, big or small, we are influenced by many factors, among them past experience, cognitive biases, age, individual differences, belief in personal relevance, and an escalation of commitment.

Past experience is obvious. People are more likely to decide in a similar way given a similar situation. We also tend (or at least hope) to avoid repeating past mistakes. If something worked once, it should work again and vice versa.

My friend Igor Grossmann, an associate professor of psychology and director of the Wisdom and Culture Lab at the University of Waterloo in Ontario, Canada, has written extensively about how people can act more wisely in their everyday lives. For him, it's not useful to think about wisdom entirely as an ideal, which is something no one can actually fulfill. Rather, he looks at how people behave in real life, showing wisdom in some contexts and not in others.

For Grossmann, understanding wisdom is about how we come up with a decision about how to handle various life situations. And that means it's about context and guiding principles, such as intellectual humility, recognition of others' perspectives, and searching for compromise between different points of view.

For example, the notion of "conflict of interest" infuses our legal system and many of our formal expectations for how relationships should be managed. A judge (such as my father was) is expected to render his or her opinions independent of personal motivations. In legal and medical settings, that's a good thing.

But in everyday life, we are unavoidably influenced by more personal, fluid, and contextual factors. We might argue vociferously with a loved one about the foolhardiness of smoking, but not even pause when helping to light a cigarette at the request of a frail older stranger.

Grossmann offers another example from research published in 2014. Study participants who were in long-term relationships were randomly assigned to reflect on a situation in which either their romantic partner cheated on them or their best friend's romantic partner cheated on the best friend. They were asked to reason about how their relationship or their friend's relationship would unfold in the future. They answered questions that were designed to measure wise reasoning, such as "How important is it for you to try to search for compromise?"

As they hypothesized, participants showed greater wisdom when reasoning about their friend's situation than those who were asked to imagine the situation in their own lives. When something dramatic or traumatic happens to others, we have the benefit (to varying degrees) of distance. We can step back and think logically, less affected by the powerful vagaries of emotion.

We like to think of ourselves as rational creatures, but we often make irrational choices based on common mental errors. We are all subject to cognitive biases. These are thinking patterns based on observations and generalizations that may lead to memory errors, inaccurate judgments, and faulty logic.

There are many cognitive biases; here are a few of the most common:

- *We tend to focus on winners, though losers may have employed the same strategies. Bill Gates and Mark Zuckerberg dropped out of school and became billionaires, but the vast majority of school dropouts are, well, not billionaires. Loss aversion is the tendency to strongly prefer avoiding losses over acquiring gains. If someone gives you $10, there's a brief moment of elation. If you lose $10, it seems to sting disproportionately. We are wired to be protective of things we already have,* *even if we don't need them. Think about that suit or pair of shoes in your closet that you never wear and know you likely never will, but still you can't bear to part with it. That leads to a hoarding tendency.*

- *The availability heuristic (a fancy word meaning an aid to learning or discovery) is our inclination to believe that the examples that come most easily to mind are also the examples that are most important. We overvalue and overestimate the impact of things we can remember and undervalue and underestimate things we forget or do not know. It's a mental shortcut that can lead us in the wrong direction.*

- *Confirmation bias is the oldest mental error of them all. It is our tendency to search for and favor information that confirms what we already believe while simultaneously ignoring or devaluing information that contradicts those beliefs. You can see it manifested large scale in the fragmented media landscape where consumers favor news purveyors who reaffirm their opinions and perspectives while avoiding, ignoring, or disparaging media that present alternative, contradictory, or opposing points of view.*

Age plays a role in how we make decisions. As cognitive function naturally declines with age, decision-making ability may follow. Studies suggest that some older people may become overly confident of their ability to make decisions—they've "seen it all"—which can inhibit their ability to apply new strategies or think outside the box. On the other hand, decision-making ability may improve with aging in people who learn and remember from their experiences.

Other individual differences are external. Socioeconomic status, for example, can limit decision-making. People in lower socioeconomic groups may have less access to education or resources, making them more susceptible to experiencing negative events. The resulting experiences may then color subsequent decisions.

People make choices most often when they believe the decision will personally affect them. People are more likely to vote, for example, when they think their vote reflects the thinking of the general population. They vote because they think their vote will count toward winning an election. It's an ironic phenomenon: when more people vote, individual votes carry less weight—at least in terms of electoral math.

The more skin you have in the game, the more important the game. Escalation of commitment refers to the increasing importance of a decision or choice based on how much you have already invested in that decision or choice. Experts refer to it as "sunk outcome." You stick with a decision because you've invested too much to change course.

Emotions obviously play a role in decision-making. The common advice mentioned earlier, "Don't drive angry," applies equally to making decisions: "Don't decide angry, either." There is much research to show how emotions impact decision-making. In one study, for example, participants were asked to consider whether to buy a car. One cohort was prepped with safety considerations, which naturally prompted negative emotions. (Who wants to think about getting into an accident?) These decision-makers were more likely to choose not to choose, or stick with the status quo.

In another study, participants who experienced "frustrated anger" were more likely to choose a high-risk, high-reward option in a lottery. And in another, participants who had been induced to feel sad were likely to set a lower asking price for an item they were told to sell. Fearful people make more pessimistic judgments of future events.

The point of all this is that wise decision-making requires balanced thinking that is not dependent primarily on one's emotions.

Decision-Making in the Brain

Neuroimaging studies suggest that the circuits implicated in decision-making emphasize different parts of the brain depending on the stage of the decision-making process, whether you're forming a preference, executing an action, or evaluating an outcome.

The first and last steps appear to involve both the limbic and PFC regions of the brain, while executing an action is more closely tied to the striatum—a region deep within the brain linked to multiple aspects of cognition, including motor- and action-planning, motivation, and reinforcement.

Every decision—and a major aspect of wisdom—is a matter of balancing choices between immediate reward versus long-term gratification or consequences. This is the yin-yang of the limbic system and PFC discussed earlier. When you choose an immediate reward, odds are the limbic regions of the brain prevailed; when you delay gratification, it's likely the influence of the PFC.

Decisions vary in difficulty and complexity, which affects how the brain tackles them. Take this well-known moral dilemma, often used in testing:

> You're at your girlfriend's wedding. That morning, you discover irrefutable evidence that the bridegroom is actively engaged in a relationship with another woman. No one else knows, and it's likely the relationship will continue after the wedding. Do you tell your girlfriend about her soon-to-be husband's infidelity, ruining her wedding day, but perhaps avoiding greater, later grief? Or do you say nothing, smile, and support your friend on "the happiest day in her life"?

It's a dilemma because there is no clear, absolutely correct answer. It's further complicated by its moral subtext. What is the morally right thing to do? The brain brings a lot of resources together to try to find an answer, with activity in the ventromedial PFC, the posterior cingulate cortex, the dorsolateral PFC, and posterior superior temporal sulcus. The amygdala is summoned too since the decision involves emotion-laden attitudes. It's a group effort, though all this activity doesn't ensure a "correct" decision or satisfaction with it.

Less is known about brain activity in terms of recognizing and dealing effectively with uncertainty. Many of the same parts of the brain involved in social decision-making and pragmatic knowledge of life are involved in coping with its unknown consequences.

Interestingly, depending on a person's predisposition to risk or ambiguity, imaging studies show different regions of the brain activate more or less. When you believe something is true—let's say someone tells you that you left your wallet in the restaurant—it becomes the basis for further thought and action, with correspondingly increased activity in the brain. If you reject the statement as false—someone says your leather wallet is an offense to all hide-bearing animals—it's just a string of words, a neurological dead-end.

These kinds of findings, which have been mapped in the brain, support a concept that the brain has multiple executive function systems, one for making decisions that are "hot," such as emotional or risky choices, and another for those that are "cold" and analytical.

Bad Is Good Is Bad Is Good

Wisdom is about making good decisions, but what is a good decision? Mark Twain opined that "good decisions come from experience. Experience comes from making bad decisions." That's very true, but there is also a Taoist parable that suggests there's really no such thing as good or bad, that good arises from bad and vice versa, making it hard to discern which is which.

Consider this particular parable, a favorite of mine. It involves a farmer and his horse. One day, the horse wanders off. The farmer is devastated. The horse was his most valuable possession. But then the horse returns, bringing with it a dozen new horses. The farmer cele-brates his equine windfall. But then misfortune strikes: the farmer's son breaks his leg while attempting to tame the new horses. But then fortune follows: the son's broken leg spares him mandatory con-scription in the army.

And so it goes; bad begets good begets bad begets good ad infinitum.

Here's a more modern example, courtesy of David Allan, editorial director of CNN Features, writer of a column called "The Wisdom Project," and someone with whom I have shared conversations on the topic. Allan describes watching speeches and news coverage in New Orleans on the 10th anniversary of Hurricane Katrina, which had devastated the city and region in 2005.

Before the notorious storm, the local high school graduation rate had been 54 percent; now it's up to 73 percent. Before the storm, college enrollment was 37 percent; now it's almost 60 percent. What Hurricane Katrina destroyed, the residents of New Orleans now strive to make better. The storm revealed horrendous inequities and lives leaden with despair, but it also provided a chance to iden-tify and fix them—or not. Bad begets good begets what?

The point of the earlier parable is that neither the farmer (nor arguably the citizens of New Orleans) can entirely celebrate the good nor bemoan the bad. They can't really know which is which because one thing always leads to another. Their only recourse is to make the best decision in the moment and see what happens.

Five Missiles, One Decision, Zero War

On September 1, 1983, a Soviet Union military interceptor shot down scheduled Korean Air Lines Flight 007, killing all 269 pas-sengers and crew. At first, Kremlin leaders denied any knowledge of the incident; then they claimed the Boeing 747 airliner was a spy plane and a purposeful provocation by the United States.

The incident inflamed international relations and became one of the tensest moments of the Cold War.

Three weeks later, Lieutenant Colonel Stanislav Yevgrafovich Petrov of the Soviet Union Air Defense Forces was working an overnight shift at a nuclear early warning command center when the satellite system reported that a missile had been launched from the US, followed by perhaps four or five more. Standing orders were clear: at first alarm, Petrov should report the missiles, initiating military protocol and a Soviet counterattack.

But Petrov paused. He wondered why the Americans would send so few missiles if this was an all-out strike, which he had been taught to expect. He also doubted the early warning system itself. The alarm had passed through multiple layers of verification too quickly. Ground radar was showing no collaborative evidence. Petrov wasn't certain the alarm was erroneous, but something just didn't seem right.

In that fraught moment, Petrov decided the alarm must be a system malfunction. He did not initiate a Soviet response. In that decision, he arguably prevented nuclear war. (As it turned out, the alarm was false, created by a rare alignment of sunlight on high-altitude clouds above North Dakota and a misreading by Soviet surveillance satellites.)

Petrov's decision could not have been easy. Disregarding orders carried harsh repercussions. But even with little time to ponder, Petrov displayed multiple elements of wise decision-making. He did not act impulsively, simply and unthinkingly behaving according to established protocol. Indeed, he later said his earlier civilian training helped him make the right decision compared to colleagues who were all professional soldiers with purely military training and more likely to just follow orders.

Petrov evaluated the situation, tapping into both his training and his critical thinking skills. He put emotions aside; this was no time for fear or panic. He acted by not acting. He couldn't know what would happen next or as a consequence, only that this was not the time nor circumstance to perhaps start World War III.

In the aftermath, Soviet authorities did not reward Petrov for his decisive inaction. He was chastised for poor paperwork in documenting the event and reassigned to a less sensitive post. He left the military in 1984, ironically getting a job at the research institute that had developed the early warning system. Notably, Petrov's story remained largely unknown and untold for decades. Petrov didn't even tell his wife about it until 10 years after the fact. It was simply something he did, in the moment, and then he moved on, quietly.

But there are other times when the effects and power of wise decisions linger. On January 15, 2009, US Airways pilot Chesley "Sully" Sullenberger III had just taken off from LaGuardia Airport in New York City. There were 155 people aboard Flight 1549. Minutes after takeoff, the Airbus A320 struck a large flock of Canada geese, and both engines lost power.

Sullenberger quickly determined he could not safely return to LaGuardia or make the nearby Teterboro Airport. Instead, he landed the plane in the Hudson River, where boats rescued all 155 aboard. Sullenberger was the last to leave the plane.

The act epitomizes many key elements of wisdom. Sullenberger was obviously decisive in the face of uncertainty. He said the moments before ditching were "the worst, sickening, pit-of-your-stomach, falling-through-the-floor feeling" he had ever experienced. He remained emotionally stable.

New York City Mayor Michael Bloomberg dubbed him "Captain Cool." He was resolved to save the lives of all those passengers and crew who depended on him.

Later, of course, there would be reviews and reconsiderations: Did Sullenberger and his flight crew act correctly and appropriately? Was there a better course of action? A 2016 movie by Clint Eastwood that portrays the story of Sullenberger and Flight 1549 depicts an adversarial confrontation between the pilot and investigators from the National Transportation Safety Board (NTSB). Reality was perhaps less overtly overwrought, though Sullenberger has said the film captures how he felt at the time, under intense media and bureaucratic scrutiny, with the professional reputations of himself and his copilot Jeff Skiles hanging in the balance.

But throughout the NTSB review, Sullenberger and Skiles remained visibly calm and supportive of each other. They explained how they made their decisions in the moment and stuck by them even after later computer simulations suggested the pilots might have safely returned to LaGuardia.

In the end, NTSB investigators absolved Sullenberger and Skiles of any wrongdoing and praised the entire flight crew for saving everyone aboard.

Sullenberger retired a year later and took up a second career as a writer and speaker, mostly on the topics of aviation safety, leadership, and living a life of integrity.

Often there is no way to know whether a decision is correct and wise. We must make it based on the best information we have at the time, critically assessed and filtered through our senses of right and wrong, fairness, compassion, and more. If events prove our decision to have been unwise, we have a new decision to make: How do we fix it?

The Inevitabilty of Unpredictability

The philosopher Daniel Dennett has described the human brain as an "anticipation machine" and its most important function as "making the future." We cannot help but contemplate the future and wonder what it will bring. It separates us from other species. It helps us build civilizations, create the previously unimagined, and sustain ourselves. Looking ahead is usually a good thing. It's how we prepare. "The power of prospection is what makes us wise," wrote Martin E. P. Seligman and John Tierney in a *New York Times* article titled "We Aren't Built to Live in the Moment."

But the problem with trying to discern events that haven't happened yet is that they, well, haven't happened. We do not like uncertainty. It makes us feel vulnerable, so we try to avoid it as much as we can. Indeed, we may endure negative effects or events in the moment just because we know what to expect. In experiments, people tend to prefer an electric shock now rather than the *possibility* of receiving one later.

Intolerance of uncertainty is a psychological term with its own scale. It has been linked to its own assortment of ailments, from persistent worry to generalized anxiety disorder. It may play a part in some emotional disorders too.

I would tweak Seligman and Tierney's comment about the power of prospection. Wisdom doesn't derive from the ability to look ahead. Wisdom is about knowing you cannot know everything, that life is fraught with uncertainties, and then deciding to carry on the best you can.

Decisional Capacity

The ability to make good decisions, even in the face of uncertainty, may be the consequence of underlying traits, such as a penchant to think before acting or to refrain from panic, but for scientists and doctors seeking to measure it, it seems less a fixed trait and more a state of mind and knowledge, dependent on a variety of factors.

We all make good and bad decisions, based on myriad factors from the nature and complexity of the topic to whether we had breakfast that morning. No one is born with immutable good or bad judgment though different people vary in their general ability to make logical versus illogical decisions.

One area where the ability to assess decisional capacity is critical is in clinical treatment and research. Many types of clinical research, such as testing an experimental drug or therapy, require participants to sign informed consent agreements—documents that acknowledge that they agree to the scope and purpose of the research and understand its possible consequences. Patients typically do something similar before a medical procedure. They must sign consent forms that describe their treatment, including surgery, in detail, with all possible known benefits and risks.

Informed consent is a cornerstone of ethical clinical practice and clinical research. There are few defensible exceptions to this goal and expectation, and there are extensive laws and regulations to ensure it is asked and given.

But here—and always—there is a conundrum: what constitutes meaningful consent? That's only possible if the study participant or patient has the capacity to effectively use disclosed information in deciding whether to accept a proposed treatment or participate in a research protocol.

Four elements comprise decisional capacity:

- *Understanding the relevant information*

- *Appreciation: Applying the information to one's own situation*

- *Reasoning: Using the information in making a rational decision*

- *Expressing the choice clearly*

Lots of things can reduce decisional capacity, such as cognitive impairment, severe psychotic symptoms like delusions, and situational factors like the complexity of the information or the way the information is disclosed. Context is important too. A low-risk decision requires lower decisional capacity than a high-risk decision.

Despite the overarching importance of informed consent and decades of debate, there is no consensus on how it should be managed. Rather, as one scientist has noted, there is "a hodgepodge of practices."

Some years ago, colleagues and I surveyed instruments used to assess decisional capacity for clinical research or treatment. To be effective, such an instrument needs to measure a person's understanding, appreciation, and reasoning of the information relevant to giving consent. A number of instruments have been created to do so. Some have been validated and found to be reliable. Most take substantial time to complete and may require specifically trained personnel to conduct the process.

Our review found that most instruments focused on the understanding component of decisional capacity—much less on appreciation and reasoning. Every instrument we looked at being used in laboratories and clinics had limitations, not least that they required considerable time to conduct. Time can be a major, practical issue when resources are limited. We found no gold standard for assessing decisional capacity. In reality, most of the so-called written informed consents for various clinical procedures and treatments are far from "informed"—they merely involve the patient signing a piece of paper without reading or knowing what they are agreeing to.

In 2007, I published another paper with a different team, describing a new decision assessment tool that we had developed and tested. Again, we scrutinized all the published scales or measurements for their abilities to assess decisional capacity regarding informed consent to clinical research (or treatment), identifying their strengths and weaknesses. Then we built our own.

Our resulting scale, called the University of California San Diego Brief Assessment of Capacity to Consent, or the somewhat less unwieldy UBACC, consists of just 10 questions based on understanding, appreciation, and reasoning. Each question is scored zero to 2. A zero reflects a clearly incapable response; 2 indicates a fully capable response; 1 is somewhere in between. The questions or statements presented are straightforward, such as these examples:

- *What is the purpose of the study that was just described to you?*

- *If you participate in this study, what are some of the things that you will be asked to do?*

- *Please describe some of the risks or discomforts that people may experience if they participate in this study.*

- *Is it possible that being in this study will not have any benefit to you?*

The UBACC takes only about five minutes to complete. We developed UBACC through our ongoing work with patients suffering from schizophrenia, a condition in which informed decision-making is obviously important but is frequently compromised. We tested its reliability and validity using schizophrenia patients and healthy comparison participants who received information about a simulated clinical drug trial.

Our published findings suggest that UBACC is a useful instrument for screening large numbers of subjects, particularly to identify those needing more comprehensive decisional capacity assessment or remediation efforts. It focuses on a few things that matter most, such as the most serious risks, and not the myriad hypothetical risks noted in the *Physicians' Desk Reference* or on a consent form. This scale has been translated into multiple languages and used in numerous studies.

Critical Thinking

Critical or wise thinking is associated with wellness and longevity. Critical thinking is a collection of cognitive skills used to think rationally in a goal-oriented fashion. Critical thinkers are "amiable skeptics," writes Heather Butler, an assistant professor in the psychology department at California State University Dominguez Hills. Butler and others have conducted research into what constitutes critical thinking. Among those key components is decision-making.

The influence and impact of critical thinking threads through both my research in wisdom and my work with people with schizophrenia. Many of the insights I have gleaned about the nature of wisdom and how to assess and improve it have come from interacting with people suffering cognitive impairment. If we can assess and improve wise thinking in these individuals, we can certainly do so in healthy people too.

In 2007, my team published an imaging study in the *Journal of Neuropsychiatry and Clinical Neurosciences* that looked at brain response and decisional capacity in patients with schizophrenia.

People with serious mental illnesses typically have a tougher time grappling with decisions—at least in a consistent way. But like mentally healthy people, there is considerable variation in their decision-making abilities. We wanted to see what was actually happening inside their brains when patients were making decisions. Did some regions of the brain activate more or less?

Twenty-four study participants with schizophrenia took a well-validated and rather long decisional assessment test called the MacArthur Competence Assessment Tool for Clinical Research (MacCAT-CR), which measured their abilities to understand and reason. We then asked them to perform a series of mental tasks—matching pairs of associated words—while lying inside an fMRI machine.

As predicted, participants with higher MacCAT-CR scores showed the greatest learning-related activation in the hippocampus, the region of the brain thought to be crucial for encoding and recognizing information. Other areas activated included the bilateral parahippocampal cortex, cerebellum, and thalamus—all areas involved in verbal learning tasks.

One takeaway: a good understanding of a consent form—or arguably any complex information—involves adequate engagement of brain systems known to be involved in encoding verbal information. This observation applies to everyone, not just people with schizophrenia. When information is shared verbally, and the brain responds appropriately, it resonates in ways different and perhaps more effective than other methods of sharing information.

Scientifically speaking, what happens in a conversation? Humans are verbal creatures; our language skills evolving along with the rest of our abilities. Language processing involves multiple, widely dispersed parts of the brain, from Wernicke's and Broca's areas to more obscure regions like the arcuate fasciculus. When people talk and listen to each other, imaging studies show that their brains metaphorically lock together, their previously differing neural activity synchronizing in mental communion.

To make good decisions, we should use every means of communication possible—communication with others and with oneself, debating internally both positives and negatives of the different options available.

Acceptance of Diversity of Values

In modern societies, with their emphasis on individual rights, conflicts between people with different perspectives are inevitable. A price of free speech is the obligation to allow others with opposing opinions and values to speak their minds—and to listen to what they have to say.

To be sure, some values are nearly absolute. It is not acceptable to cause harm or death to another person without strong justification, such as self-defense or defense of loved ones, but the world is fraught with values that shift with time, cultures, and circumstances. A person may consider it morally wrong to eat meat, but also consider it unethical to impose that belief on others. Parents may support government prohibitions against underage drinking, but still allow their own 20-year-old son or daughter a sip of champagne at a family party.

Practical considerations come into play. American society embraced alcohol consumption until the advent of Prohibition, and then changed the laws again when it became obvious that banning alcohol was impractical and impossible. The therapeutic use of stem cells or gene editing arouse concerns and opposition, but these diminish as tangible benefits to patients and society take form.

Wisdom is characterized by acceptance of this diversity of value systems. It seeks to learn and understand from what might appear at first as simply different, strange, or off-putting. Wisdom is a balancing act of embracing and acting according to one's deeply held values while at the same time acknowledging and perhaps even celebrating that others hold different values just as deeply.

Decision-Making Techniques

There may be almost as many ways to make a decision as there are decisions to be made. Broadly speaking, decision-making techniques can be lumped into two categories: group and individual.

Group decisions obviously involve more than one person. Some standards are voting (majority or plurality); finding a consensus, in which the majority determines a course of action with minority consent and input (avoiding winners and losers); the Delphi method, which we used to develop our experts' definition of wisdom; and participative decision-making, often used by organizations or authorities to engage members in the decision-making process.

Individuals have their own decision-making tools. Plato and Benjamin Franklin were both big fans of decisional balance sheets: writing down the pros and cons, benefits and costs of a choice. A solitary decider can choose between utility (what choice provides the greatest benefit or satisfies the most urgent need) and opportunity cost (what is the cost of not choosing an option). And there are the less refined alternatives of flipping coins, cutting decks of cards, doing the contrary to what everyone advises, or reading tarot cards—none of which seems very wise.

In the next chapter, we discuss three additional components of wisdom: self-reflection, that particularly human capacity to examine our inner self; curiosity or openness to new experiences; and humor, including why laughter really is good medicine even if we don't always understand the joke.

Each of these plays a role in making wise decisions in daily life.

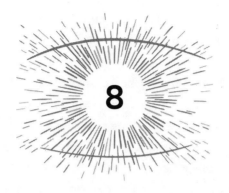

Self-Reflection, Curiosity, and Humor

What lies behind us, and what lies before us,
are tiny matters compared to what lies within us.
HENRY S. HASKINS, *Meditations in Wall Street*

I have no particular talent. I am merely inquisitive.
ALBERT EINSTEIN

A little nonsense now and then is
relished by the wisest men.
ROALD DAHL, *Charlie and the Chocolate Factory*

I FIRST MET ELYN SAKS in the early 1990s. I was doing research on ethics and decision-making related to patients with mental illness, and a colleague had recommended reaching out to Saks. She was a Yale-educated professor of law at the University of Southern

California. She had written extensively about law and mental health, including the ethical dimensions of psychiatric research and forced treatment. She was widely admired, with a gleaming reputation. In the years to come, among her many honors, there would be a MacArthur Fellowship, the so-called Genius Grant.

So I wrote to Saks, introducing myself and my work. I followed up with a call. Our interests and aspirations were mutual, and we quickly became colleagues who, over the next decade or so, would coauthor numerous published studies and papers.

One day, several years after we began collaborating, Saks called to ask if we might speak in person. She sounded nervous. We met and she got straight to the point: she had been diagnosed with schizophrenia. It wasn't a new diagnosis. She experienced her first symptoms at 8 years old. And one day when she was 16, she walked out of school without reason, without telling anyone, and headed toward her house five miles away. It proved a terrifying journey during which, she believed, houses she passed in her neighborhood were beaming hostile and insulting messages directly into her brain. "Walk," the houses said without voice or words. "Repent. You are special. You are especially bad."

It was her first experience with psychosis, but not her last. Five years later, while a fellow at Oxford University in England, she suffered her first complete, official schizophrenic break. There would be still others.

Saks describes living with schizophrenia as living within a nightmare. During psychotic episodes, there are bizarre images, voices, and sounds. The experience is utterly disorienting and profoundly frightening. What is real and what is not can be impossible to discern. And unlike an ordinary nightmare, there is no relief in awakening. On even not-so-bad days, she says, life with schizophrenia can be a jumble of chaotic, disorganized thinking with thoughts sprayed out as incomprehensible word salads.

The disease has both "positive" and "negative" symptoms. "A positive symptom is something you have that you don't want, and a negative symptom is something you want but don't have," says Saks.

Delusions are positive symptoms, which became fixed in her mind. She would imagine, for example, with total conviction, that she had killed hundreds of thousands of people with her thoughts. Or that someone had detonated a nuclear bomb in her brain.

Negative symptoms are things people with schizophrenia frequently lack, such as emotional regulation or the ability to sustain relationships or hold down a regular job.

Saks says she's mostly been spared the condition's most malignant negative symptoms. The first years of her illness were the worst, with treatments often harsh and sometimes forced. She spent many days in psychiatric hospitals, occasionally in physical restraints, though she never threatened anyone. She was given many medications.

But that had been long ago, she told me on the day of this meeting. She was better now. She enjoyed deep support from her husband, family, and friends. She was not only managing, but excelling, in life. And now, she said, she no longer wanted to hide her disease from the world—or the horrors she had experienced, both from her condition and from those who would remedy it. She wanted to write honestly about schizophrenia and her "journey through madness," a phrase that would become part of her autobiography *The Center Cannot Hold*.

But she feared coming out would come at a cost.

"I'm worried that you will no longer want to collaborate with me," she said.

My reaction was quite the opposite. I congratulated her on the decision to let the world know about her condition. I appreciated the courage it took. The stigma of mental illness persists in ways large and small, obvious and subtle. Going public about her condition must have been terrifying, fraught with uncertainty. I told her I would support her in whatever way I could.

Saks and I have continued to be colleagues, friends, and collaborators. And when I think about her today in the context of wisdom, I am reminded again and again that wisdom is not restricted to the healthiest people. Some of the wisest among us—and in that group I would include Saks—have earned the distinction through enormous struggle.

Take a Look at Yourself

Not least among the many traits that make Saks wise is her ability to self-reflect, to look within herself, to learn and change with the revelations. Her books and papers—and indeed her life—are tangible testaments.

But self-reflection is hard to do. You have to be honest with yourself, perhaps brutally so. Otherwise, you're simply cheating yourself, and what's the point of that? When I do something that doesn't work, that's okay. "Failure is not fatal," Winston Churchill once said. We learn more from failure than we do from success. When I try to do it again, and it still doesn't work, I begin looking for a pattern or clue to what I am doing wrong. If I try the same thing for a third time and again fail, I know I must do it differently. I must change my thinking.

Self-reflection seems to be a uniquely human trait. It is something beyond self-awareness, which is not unique. In the 1970s, psychologist Gordon Gallup Jr. devised a mirror test to determine if other animal species possessed the ability to recognize themselves as individuals separate from others and from their environment.

To conduct the test, Gallup—and later, other researchers—would visually mark an animal's body, usually with a dab of scentless paint or a sticker, and then watch what happened when the animal was placed in front of a mirror.

Animals that passed the mirror test typically noticed the marking almost immediately. They adjusted their bodies to get a better look at it. They tried to touch it or remove it. It was an obvious object of fascination or concern.

Such behavior suggested mental complexities beyond just reacting to the sight of a similar-looking animal, which lots of species do. Placed in front of a mirror, they react as if seeing another of their kind. The response may be aggression or affection, but it's obviously mistaken. Marked animals who see themselves in a mirror and recognize that what they see is visually different from what they know suggests a deeper, innate sense of themselves. They know what they look like and that dab of paint or sticker is not a normal part of them.

Humans pass the mirror test at around 18 months old, but several other animals do as well at relatively later ages, such as Asian elephants, great apes, bottlenose dolphins, orca whales, Eurasian magpies, and remarkably, ants.

Even so, self-awareness appears to be rare among the world's myriad species, and self-reflection seems to be limited to just one species—ourselves. It is the human capacity to see ourselves in a mental mirror and ponder what we see.

Self-reflection is the exercise of introspection, the examination of our own mental and emotional processes to better understand their fundamental nature, purpose, and essence. It's a profoundly important and obvious element of wisdom. "The unexamined life is not worth living," wrote Plato in *The Apology of Socrates*, a recollection of the speech his mentor gave at his ill-fated trial.

Reflection gives the brain time to pause, to untangle and sort through the myriad observations and experiences that wash over and through it every second of every waking hour—and perhaps in many sleeping hours as well. It provides time to consider multiple interpretations and create meaning, which in turn becomes learning and shapes our future thoughts and actions.

Self-reflection is critical to learning. Rather than simply go from task to task, humans can pause to review what they have done, the processes involved and the outcome, to extract new value or relevance and improve performance in the future. Throughout her life and career, this is what Saks has done, producing remarkable insight and knowledge that has helped her not only manage her schizophrenia, but also to help many others as well.

Self-reflection leads to a greater understanding of one's own emotions, cognitions, and behaviors, what the philosopher Daniel Dennett describes as the ability to experience ourselves and be the "author of our own lives."

But it also plays a role in how we understand the lives and perspectives of others. When you ask yourself, "What would I do if that were me?" it can provide insights into the thinking of others, into what they are, in fact, asking themselves.

The Reflection Section

The act of self-reflection occurs in the medial prefrontal cortex (mPFC) of the brain, right behind the forehead. When the brain shifts into default mode, periods when it's not actively engaged in a task, metabolic activity remains high in the mPFC—the result of your brain simply thinking about you or ruminating about life or the future.

Autobiographical memories activate the mPFC, as do tasks that involve self-judgment. At such times, the mPFC, in collaboration with other brain structures like the cingulate cortex (both anterior and posterior), gets to work. Depending on age and experience, these other parts of the brain play larger or lesser roles. Adults lean more on the posterior precuneus, tucked farther back in the brain and involved in self-consciousness and memory, while children activate both the posterior cingulate, the backmost part of the cingulate cortex, and the anterior precuneus.

Such variation provides insight into how humans of different ages think about and view themselves. Older children activate the mPFC less intensely than younger children or adults because at that age they resort to introspection less often.

Young children don't yet have the wealth of specific skills that adults do, so they show greater activation during spatial tasks. This illustrates the idea that with increased expertise in a task, there is less activity in the part of the brain dealing with broad spatial parameters—the *how do I do this?*—and more focus on specific performance—the *how well am I doing this?*

The importance of the mPFC is particularly noticeable when it is damaged or dysfunctional due to injury or disease. An example of the latter is frontotemporal dementia (FTD) where self-awareness and self-identity may be lost. Or in narcissistic personality disorder, in which people have highly grandiose views of self and simply cannot see themselves as others do.

No Time to Think

While humans possess the power of self-reflection, that doesn't necessarily mean everyone uses it—or uses it willingly. We may like to believe that we think a lot, but there's plenty of evidence to suggest that's not quite true.

In 2014, for example, scientists at the University of Virginia conducted a series of experiments in which participants were placed in situations where they would be left alone with nothing but their own thoughts. Most participants found the experience to be unpleasant after just 6 to 15 minutes.

Indeed, some participants went to surprising lengths to avoid thinking. In one experiment, for example, 64 percent of men and 15 percent of women began self-administering low-level electric shocks when they were left alone to think. Previously, the same participants had told researchers they would pay money to avoid receiving unpleasant jolts.

The urge to not reflect was the same whether the experiments were conducted in labs or in participants' homes. It didn't help when researchers provided suggestions about what to think about, such as an upcoming vacation.

Humans are problem solvers and meaning makers. These traits help us survive and thrive. But they may also have negative consequences. When left to our own thoughts, we may think about unresolved issues, difficult relationships, money problems, health concerns, personal or professional failures—whatever is stressing us in the moment or a source of chronic concern.

This is particularly true for younger people. With age and experience, as people tend to become wiser, they forget or pay less attention to negative events or emotions. As I discussed in an earlier chapter, negative or stressful experiences adhere to younger minds like Velcro. Older adult minds are more like Teflon: the same experiences don't stick or just peel away.

Younger people value action more than thinking. "It's like we're all in this addicted family where all this busyness seems normal when it's really harmful," said Stephanie Brown, a psychologist in Silicon Valley and the author of *Speed: Facing Our Addiction to Fast and Faster—and Overcoming Our Fear of Slowing Down.* "There's this widespread belief that thinking and feeling will only slow you down and get in your way, but it's the opposite."

The Benefits of Self-Affirmation

Thinking about bad stuff is tough. It can be depressing and anxiety inducing. No one relishes doing it, but trying to suppress negative feelings and thoughts may be worse. The act of suppression imbues negative thoughts with more power, which in turn leads to greater intrusion and even more effort required to further suppress them.

Psychologists call it the ironic process theory or "the white bear problem," a nod to a line by Fyodor Dostoevsky in *Winter Notes on Summer Impressions*: "Try to pose for yourself this task: not to think of a polar bear, and you will see that the cursed thing will come to mind every minute."

The constant cognitive strain of not thinking about something can contribute to a host of psychological ills, including obsessive-compulsive disorder, anxiety, depression, panic attacks, and numerous addictions. It's also associated with stress-worsened physical ailments such as eczema, irritable bowel syndrome, asthma, and headaches.

The opposite of dwelling on the negative—or forever trying to avoid thinking negative thoughts—is self-affirmation, which plays a positive role in wisdom and in life in general. When you seek and focus on sources of meaning and purpose in life, you naturally improve your own.

In my research, I study the effects of meaning or purpose in life, both in healthy people and in those with schizophrenia. In both groups, having a purpose or meaning is associated with better mental and physical health. Other scientists have shown that meaning even predicts the rate of biological aging.

Self-affirmation activates the reward centers of the brain, including the ventral striatum and ventromedial prefrontal cortex. These are the same neural structures involved in pleasurable experiences, such as eating a favorite food or winning a prize. When these reward circuits are triggered by affirmation, they can mitigate or dampen negative emotions or reinforce positive convictions.

Affirmation also activates the mPFC and posterior cingulate, both connected to the act of thinking about ourselves. This suggests that self-related processing acts like a kind of emotional buffer to painful or negative or threatening information.

Interestingly, the beneficial effects of self-affirmation may be stronger when related to future events than to those of the past. In neuroimaging studies, when participants were asked to think about career successes of the past versus anticipating future achievements, the act of looking ahead triggered more self-affirming brain activity.

Finding Your Own Way in Your Own Way

According to Google statistics, roughly one hundred million selfies are taken every day—and that's probably an under-estimate. One poll found that every third photo taken by someone aged 18 to 24 is a selfie, and that the average millennial (people born between, roughly, the early 1980s and the mid-1990s) will take more than twenty-five thousand selfies over their life span, or close to one selfie every day of their lives.

Selfies are "a kind of self-definition," said psychologist and author Terri Apter. "We all like the idea of being sort of in control of our image and getting attention, being noticed, being part of the culture."

But selfies reflect only the superficial, and even then, it's usually a carefully calibrated and curated representation intended only for an external audience. Do selfies tell the selfie-takers anything about themselves?

Self-reflection requires more than a cell phone and a stick. It's a process of asking yourself sometimes-difficult questions about your beliefs, behaviors, past acts, and future goals. What lies inside me? Why? What should I keep and what should I change?

During his psychiatry residency in 1974, Alan Green suddenly became ill with systemic cytomegalovirus (CMV). Most CMV infections lie dormant and never cause problems. In fact, the Centers for Disease Control and Prevention estimates that half to 80 percent of all adults are infected with CMV by age 40; most will never show signs or symptoms.

But in Green's case, the viral infection was devastating. It wreaked havoc in his body, causing high fevers, an enlarged spleen, and anemia. For five years, he was so ill that he could do little more than read (often books "about people . . . confined against their will") and think. In that time, frequently bedridden, Green considered himself and his fate, ultimately vowing that if he recovered, he would dedicate himself to an active life in medical research.

And he did. Today, Green is chair and professor of psychiatry at Dartmouth's Geisel School of Medicine, with a career of highlights and accomplishment. He is a colleague, friend, and inspiration.

We should look, of course, for inspiration everywhere, but action truly comes from looking within.

Benjamin Franklin is celebrated for many things: a founding father of the United States, printer, diplomat, scientist, inventor, musician, traveler, author, and athlete. (He's in the International Swimming Hall of Fame!) He helped inspire the idea of the "self-made man."

In 1726, at the age of 20, Franklin set perhaps his loftiest goal: the attainment of what he called "moral perfection" in his autobiography:

I conceiv'd the bold and arduous project of arriving at
moral perfection. I wish'd to live without committing

any fault at any time; I would conquer all that either nat-
ural inclination, custom, or company might lead me into.

As I knew, or thought I knew, what was right and wrong, I
did not see why I might not always do the one and avoid
the other. But I soon found I had undertaken a task of
more difficulty than I had imagined. While my care was
employ'd in guarding against one fault, I was often sur-
prised by another.

Over time and with much rumination, Franklin compiled a set of 13 virtues, from temperance and sincerity to humility and resolution. He then carried around a small book in which he charted and evaluated his efforts. It was self-reflection writ daily: "I enter'd upon the execution of this plan for self-examination, and continu'd it with occasional intermissions for some time. I was surpris'd to find myself so much fuller of faults than I had imagined; but I had the satisfaction of seeing them diminish."

Franklin said he "never arrived at the perfection" that he so ambitiously sought but was "a better and happier man than I otherwise should have been if I had not attempted it." Few of us are or will rise to the stature of Benjamin Franklin, but we can all be better selves by ourselves.

In some ways, self-reflection is as fundamental and important to wisdom as more obvious traits like empathy and compassion. In the pursuit of greater wisdom, it might be more important. The poet Carl Sandburg wrote on this topic:

A man [or woman] must find time for himself. Time is
what we spend our lives with. If we are not careful we
find others spending it for us. . . . It is necessary now and
then for a man to go away by himself and experience

loneliness; to sit on a rock in the forest and to ask of himself, "Who am I, and where have I been, and where am I going?" . . . If one is not careful, one allows diversions to take up one's time–the stuff of life."

But self-reflection—what Socrates might call "the examined life"—must be clear-eyed and honest, sometimes brutally so. We've all taken those popular magazine tests claiming to assess everything from our sense of style to our inner beauty. It's tempting to be easy on ourselves, angling for a "better" score. That's fine for such tests, which aren't at all serious. But if we are to truly improve ourselves, we must know where we stand—and who we are—so that we can take the appropriate steps and look back with great satisfaction and greater wisdom.

Not Thinking at All

While many of us—or maybe all of us at one time or another—try to avoid being alone with our thoughts, there are times when not thinking is a good thing. Proverbs 16:27 warns that idle hands are the devil's workshop, but an idle mind can be a source of inspired busyness. There is considerable evidence indicating that innovation often arises when minds wander.

Seemingly unfocused mental meandering has traditionally been viewed as a cognitive waste of time or even a lack of mental control and ability. But experts are rethinking the notion. When minds wander away from their conscious target, they are more likely to discover new thoughts or insights. Research shows that when people let their minds rest, as in daydreaming, it helps strengthen memories of events and retention of information. The right kind of mental rest can boost future learning and effective wisdom.

A variation of this is to, metaphorically, do a little mental unlimbering or cooling down. After completing a really challenging cerebral task, take a moment to review what you've just accomplished. Do it during a stroll to get some physical exercise at the same time. Brain scans have found that people who used time after learning something new to reflect on what they had just learned did better on tests of that knowledge later.

"We think replaying memories during rest makes those earlier memories stronger, not just impacting the original content, but impacting the memories to come," said Alison Preston, associate professor of psychology and neuroscience at University of Texas at Austin.

Common Curiosity

I am an immigrant from India. Voluntary immigrants have been found to have high levels of striatal dopamine, which is associated with greater curiosity and openness to new experience.

As I mentioned in the introduction, my primary reason for moving to the United States was to conduct research. In India, I learned to conduct clinical research in psychiatry, most notably with Drs. N. S. Vahia and D. R. Doongaji, who were pioneers of psychiatry in that country.

The discipline of research fascinated me. Although a scientist usually has some notion about what he or she is likely to find, some research results are always surprising. One must be open to getting unexpected results, and for me, that was intensely exciting. When you are awaiting data from a study, it is a period of anxious expectation. You are keen to see how the investigation turned out and what you can make of the results. It is like an expectant mother who doesn't know if she is going to have a boy or a girl or how healthy the baby will be.

When I lived in India, most of the clinical research I could do was epidemiological, that is, studies of hundreds of patients with schizophrenia or depression or epilepsy. Epidemiology is the study of the distribution and determinants of health-related states or events, such as the prevalence of certain toxins in the air, specific ailments afflicting a community, or local health-care practices and how this knowledge can be used to control diseases and other health problems. After a few years of doing this, I wanted to explore other frontiers of research, what is inside of people, especially biological investigations involving the brain. I had learned that the best place for psychiatric research was the National Institute of Mental Health, one of the agencies that comprise the National Institutes of Health (NIH) in Washington, DC.

Beyond that, I knew little, and so a decision to move permanently to America was risky. I was giving up my stable home environment and an almost assured professional career for an entirely new culture fraught with lots of unknowns. But inside myself, I felt I had no choice. Only in the United States could I satisfy my personal and professional curiosities.

After completing a mandatory one-year residency in psychiatry at New Jersey Medical School and then two years at Cornell University, I joined the NIH. It was a dream come true. Top experts in practically every area of science work at the NIH. The world's largest medical library—the National Library of Medicine—is there. Every state-of-the-art technology is available. I learned so many new things, got involved in numerous studies, and published lots of papers. After several years, I felt it was time to take new risks by leaving the unique research haven of NIH and venture out into the world where I could set up my own lab and develop my own research and training programs. Once again, it was exciting but fraught with risks.

At a young age, openness to new experience and risk-taking are normal. As one gets older, this craving has to be balanced by the need for stability. After looking at several universities, I chose the University of California San Diego. It was a wise decision. I have been at UC San Diego now for over three decades. In terms of my physical and family environment, it is the epitome of stability. At the same time, I am continuing to explore new areas of research to satisfy my unquenched curiosity.

Curiosity is a basic element of cognition. It is the motivator for learning and is influential in decision-making. It drives human development at all scales, from individuals to entire cultures and societies.

Curiosity is also pervasive, so much so that we can be almost oblivious to it. We marvel at the overt curiosity of children whose minds are like blotting paper, eager to suck in any and all material, but it's there in adults too. Witness our insatiable desire for information and novelty. You pause, for example, to peruse headlines and magazine covers at a newsstand or to check out what's happening on the wall of screens inside a big-box store selling televisions or to see why everybody is slowing down on the freeway (even as you rant about drivers slowing down on the freeway). And when did you last check your smartphone for emails, texts, a photo or video from a friend, or for the latest news alert?

A 2015 study by the consulting firm Deloitte estimated that Americans collectively check their smartphones upward of eight billion times per day—or about 46 times per person per day, up 13 from the previous year. Of course, that's the estimated average. The younger the person, the more peeks at the phone.

If self-reflection is about looking and wandering within, curiosity is about looking and wondering without. It's a complex and nuanced trait. The late Canadian psychologist Daniel Berlyne and others have described four kinds of curiosity:

- *Perceptual curiosity, which is aroused by new, ambiguous, or puzzling sights*

- *Specific curiosity, when you seek a specific piece of information*

- *Diversive curiosity, which is the attraction to novelty of any sort and what encourages us to explore new places, people, and things*

- *Epistemic curiosity, an appetite for knowledge*

Humans possess all of these versions in varying degrees.

George Loewenstein, an economist and psychologist at Carnegie Mellon University who is credited with cofounding the field of behavioral economics, explains curiosity with his "information gap theory." Curiosity happens, he says, when the world works in ways incompatible with our understanding of it, when we try to reconcile reality with expectation. If a ball bounces the wrong way or a person does the unexpected, we take notice and wonder why.

There are other ways to define curiosity, including using the term *openness to experience*, which is one of the domains in the Five-Factor Model describing human personality. The others are agreeableness, conscientiousness, extraversion versus introversion, and neuroticism. The last domain refers to a person's penchant for moodiness or feelings like anxiety, fear, worry, anger, frustration, envy, jealousy, guilt, or loneliness.

Researchers typically measure openness to experience with self-report tools in which participants agree or disagree with statements or descriptive phrases, such as these:

I like poetry.

I have a vivid imagination.

I don't avoid philosophical discussions.

If you think these statements honestly describe you, you are likely open to experience. The more strongly you agree, the more open you are. If you disagree with the statements, if they don't really describe you, then you are less open to experience. Most people score moderately on measures of openness, with outliers at both extremes. People who score low are considered closed to experience. They tend to be conventional and traditional, preferring familiar routines and expressing narrower sets of interest. People who score high are considered to be artistic, creative, or risk-takers.

The Curious Path

In 2009, researchers at the California Institute of Technology (Caltech) conducted a novel imaging study to identify the neural pathways of curiosity. Nineteen participants were placed in an fMRI machine and presented with 40 trivia questions on various topics. Some of the questions were quite broad and presumably easy; others required more specific knowledge or interest.

Here are two examples:

What is the name of the galaxy that the Earth is part of?

What instrument was invented to sound like a human singing?

Participants were asked to read a question, answer or guess an answer if they didn't know, rate their curiosity to learn the correct answer, and indicate how confident they were that their guesses were correct.

Neuroimaging showed that self-reported high curiosity activated the left caudate, part of the dorsal striatum and the prefrontal cortex. Both regions are linked to rewarding stimuli. The finding confirmed that a thirst for knowledge triggers the brain's reward circuit, but not all of it. Correct answers energized regions of the brain associated with learning, memory, and language, such as the inferior frontal gyrus. Interestingly, brain structures were activated more strongly when participants learned they had guessed wrong. These revelations seemed to enhance participants' memories, and when asked later about the questions and answers, they showed better recall of those missed questions and answers.

It should be no surprise that curiosity benefits learning. When people are highly curious about the answer to a question, they are also better at learning and remembering the relevant information. Also, in numerous studies, highly curious people tend to do better at learning unrelated information. Part of this phenomenon is visible in neuroimaging studies, which show that learning motivated by curiosity stimulates activity in the hippocampus, boosting the formation of new memories and connections with the brain's reward circuit.

Curiosity is its own reward. New discoveries make you feel good. Internal motivation—there's a boost in dopamine levels when you're curious—promotes external motivation. One new bit of information or discovery fuels the desire to seek more information and innovation.

And because you're curious, the answers to the questions above about which galaxy the Earth is found in and what musical instrument sounds like human singing are the Milky Way and the violin.

Laughed but Not Least

Mark Twain once observed that genuine humor is replete with wisdom. He's right, but I (and many others) think there's more to it. Humor is part and parcel of wisdom, both informing it and reflecting it. One cannot survive or thrive without being able to laugh. "Humor," wrote Roger Shattuck in his history *The Banquet Years: The Origins of the Avant-Garde in France—1885 to World War I*, "demands that we reckon with the realities of human nature and the world without falling into grimness and despair."

In 2002, a psychologist named Richard Wiseman at the University of Hertfordshire in England wanted to find the world's funniest joke—or at least the joke that provoked the most laughter. So he launched a website called LaughLab where anyone could submit a joke or rate jokes submitted by others. There were more than forty-one thousand entries.

In the end, Wiseman and colleagues declared a winner—you can Google it easily enough—but in truth, there is no universally funny joke at which everyone laughs. Humor is influenced by geographical location, culture, maturity, level of education, intelligence, and context. Westerners regard humor as common and positive: everyone is at least potentially funny. Conversely, some cultures regard humor as a special disposition possessed only by a few.

A Caveman Walks into a Cave . . .

Humor is dictated by individual experience and taste. It's a bit like pornography: we know it when we see or hear it, but it can be hard to define.

Without humor, life and human behavior are often inexplicable, strange, and irrational. The ability to find humor, to laugh with or at someone or something, is distinctly human, though its origins and nature are not well understood.

Humor has both cognitive and affective, or emotional, elements. Cognitive processes are involved to detect and understand what's funny. Affective processes allow us to enjoy the joke. There are multiple theories about what constitutes humor. Perhaps the best known, originally postulated by Aristotle himself, is the incongruity model, which suggests that our brains are always trying to anticipate what will happen next, to marshal the appropriate resources and response. Humor happens when what we expect doesn't happen.

Other theories suggest that we laugh at others because it makes us feel better about ourselves or to reduce tension, relieve fear, overcome inhibitions, reveal suppressed desires, or deal with confusion. All of these theories explain some kinds of humor, but not all. Humans also laugh at strange noises. We are capable of laughing at things nobody else sees or hears.

The Joke's in You

The author E. B. White, whose talents spanned the children's classics *Stuart Little* and *Charlotte's Web* to his timeless guide to the English language, *The Elements of Style*, once said, "Humor can be dissected as a frog can, but the thing dies in the process and the innards are discouraging to any but the pure scientific mind."

White was right. If you need to explain a joke, break it down into its component elements, it may no longer be funny. On the other hand, what happens inside your brain when you hear a joke is fascinating.

Here's what some scientists think happens:

A guy shows up late for work. . . .

Hearing those words, your brain recognizes a joke in the offing. Various neurocircuits begin firing: the frontal lobe to process incoming information; the supplementary motor areas to direct motor activities, such as movements associated with laughter; the nucleus accumbens to trigger reward circuits when you hear the punchline.

A guy shows up late for work.

The boss yells at him, "You should've been here at 8:30!"

"Why," replies the guy, "what happened at 8:30?"

Jokes are funny because they surprise. They defy expectation. Our brains—and in particular, our frontal lobe—is constantly looking for patterns, endlessly attempting to anticipate what will come next. When you listen to a friend, you're not only hearing the words streaming from her mouth, but predicting what words will come next and how you will respond to them.

The unexpected punchline—"What happened at 8:30?"—momentarily throws everything off-kilter. Your brain shifts from information processing toward an emotional response linked to the nucleus accumbens. What did you say? the brain asks. The PFC reexamines the punchline, assesses the information anew, pulling in more conscious resources. If it "gets" the joke, the brain shifts back to the nucleus accumbens and its pleasure-and-reward circuity. You smile. You laugh.

A few years ago, researchers at the University of Southern California went looking to trace where jokes come from in the brain. They asked a group of amateur and professional improvisational comedians to write funny captions for blank cartoons from *The New Yorker* magazine while lying in an fMRI machine.

When amateur comedians wrote captions, the mPFC and temporal association cortex (TSC) were activated. The mPFC is involved in retrieving and consolidating remote long-term memory. It helps us respond to social situations. The TSC is linked to memory as well, but it's also involved in recognizing complex stimuli like human faces and speech.

More experienced comedians showed heightened activity in their temporal lobe and less in the PFC. This makes sense because the temporal lobe is known to process semantic and abstract information while the PFC is more focused on top-down decision-making. The best gags are spontaneous, the product of surprise and novelty. They aren't worked out by the logical PFC.

The same kind of brain activity appears when people study masterpiece paintings or gaze at beautiful vistas. It involves cortical regions responsible for visual processing that also have a high density of opioid receptors, which are part of the brain's reward system. A magnificent work of art, a good song, view, or joke all provide neural pleasure, though repetition (not unlike the dulling addiction of opiates) invariably reduces the thrill. We crave newness. A good joke heard again and again loses its humor.

The Best Medicine

Humor is linked to health. Studies have found that people prone to humor have stronger immune systems (based on the presence of key biomarkers), higher pain tolerances, lower blood pressure, and fewer psychological ills, such as persistent anxiety.

In one clever experiment, for example, study participants were told they would be given a mild electric shock after a period of time. Half of the group was then exposed to humorous content while waiting for the shock to come; the other just waited. Participants had their heart rates continuously measured, and they were asked to rate their anxiety levels. Everyone also took a test to measure their sense of humor.

People who scored high on the sense of humor assessment reported less anxiety, both in the group that was entertained and in the group that was not. People who were exposed to humorous material but had rated low in terms of their own sense of humor also reported less anxiety. Heart rate did not vary significantly among the groups. Bottom line: having a good sense of humor—or being exposed to humor—can help take the edge off in life.

Humor improves the aging process in important ways. It provides a sense of better health. It boosts social communication. And it generates a feeling of satisfaction with life. Higher self-esteem and lower levels of depression, anxiety, and perceived stress are associated with humor. Even older people with specific diseases have shown improvement in their health and demeanor if they use humor.

Curiosity and humor may not play as grand a role in wisdom compared to, say, compassion or decision-making, but neither are they bit players in the drama of life. Each has something to say about who you are and how wise you can be. Without curiosity, people cannot maximize learning or share what they have learned. Without humor, people may not share wisely. Humor leavens difficult truths. It helps us find commonality with others or get through the sticky patches of life.

"If fate doesn't make you laugh," said Australian author Gregory David Roberts, "you just don't get the joke." And we all want to get the joke.

Higher Callings

"To make God laugh, tell him your plans."

It's an old Yiddish witticism, though the universal truth of it, through several variations, has been attributed to many authors from Woody Allen to Mother Teresa. It alludes to the belief in someone or something larger than life or even the universe. The traits of religiosity and spirituality have figured strongly in my search for a scientific description of wisdom, though there wasn't enough consensus among experts to solidly make either a primary component of wisdom.

But many wise people are religious, spiritual, or both—at least they appear to be. But what does that mean in terms of becoming wiser faster? There is evidence of a neurobiology of spirituality similar to that of other components of wisdom. Scientists have written about a "God spot" in the brain. In the next chapter, we go looking for these answers. We examine religiosity versus spirituality (they are not the same thing) and how to measure each. To look upward, we must look inward too.

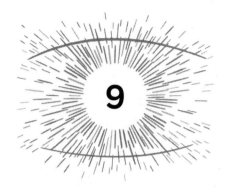

Spirituality

*Science and religion are two vividly different realms
of the human mind. They work differently at the
molecular level, but the purpose of both is alleviation
of the mind from the darkness of ignorance.*
ABHIJIT NASKAR, *Love, God and Neurons*

*The possession of knowledge does not kill the sense of
wonder and mystery. There is always more mystery.*
ANAÏS NIN, *Diary of Anaïs Nin*

I GREW UP IN a moderately religious family. Everyone in my family—
indeed like all of the families I knew—believed in the traditions of
Hinduism, including specific gods and goddesses common to the
part of India where we lived, then called Bombay state, now known
as Maharashtra state.

In India, almost 80 percent of the population belongs to the
Hindu religion. The largest minority is Muslim (14.2 percent).

Christians make up 2.3 percent of the population, followed by Sikhs and Buddhists, according to the 2011 national census. Most Hindus share some common gods and goddesses, but there are also many other deities worshipped in specific regions.

My family was not at all fastidious about our religion. We were accepting of other faiths. However, we observed many of the prevalent religious traditions. Our home contained images of gods; we went to temples when we could, but not in a compulsive way.

As a child, religion was associated with positive feelings. When we performed a pooja in our house, we would invite several friends and neighbors. The purpose of the pooja was to invoke the deities, praying to them to deliver us good fortune. These were festive occasions, with fasting in the morning until the religious function was completed, then a specially cooked, delicious lunch and mouthwatering desserts. Excitement and anticipation built in the days before the pooja. It was a social function as much as a religious one.

My unquestioned faith in religion as a child provided a magical feeling that the world was orderly and that if you did the right things like working hard and worshipping the gods, you would succeed in school and in life. Of course, I knew that only worshipping without studying was not going to help, but studying without worshipping was not appropriate either.

The town of Poona (now Pune), where I went to school, followed by college and medical school, was not a cosmopolitan city like Bombay (now Mumbai) at that time. I knew only a small number of people from other religions, and they too were involved in larger annual religious events that were a part of the entire society.

Once a year, for example, the Ganesh festival occurred, a 10-day event that involved everyone in town. Ganesh is a Hindu god, but Muslims and Christians also participated in the festival. To me, my beliefs and the ancient scriptures they were based on were universal truths. Later, when I moved to Bombay for psychiatric training, I discovered others had different religious beliefs, but even as I accepted them in others, they raised no doubts about my philosophy of life.

Things began to change after my wife and I immigrated to the United States to begin my psychiatric residency training. During the first few months, we mingled mostly with Indian compatriots. There was a sense of comfort being among others with similar beliefs, though we still experienced the culture shock of living in a place thousands of miles from our homeland—and very much different.

Gradually, I began to realize that most people in the United States had markedly different religious beliefs from my own, and even from each other. Their history and understanding of the world were quite distinct from what I had learned as a boy. For the first time, I found that many of my new American friends and colleagues, who were as nice and helpful as those we knew in Poona and Bombay, thought my beliefs were exotic, even strange. They couldn't comprehend how there could be multiple gods and goddesses or that hundreds of millions of people would worship a god with an elephant head named Ganesh.

It took me a while to not take such comments and attitudes personally. I came to understand that some people from different religions possessed quizzical views of belief systems in other religions.

I learned something else: every religion has its extremists, but most adherents of most religions in the world share compassion and empathy toward others, even when they strongly retain beliefs in their own scriptures and traditions. One can believe in one's own religious system (or in none at all) while accepting others' right to have their own.

That is when I began to think more about the nature of spirituality and less about religiosity. While specific religious and cultural
beliefs are distinct, I increasingly uncovered a common value
system shared in an unspoken way. Most people believe in something larger than themselves: a universal or cosmic entity. For most,
this entity is a god (or goddess), and their connection is intensely
personal or emotional. For a minority, their belief system is more
intellectual. It's a realization that humans are but a tiny part of
the universe.

Whether or not *Homo sapiens* is a unique species in the universe, we accept as fact that the Earth is just one small planet in one
medium-sized galaxy among untold numbers of galaxies extending
infinitely in all directions. It is this understanding—emotional and/
or intellectual—that provides humility and reinforces our desire
to go beyond selfish needs in order to help others. That, to me, is
spirituality.

In my years of pondering the meaning and value of spirituality
(which includes but extends beyond religiosity), I wondered about
the reason for its near universality. Why are most humans spiritual?
Does it have evolutionary value? Is it useful for the survival of our
species, and if so, is it biologically rooted? These are the same questions I had about wisdom. So, it was natural to combine them: is
spirituality a component of wisdom?

I and many others (but not everyone) believe the answer is yes.

Religiosity "Versus" Spirituality

People often use these words as if they are interchangeable. Certainly,
the abundance of definitions can confuse matters. I like the definitions used by my friend Dan Blazer, a distinguished expert in aging
and mental health at Duke University. He defines religion as an organized system of beliefs, practices, rituals, and symbols designed to

facilitate closeness to the sacred or transcendent. Spirituality, on the other hand, is something that encompasses religion but expands on its definition to include an understanding of answers to ultimate questions about life, meaning, and relationships with the sacred or transcendent.

I also believe that spirituality can exist in the absence of religiosity.

Dozens of major religions exist today, and within them scores, hundreds, even thousands of subgroups, denominations, or sects. Their total number, not to mention estimates of religions that have come and gone throughout human history, is a matter of debate. Let's just say we're talking about big numbers.

The concept of religion as a way to organize society and the world has been much dissected and discussed, from the ideas of Emile Durkheim and Mircea Eliade, who described religion as splitting human experience into the sacred and the profane, to Sigmund Freud and Karl Marx, who, respectively, argued that religion was merely a kind of mass neurosis or an "opiate of the masses."

I'll not debate any of these notions here. We are all entitled to our beliefs and religious practices as long as they do not harm others. At its essence, religion in its most generic form seems designed to give meaning to life by advocating for the existence of a protective creator or divinity, by helping make sense of crises, and by universalizing problems, as in we're all in this together.

Religion is something most people are familiar with. It is often a part of growing up. Going to church or synagogue or mosque or temple or someplace similar provides measurable, documented benefit. For example, attendees enjoy regular opportunities to socialize with people like themselves, a fundamental human need. They hear and learn explanations, stories, and advice for addressing many, if not all, of life's dilemmas and conundrums, which can provide emotional support and strength for coping with adversity or simply boost one's optimism and resilience.

Regular church attendance requires discipline and appropriate social behaviors, creating useful and beneficial habits for the rest of life. It provides a chance for self-reflection and meditation. And last but not least, a church, mosque, or temple is often simply a healthy place to hang out: nobody smokes or drinks inside a place of sanctity.

In places of sanctity, people can flourish.

What is flourishing? In broad terms, to flourish simply means to grow or develop in a healthy or vigorous way. That's a good description for a robust plant. For people, it has more, and more deeply nuanced, meanings. Flourishing is a state in which people experience positive emotions and positive psychosocial functioning.

In 2017, Tyler VanderWeele, a professor of epidemiology at the Harvard T.H. Chan School of Public Health, published a paper (aptly titled "On the Promotion of Human Flourishing") that both expanded and refined this idea. Flourishing, he wrote in the *Proceedings of the National Academy of Sciences*, should include doing or being well in five broad domains of human life: happiness and life satisfaction, mental and physical health, meaning and purpose, character and virtue, and close social relationships.

VanderWeele wrote that each of these domains meets the criterion of being a universally desirable outcome. We all desire each and every one of them. But something else is needed too: the stability of financial and material resources to sustain flourishing over time. It is hard to be happy if you're hungry or to find meaning when you can't find a job.

VanderWeele reviewed the scientific literature (longitudinal, experimental, and quasi-experimental studies) to identify the major determinants of human flourishing. He found four common paths: family, work, education, and religious community. Let's look at the last one.

In 2012, the Pew Research Center estimated that approximately 84 percent of the world's population reported some sort of religious affiliation. Within the United States, according to a Gallup poll three years later, 89 percent of Americans said they believed in God or a universal spirit, 78 percent considered religion to be a very important or fairly important part of life, 79 percent identified with a specific religious group, and 36 percent reported having attended a religious service within the previous week.

There is fairly good evidence that participation in a religious community is longitudinally associated with the various domains of flourishing. A number of studies have found that attending religious services is linked to better health. Although much of this literature is methodologically weak, several well-designed longitudinal studies suggest regular attendance at religious services is associated with greater longevity, a 30 percent lower incidence of depression, a fivefold lower rate of suicide, longer survival with cancer, and other positive outcomes.

Importantly, the evidence underscores that it is the act of attending religious services that is strongly predictive of health. It is the communal form of religious practice that appears to bring about better health outcomes.

Religion is commonly equated with virtue. Righteousness equals virtuousness. Again, the science here is a bit vague, largely dependent on cross-sectional studies with inherent limitations, but nonetheless there have been some randomized priming experiments (in which a stimulus to one implicit or unconscious memory influences a person's response to another stimulus) to suggest at least some short-term effects of religious prompts on prosocial behaviors. Put another way, some lessons unconsciously learned at church or temple or mosque appear to influence or guide later behaviors in beneficial ways.

There is evidence that people who attend services are subsequently more generous and more civically engaged and that encouragement to pray increases forgiveness, gratitude, and trust. And finally, attending religious services improves connections between people, boosting the likelihood of making new friends, building social support networks, and getting and staying married.

Of course, organized religion is often maligned. It's a commonly heard assertion that religion has killed more people than war. This is not exactly true. While many conflicts of the past and present have been and are fueled by theologies, far more have been caused by simple grabs for power or resources. But the point is duly noted. Humans do harm and kill their fellow humans in the name of a belief system.

A number of people consider themselves spiritual but not religious. Saying you're spiritual places emphasis on the well-being of your mind, body, and spirit rather than declaring support for an organized religion or like-minded group that might seem problematic.

Measuring Religiosity and Spirituality

There are many scales available to measure degrees of religiosity and spirituality. For example, one systematic review in 2010 by Swiss and American researchers looking at measures of spirituality in clinical research identified 35 different tools used to assess general spirituality, spiritual well-being, spiritual coping, and spiritual needs. However, many of them use *religiosity* and *spirituality* synonymously.

Scientific efforts to measure spirituality typically depend on self-reporting. That is, study participants are asked to describe themselves by agreeing or disagreeing with specific statements. My colleagues and I used self-reports in a 2011 study measuring the "correlates of spirituality in older women." We constructed a five-item measure derived from larger scales. First were two questions asking how often a person attended church or synagogue or other place of worship and how often she spent time in private spiritual activities. Those questions were followed by three statements:

In my life I experience the presence of the divine.

My spiritual beliefs lie behind my whole approach to life.

I carry my spiritual beliefs into all other dealings in life.

Self-reporting has some obvious limitations. There's an inherent bias when people describe themselves. They might go easy on themselves, avoiding truly realistic assessments, or answer in a way that they think others will like or approve of. Also, they may not fully understand the statements or may comprehend them in a way different from others.

While it's possible to surmise religiosity to some degree based on concrete external measures like attendance at church or other places of worship, there are no validated, objective measures of religiosity or spirituality at the moment. But done correctly, with careful crafting and rigorous review, self-reports do provide a glimpse into the human psyche. They offer a rough idea about an individual's level of religiosity or spirituality.

The Nature of Spirituality

No discussion of spirituality is complete without at least a mention of the role nature and the natural world play. Our first level of experience involves our connection to the environment, good and bad.

Humans have always drawn inspiration from the natural world in all its forms: honoring, revering, and celebrating other animals, rivers, mountains, trees, the sun, the moon, everything around us and all we can sense. The beauty of nature can leave us breathless. Its scale and complexity, from virus to cosmos, reminds us that we are part of something far larger than ourselves and grand beyond imagination. We are a part of nature and yet, empowered with unrivaled minds, able to step back to more fully appreciate it.

Spirituality in Wisdom

Religious traditions in Buddhism, Christianity, Hinduism, and Judaism stress religiosity—or at least spirituality—as a characteristic of wise people.

As I mentioned in chapter 2 on the neuroscience of wisdom, with UC San Diego colleague Trey Meeks and several outside collaborators (Monika Ardelt, Dan Blazer, Helena Kraemer, and George Vaillant), I went looking for a scientific definition of wisdom. We conducted a survey of international researchers in wisdom in 2010, asking them to define the characteristics of wisdom compared to those for intelligence and spirituality. We started with 53 conceptual statements, grouping and paring as commonalities and differences emerged.

Wisdom differed from intelligence on 49 of the 53 conceptual characteristics. The only overlap contained skepticism, desire to learn or possess knowledge, and the (unimportance of) participation in religious services, rituals, and membership in a faith community.

The experts found greater commonality between wisdom and spirituality than they did between wisdom and intelligence. Sixteen items were rated as important to both: altruism, "other-centeredness," a willingness to forgive others, ego integrity, a sense of peace with eventual death, humility, gratitude, self-compassion, mindfulness, reverence for nature, nonviolence, ethical conduct, calmness, a sense of purpose in life, life satisfaction, and a general sense of well-being.

Another characteristic common to both wisdom and spirituality, said the experts, was that both were fundamentally traits.

They weren't present or absent, but rather present to some degree in anyone deemed wise or spiritual.

At the same time, wisdom and spirituality were not considered synonymous. For example, the experts said a rich knowledge of life, realism, value relativism, learning from experience, and acceptance of uncertainty in life were more characteristic of wisdom than of spirituality. Resilience and successful coping strategies were thought to be components of wisdom more than of spirituality or intelligence. Conversely, a sense of higher power, connection with a wider universe, and nonattachment to the material world were characteristics of spirituality more than of wisdom.

Living and Dying with Spirit

The rabbi Sharon Brous is celebrated as one of America's most influential religious leaders, in particular for cofounding IKAR, a postdenominational congregation based in Los Angeles that embraces all of the different Jewish groups that have developed since ancient times. Brous remains its rabbi.

IKAR was founded in 2004, a time when the world seemed particularly aflame with violence, from wars in Iraq and Afghanistan to terrorist attacks around the globe. Brous was a new mother, and fearful. "I remember thinking, 'My God, what kind of world did we bring this child into?'" she recalled in a 2016 TED Talk.

Religion had become (again) a principal battlefield for people, cultures, and ideologies. Religious extremism had taken many forms, all of them bloody and vindictive. The promise and benefit of organized religion, a life of connectedness and contentment, was vanishing, or so it seemed to Brous.

So Brous, with others, set out to reclaim and reinvent her religion by founding IKAR, which means "the heart of the matter." If all sacred traditions contain the raw material to justify violence and extremism, she said, they also contain the raw material to justify compassion, coexistence, and kindness.

The basis of IKAR—and similar efforts by others and other denominations—rests on four specific commitments:

WAKEFULNESS. This is the idea that we need to be aware of what is happening around us and, if appropriate and necessary, take action. It's hard to do. It's easier to become psychically numb, shut ourselves off from external pain and discomfort, and convince ourselves there is nothing we can do. Of course, if we do nothing, nothing is done.

HOPE. Hope is neither naïve nor an opiate. It is an act of defiance against the "politics of pessimism and the culture of despair," said Brous, who recalls attending an African American church service on the South Side of Chicago in the summer of 2016. More than three thousand people had already been shot in that city in just half a year. Brous remembers listening to the sermon and then a choir, which sang of love and need. "I realized in that moment that this is what religion is supposed to be about. It's supposed to be about giving people back a sense of purpose, a sense of hope, a sense that they and their dreams fundamentally matter in this world that tells them that they don't matter at all."

MIGHTINESS. There is strength in numbers, but individuals are not without power. Every person can love, forgive, protest, be part of the conversation, push the envelope—even if it's just a little.

INTERCONNECTEDNESS. Brous tells the story of a man walking along a remote Alaska beach in 2012 when he discovered a soccer ball washed ashore. It had some Japanese writing on it. The man posted a photo of the ball on social media, and a Japanese teenager contacted him. The teen had lost everything in a notorious tsunami that had devastated his country one year earlier, killing almost twenty thousand people. The Alaska man later returned the ball personally, along with a volleyball that had also washed ashore with similar writing that belonged to another Japanese teenager. The world is not so big, and we are not so far apart as we imagine.

In my work, I have written about people on the cusp of dying, asking them what they have learned about life and the nature of wisdom. Theirs is a unique perspective, though obviously one we will all experience.

Many people seek comfort in religion, in familiar rites and rituals that help push back the myriad fears surrounding death in favor of a belief in a bigger and better existence beyond. "I have a relationship with God, and if I need something, I ask Him," one person told me.

Others seek strength and solace in less formal ways, perhaps described as more spiritual than religious. They find renewed joy in sunsets and just waking up to another day. They find strength and solace within.

"Wisdom is the inner voice that we're given at birth," said another person, "but most people seem to seek exterior forces and people, places, and things in order to make them happier, but to me wisdom itself emanates from within us. We just have to slow down long enough to find it."

The Body of Spirit: Health Outcomes

Numerous studies have found a correlation between the use of religion as a positive tool for coping with life's challenges and positive health outcomes. Spirituality can be predictive of better physical and mental health outcomes—and vice versa. Low spiritual well-being and religious struggle have been associated with more severe depression, hopelessness, suicidal ideation, and even higher mortality rates.

But for many practicing physicians, religiosity and spirituality are sensitive subjects. They may know little or nothing about a patient's religion, sense of spirituality, or inner life. They may not consider it their business, but a better understanding or greater insight might benefit treatment and prognosis.

My colleague, Douglas Ziedonis, associate vice chancellor for health sciences at UC San Diego, suggests asking three basic questions: What helps you get through tough times? Who do you turn to when you need support? What meaning does this experience have for you?

Most studies of spirituality and health have focused on specialized populations, such as patients who are ill or people who have experienced recent personal loss. It's harder to meaningfully incorporate spirituality into models of well-being and healthy aging.

That's what we did in our 2011 study of older women. We wanted to see how spirituality correlated with measured domains of self-reported successful aging, including health-related quality of life and levels of depression.

We looked at 1,942 women, aged 60 to 91 years, who were living in San Diego County and were part of the largest national study of women supported by the National Institutes of Health, called the Women's Health Initiative. We asked about religious attendance and spiritual beliefs and then compared those answers to self-assessments of how well the women thought they were aging.

Just over 40 percent said they attended a religious service more than once a week. Fifty-six percent said they carried their spiritual beliefs into all other dealings in life. And 55 percent strongly agreed with the statement, "In my life, I experience the presence of the divine."

Our findings supported our hypothesis that spirituality is associated with successful cognitive and emotional aging. Greater spirituality correlated with higher resilience and higher optimism. Higher spirituality or religiosity also correlated with faster recovery from medical illnesses.

One particular surprise was that spirituality was associated with lower education, lower income, and lower likelihood of being in a marital or committed relationship. The reasons aren't clear, but one likely explanation is that increased spirituality offers a coping strategy to negative life events and for grappling with inevitable uncertainties, especially for people in socioeconomically disadvantaged situations.

Possible Neurobiological Roots of Spirituality

Several scientists have suggested that religious and spiritual beliefs have a neurobiological basis. Medical literature brims with carefully documented accounts of what Oliver Sacks, the late British neurologist and poet laureate of medicine, has called "life-altering religious experiences," moments of overwhelming intensity often accompanied by a sense of supernatural bliss and rarified ecstasy. He believed that these were products of temporary brain dysfunction.

In 1970, Kenneth Dewhurst and A. W. Beard, a research psychiatrist and psychologist, respectively, in the United Kingdom, published a widely noted series of case studies describing sudden religious conversions following epileptic seizures.

In one case, they recount the story of a bus conductor unexpectedly overwhelmed by a feeling of elation while collecting fares. "He was suddenly overcome with a feeling of bliss. He felt he was literally in Heaven. He collected the fares correctly, telling his passengers at the same time how pleased he was to be in Heaven," they wrote in the *Journal of Neurology, Neurosurgery, and Psychiatry*.

"He remained in this state of exaltation, hearing divine and angelic voices, for two days. Afterwards he was able to recall these experiences and he continued to believe in their validity."

Three years later, the conductor suffered three epileptic seizures on three successive days. He experienced feelings of elation again, but this time he said his mind "cleared." Now, he no longer believed in heaven and hell or in an afterlife or in any divinity.

Sacks suggested that the reason hallucinations seem so real is that they deploy the same systems of the brain used for actual, normal perceptions—the auditory pathways for voices heard, for example, or the fusiform face area for faces seen.

There is a field of scientific endeavor called neurotheology or spiritual neuroscience, which seeks to understand the relationship between the human brain and religion. Andrew Newberg and others have reported on brain scans of religious and nonreligious people—nuns, monks, people speaking in tongues, atheists—to see if there are in fact differences between the brains of believers and nonbelievers. And they have found some.

For example, the brains of people who have practiced meditation or who have prayed regularly over many years exhibit increased activity and greater tissue mass in the frontal lobes, regions associated with attention and reward.

In other experiments, researchers have found that when religious people prayed to God, it activated the same parts of the brain triggered when they talked to their next-door neighbor. "In other words," Newberg explained to *Scientific American* in 2012, "in the religious person's brain, God is just as real as any object or person."

Research also suggests that brain chemistry plays a role. One study found that believers were much more likely than skeptics to see words and faces on a jumbled screen where there were none, while conversely, skeptics were more likely to not see words and faces that actually were on the same jumbled screen.

When skeptics were given the drug L-dopa, a hormone that increases the activity of the dopaminergic system associated with attention and motivation, they were just as likely as believers to interpret jumbled patterns into words and faces.

Similarly, the brain chemistry of people is different after attending a seven-day religious retreat. Postretreat scans revealed decreases in dopamine and serotonin transporter binding, meaning more of these neurotransmitters were available in the brain. Both are associated with positive emotions and spiritual feelings.

Hallucinogenic drugs, such as LSD and peyote, affect the brain's serotonin system. These psychedelic drugs work by temporarily erasing the mental divisions between individuals and the world around them. Users report their sense of self becomes diminished or completely dissolved, resulting in a moment of expanded awareness and connection with their surroundings.

Certainly, we are far from knowing the exact neurobiology of religiosity and spirituality. It's notable that some of the same brain regions and neurotransmitters discussed earlier in connection with the neurobiology of wisdom show up here too, mainly the prefrontal cortex and dopamine.

At the same time, however, a few other brain components appear to get involved in religiosity and spirituality—the temporal lobes and serotonin. This is not to suggest that differences between religious versus nonreligious people or spiritual versus nonspiritual individuals are a result of differences in their brain structures.

It is more likely that behaviors and activities such as meditation or prayer produce measurable, physiological changes in the brain.

Enhancing Spirituality

During World War I, at a memorial service for a fallen soldier in Devon, England, a speaker read a letter from an unnamed chaplain serving on the front. In part, the letter said, "Tell the Territorials and soldiers at home that they must know God before they come to the front if they would face what lies before them. We have no atheists in the trenches. Men are not ashamed to say that, though they never prayed before, they pray now with all their hearts."

That statement ("We have no atheists in the trenches") would take on a life of its own. A version of it would circulate a generation later during World War II: "There are no atheists in foxholes."

In recent years, researchers of all stripes have explored how enhancing spirituality might directly improve well-being, physical and psychological. The work is ongoing; in many ways and areas, it is still very early days. But there is much to intrigue and encourage. Interventions to enhance spirituality and other components of wisdom are discussed in the next chapter. Here I will narrate just a few.

In a 2011 randomized clinical trial—the gold standard for such things—a team of Canadian and American researchers investigated whether a spiritual teaching program could effectively treat major depression. They divided a group of participants with diagnosed mild to moderately severe depression into two groups: one received an eight-week, home-based spirituality teaching program and the second was put on a waiting list—that is, no intervention until week nine, when they too would receive the spirituality teaching program. The use of drugs, herbal remedies, or psychotherapeutic treatments was prohibited during the study period.

The spiritual teaching program itself was fairly simple, originally developed by a psychiatrist for use in workshops. Each week, participants listened to different 90-minute audio CDs, followed by a guided visualization practice. There was also a daily 15-minute taped progressive relaxation exercise. The CDs contained lessons and stories with spiritual themes and messages on topics like transcendence, connectedness to others, nature or the divine, forgiveness, and compassion. The discussions were nondenominational, so everyone could participate in their own way.

At the end of the eight weeks, study participants took a test to measure the degree of their depression, which was compared to results from the same test they had taken before the study began. The differences were significant: For those who had taken the spirituality program, their mean score on the depression scale dropped from 20.4 at baseline to 11.9 at eight weeks. When they were tested again at 16 weeks and at 24 weeks, mean scores had continued to decrease to 10.7 and 10.4, respectively.

In the waiting list control group, the mean depression score decreased slightly from 20.3 at baseline to 18.0 at eight weeks, but after they received the spiritual intervention treatment, their mean depression scores dropped to 12.0 at 16 weeks and 10.1 at 24 weeks.

These response rates are similar to those produced by pharmacological and psychological interventions. Most antidepressant drugs take two to three weeks (or longer) to begin working, and their effectiveness is often compromised by side effects, high costs, and when people simply stop taking them. Psychotherapy is an option without side effects, but its availability is currently limited by costs, time constraints, and available resources.

The literature is rich with other studies in which religion and spirituality have been tested as treatment aids for a variety of ailments, from generalized anxiety disorder (GAD), characterized by excessive, uncontrollable, and often irrational worry (in a given year, roughly 2 percent of American adults experience GAD), to migraines, cardiovascular disease, and even breast cancer.

The impact, not surprisingly, varies. In GAD case studies, the introduction of spiritual activities like deep-breathing exercises while focusing on a religious mental image or the use of coping statements like "God will not give me more than I can handle" has measurably decreased severity of worry symptoms.

For study participants with cardiovascular disease or breast cancer, spiritually themed practices and interventions didn't directly improve their physical conditions, but they did seem to make things more tolerable; patients' quality of life improved.

For example, in a 2011 pilot study investigating the influence of spirituality intervention on quality of life, depression, and anxiety in adults with cardiovascular disease, participants practiced different forms of meditation to promote self-discovery, forgiveness, and appreciation of others and better awareness of the world around them.

One transformed patient later wrote in a journal: "I have lived here for 25 years but rarely really look at my environment. Lately, I have been watching the maple tree we planted when we first moved here. How it has grown over the years. I watch as it bends, but remains tall and strong through rainstorms. I feel a special bond with this tree and can learn something about inner strength from it."

We all can. We need security, support, and stability too, especially within ourselves. For many people, spirituality and religion are at least part of the answer, providing both a sense of rootedness and something more ethereal, a warmth and vision not unlike golden sunshine falling upon the canopy of a tree.

Part III

*Enhancing Practical and
Societal Wisdom*

This final section of the book is both the most pragmatic and the most speculative. I discuss two kinds of wisdom: practical and societal. Wisdom should be practical and not just theoretical. There's no point to being wise if one can't effectively use it in life and living. And so, in chapter 10, I share tips and observations, based on research by myself and others, that you can apply in your own quest to become wiser faster. It's all part and parcel of a larger, emerging concept called positive psychiatry.

I then explore the future of wisdom, or more specifically, the possibilities of incipient technologies and treatments to alter the acquisition of wisdom, from brain games to smart pills, or even further beyond, the notion of "artificial wisdom" and the possibilities that machines/robots might be programmed to possess traits like compassion, self-reflection, humor, curiosity, decisiveness, and more.

Finally, though we tend to think of wisdom in terms of individuals, there is such a thing as societal wisdom. Wisdom is universal in its basic biology and concept, but its level and manifestations may vary to some extent in different societies and at different time periods. Is the modern society wiser or less wise than it was in the past? Arguments can be made on both sides. While the global society has made tremendous progress on several fronts, we are also currently facing new behavioral epidemics of suicides, drug abuse, and loneliness. Some cultures are faring better than others. Are some societies wiser than others? If so, how do we know and, more to the point, how do we help our own society become wiser?

Becoming Wiser Faster

A wise man changes his mind sometimes,
but a fool never. To change your mind is the
best evidence you have one.
DESMOND FORD, Australian theologian

Do you want to know who you are? Don't ask. Act!
Action will delineate and define you.
WITOLD GOMBROWICZ, Polish author

AS A PHYSICIAN, and specifically as a psychiatrist, I have felt for many years that the fields of medicine, including psychiatry, have been too narrowly focused on illnesses, pathology, risk factors, and treatment of symptoms. Psychiatry is traditionally defined as a branch of medicine that focuses on the study and treatment of mental illnesses. I find this conceptualization both limited and damaging. Medicine and psychiatry must be broadened to include health, including mental health, and not just diseases.

Physicians need to treat illnesses and relieve suffering, of course, but they must also study and promote positive protective factors like resilience, optimism, and wisdom, and positive health outcomes such as well-being. They must seek not only to reduce symptoms, but also to prevent illnesses. When I became president of the American Psychiatric Association (APA) in May 2012, one of my main tasks was to finalize the new version of what is (erroneously) called the "Bible of Psychiatry"—a revised (the fifth) version of the *Diagnostic and Statistical Manual*, which was originally published in 1952. The APA is the largest psychiatric organization in the world and the oldest national medical society in the US, founded in 1844. Benjamin Rush, a signer of the Declaration of Independence, was the founding president of the APA. The *DSM-5* is an update of diagnoses and diagnostic criteria for all listed psychiatric disorders. It was a decade-long, multimillion-dollar effort that involved hundreds of psychiatrists, psychologists, and various other clinicians and researchers from different continents. Not surprisingly, there were several controversies associated with it too. I am proud of my role as the APA president in ensuring a successful final phase of the approval and publication of the *DSM-5*. However, personally, I wanted to go beyond the *DSM-5*. I made positive psychiatry the theme of my presidency.

Whereas positive *psychology* is a popular term even among the lay public, thanks to pioneering work by Martin Seligman and others, I found that there was very little coverage of factors like resilience, optimism, and social support in psychiatric literature or practice. A Google search for positive psychology in 2012 yielded thousands of results, while a search for positive *psychiatry* yielded none—that is right, zero. In my 2013 APA presidential address, I emphasized the need for studying and implementing enhancement of patients' well-being and happiness through promotion of positive psychosocial factors. I called it positive psychiatry. Colleagues and I published two books and wrote several papers on this topic. In recent years, a number of sessions have been held on this topic at international conferences, and this new subfield of psychiatry is growing. There is growing evidence that positive psychosocial factors significantly reduce morbidity and improve longevity. In my own research with people suffering from schizophrenia—who have a significantly higher disease risk and a 15- to 20-year shorter life span than the general population—patients who described themselves as happy tended to have greater resilience, wisdom, and social support and were also healthier. We obtained similar findings in people with cancers and those with HIV/AIDS. Positive psychiatry is really positive medicine. Traits like wisdom impact not just mental but also physical health and even longevity.

Science Looks to Intervene

Wisdom is malleable. Most personality traits are only partially inherited—35 to 55 percent—which means the remainder is subject to external forces and our own behavior. Wisdom can increase with age and personal experience, good and bad. It can be adversely affected by physiological effect or illness, such as brain trauma or frontotemporal dementia. But can it be purposefully modified and enhanced through positive, proactive means, such as behavioral interventions?

Colleagues and I went looking to see if anyone had attempted a science-based intervention directly targeting wisdom, or more plausibly, one of its components, such as empathy or emotional regulation or spirituality.

Of the hundreds of articles that emerged, just 57 were deemed relevant to our investigation. That is, each qualifying paper described a randomized controlled trial that sought to enhance a component of wisdom, was published in English, and had a minimum sample size of 40 individuals. Moreover, it had to use a published and tested measure to assess that component and present data in a way that allowed us to calculate the magnitude of change. Of the 57 studies that met our strict criteria, 29 had focused on prosocial behaviors like empathy and compassion, 13 on emotional regulation, and 15 on spirituality. The study samples (the total number of people included was 7,096) included people with psychiatric or physical illnesses and those from the general community. Forty-seven percent of these studies reported significant improvement with medium to large effect sizes—a technical term used to describe magnitude of improvement. Thus, interventions to enhance spirituality, emotional regulation, and prosocial behaviors were effective in nearly half of the people with mental or physical illnesses and from the community.

There were, of course, several limitations to these published studies. Sample sizes in individual trials were generally small to medium. Information about the people included, outcomes, and statistics used was variable across the studies. Importantly, most of them did not include a broad measure of overall wisdom.

But this fact stood out: in nearly one-half of the interventions to enhance prosocial behaviors, emotional regulation, or spirituality, people with mental or physical illnesses or those from a community at large experienced benefit. By attempting to improve elements of wisdom, some people accomplished their goal. It's a fundamentally important point, not just in the context of bettering ourselves as individuals, but also as a society wrestling with behavioral epidemics like loneliness, suicide, and opioid abuse—all issues we will discuss in greater detail in chapter 12.

The only wisdom-focused intervention was a pilot study involving nine older Vietnam veterans (aged 61 to 70) participating in a larger group counseling program for people suffering from posttraumatic stress disorder (PTSD). These participants went through a structured process in which they consciously and purposefully reviewed their lives through group discussion, writing, and the like. Reminiscence and integrating memories into new life narratives has been found to boost morale, self-esteem, and life satisfaction, especially in older adults who may increasingly feel a loss of control or relevance. In this case, life review prior to PTSD group therapy seemed to help reduce symptoms of depression among the participants. More to our point, when participants were asked to self-assess their levels of wisdom, they said the process had made them wiser. But this was a very small study. Its structure made it difficult to draw grand conclusions. However, our group has, subsequent to the review mentioned above, completed a new clinical trial that showed increase in resilience and wisdom and reduction in subjective stress with a group intervention in five retirement or senior housing communities located in three US states (California, Nevada, and Illinois). There were 89 adults over age 60 residing in independent living sectors of these senior housing communities. We studied the effects of a novel one-month group intervention that incorporated savoring, gratitude, and engagement in value-based activities. It was administered not by our research staff, but by unlicensed residential staff in those facilities who were trained by researchers. There was a one-month control period without any treatment, followed by the one-month intervention, and then a three-month follow-up without intervention.

We used validated self-report measures of resilience, perceived stress, well-being, and wisdom (the San Diego Wisdom Scale, or SD-WISE, described earlier) collected at months 0 (baseline), 1 (pre-intervention), 2 (postintervention), and 5 (follow-up).

Treatment adherence (compliance) and satisfaction with the intervention were high. Compared to the no-treatment control period, wisdom and perceived stress improved from month 1 to month 2, while resilience improved from month 1 to month 5.

The magnitude of change (effect size) was small in this sample, which is not surprising because the participants had relatively high levels of resilience and wisdom at baseline.

This study demonstrates feasibility of conducting pragmatic intervention trials in senior housing communities. The intervention resulted in significant improvement in wisdom, subjective stress, and resilience despite having relatively high levels of wisdom and resilience to start with. Future studies are warranted, particularly in samples with lower baseline scores on scales for wisdom and resilience and for people residing in assisted living facilities. Nonetheless, the feasibility of increasing levels of wisdom and resilience with a behavioral intervention is exciting.

Our review underscores the idea that it is eminently plausible to enhance parts of wisdom and, in doing so, improve wisdom overall. You build a house brick by brick. You take a journey one step at a time. It's the same with improving wisdom.

What does the literature on wisdom interventions tell us about increasing our level of wisdom in everyday life—that is, becoming wiser faster?

Practical Wisdom Means Wise Decision-Making in Daily Life

As mentioned earlier, the ancient Greeks talked about two types of wisdom: theoretical or transcendental (*sophia*) and practical (*phronesis*). The former is a kind of "scientific knowledge, combined with intuitive reason, of the things that are highest in nature," wrote Aristotle in his *Nicomachean Ethics*.

Of course, most people are more interested in the practical type of wisdom because it's the kind that can be applied to actual life and help make living it better. Unlike theoretical wisdom, whose definition suggests profound and momentous rumination, making wise practical decisions is mostly about making them often and as second nature. It's about decisions, large and small, made daily. It's about forming a habit.

Part of why I like to read ethics or advice columns is to see what my recommended response might be, if anybody asked. It's a good way to challenge yourself—and your ability to make decisions—without having to actually experience the unfortunate real-life scenarios. You can do it alone or in discussion with family or friends. Read the letter or column, but not the answer. What would you do? Think about solutions. Talk about them. Then read the expert's answer to see how yours compares.

Also, remember that the expert's opinion may not be the right solution for you, so differing from the expert doesn't make you wrong. What is important is to understand the logic behind different suggested solutions. Actively participating in discussions or friendly debates, and thus engaging your brain, can help keep your cognitive skills sharp and ready.

Of course, making good decisions can be hard, and not just because the topic or choices are difficult or the solution unclear. When you focus on a specific task, issue, or problem for an extended period of time, you are flexing your executive "muscle," and like actual muscles in your body, executive function has a limited capacity. It can become tired, hindering further activity. There is abundant research to illustrate this point. Studies have shown that students who take the SAT find it harder to focus on subsequent activities for a period of time.

It doesn't even have to be something as mentally taxing as taking the SAT. University of Minnesota researchers have found that study participants who made more choices in a mall were less likely to do well when solving simple algebra problems, and college students asked to mark their course preferences to satisfy degree requirements were much more likely to procrastinate on preparing for an important test. Instead of studying, their "tired" minds turned to more relaxing, less taxing activities.

Psychologists call moments when you're too tired to think "decision fatigue." It can happen when you're called on to make very tough decisions or when you find yourself having to make many smaller choices, one after another: what to eat, which shirt to wear, how best to get to work, what emails to answer first, and so on. Decision fatigue is the declining ability to make quality decisions over a period of time in which you make many decisions.

The result may be that your brain starts looking for shortcuts. In her Psych Central blog, *The Exhausted Woman*, Christine Hammond writes that the well-worn paths of past poor decisions become easier to follow again.

You need to take this into account when making decisions. You need to pay attention to how you feel physically, emotionally, and psychologically. Our bodies follow 24-hour circadian rhythms of sleep and wakefulness. We all have periods when we are particularly alert or just the opposite: those of us who pop awake with the dawn's first light and those who happily burn the midnight oil, morning people versus night owls. Don't make big decisions at your lowest ebb.

And stay in the moment. Step back. If you've been focused on a task, exercising self-control, or just making lots of small choices, don't just turn around and make a big one in a rush.

"Intelligence is knowing the right answer," observed Tim Fargo, author and cofounder of one of the biggest insurance fraud investigation companies in the country. "Wisdom is knowing when to say it." Or in this case, when to decide to act.

Self-Reflection

Wise decisions involve all of the components of wisdom, in varying degrees, but the first step to adopting wise decision-making as a habit is to have a realistic understanding of where you stand in terms of these components. Wisdom demands honest self-reflection; anything less defeats the purpose.

You need to know which components of wisdom you are strong in and which you are not. If you can't take a hard, honest look at yourself, if you can't seriously and without varnish consider your strengths and weaknesses, then you have no real foundation on which to build a better, wiser you.

Self-reflection helps facilitate better decision-making. We are all burdened by biases that influence our choices. We jump to conclusions; miss the forest for the trees; suffer from "hammer syndrome," the idea that if all you have is a hammer, then every problem looks like a nail. We are prone to defer to people of authority or go with whatever the majority is doing. Or we can be overconfident.

Self-reflection is part of the antidote. It makes us consider decisions in the context of ourselves and the environment, good and bad. That's not to say that wisdom requires maximum scores in every component. There can be too much of a good thing. Excessive self-reflection might result in too little attention paid to anyone else. Too much empathy or an unwillingness to accept uncertainty may be paralyzing and lead to more hand-wringing than needed action.

As with most things, the key is moderation and balance. One doesn't need or even want to score a maximum 5 on every category of the Jeste-Thomas Wisdom Index. A score of 4 or even a 3 might be better in the context of other components or in particular situations.

A lack of time is usually the first reason cited for why people can't take a moment to reflect on their lives and selves, but there are other reasons: They may not know how. They may not like the process. They may think it's not a good use of time, or they're biased toward action.

Here are some tips to help you become more reflective:

- *Identify important questions, but don't try to answer them just yet.*

- *Find a reflection process that works for you. It could be writing down your thoughts, talking with a trusted friend, or long walks alone.*

- *Schedule time. It can start with as little as a few minutes each day. Then just do it. Go back to your questions. Think. Be still. Consider possibilities and perspectives. Look beyond the obvious. You don't have to like or agree with what you're thinking. You only need to examine it.*

We are all burdened with egocentric biases. Nothing grabs our attention more than things that grab at ourselves, that affect us. One way to resolve truly difficult personal problems or dilemmas is to step away from yourself. Think about issues in the third person, or using your name rather than "I." It's something you do naturally when a family member or friend comes to you for advice. Do it for yourself. Think about a problem as if it were someone else's, and then take your own best advice.

Empathy and Compassion

You can be wise without being funny or with varying degrees of decisiveness. You cannot be wise if you lack empathy and compassion—for others and for yourself. Compassion and self-compassion should be balanced.

The historian Jon Meacham has noted that Franklin Delano Roosevelt possessed a remarkably robust ego, but it was tempered by "gifts of self-knowledge and a compassion for the plight of others, saving graces that enabled him to become one of a handful of truly great and transformative presidents."

Roosevelt frequently shows up on lists of wise people. He was capable of bringing together and guiding a nation through the Great Depression and a world war (despite being constrained by a wheelchair for most of his adult life due to polio and Guillain-Barré syndrome). He led millions of people, and his example, in this context, should be obvious: if you do not possess an abiding affinity and appreciation for others, known and unknown, then you are alone—and lost.

Traditionally, psychosocial interventions have sought to alleviate negative emotional states, but there is growing interest and realization that it's important to cultivate positive emotional states and qualities too. A patient with deep-seated anger is far better served if that more difficult emotion is not merely moderated, but replaced with a filling sense of contentment, equanimity, and even joy.

In recent years, it has become increasingly clear that compassion can be trained. You aren't born with all the compassion you will ever have. You can learn how to have more—and with it, greater wisdom.

In 2012, a group of researchers at Stanford University recruited a community sample of 100 adults who were randomly assigned to a nine-week compassion cultivation training program or to a control group on a waiting list. The goal of the study was to determine whether regular, everyday folks could be taught to be more compassionate.

Before and after the nine-week training period, participants completed self-reports measuring their compassion for others, how much compassion they received from others, and self-compassion.

The Stanford study found that compassion training, which relied substantially on guided meditation courses, improved all three domains of compassion in participants. They felt greater compassion for others. They received more from others. And they were more self-compassionate. The more participants practiced formal meditation, the greater their compassion.

Among the more popular ways to boost compassion and empathy for yourself and others is a form of meditation called lovingkindness meditation (LKM), originally taught by Buddha, and mentioned briefly in chapter 5. It is intended to open and sweeten the mind, and thus life itself.

In essence, lovingkindness meditation involves finding a quiet time and space, clearing your mind of contemporary thoughts and stresses, and replacing them with warm, caring, and grateful thoughts about others, whether a respected and beloved family member, mentor, someone you barely know, or an erstwhile enemy. By focusing entirely on positive thoughts and repeating mantras like "May you live with ease. May you be happy. May you be free of pain," your own sense of well-being is lifted and strengthened.

Does it work? Many believe so. The 2016 study conducted by researchers at Cardiff University in the UK was a randomized controlled trial of lovingkindness meditation using mixed online methods. They recruited 809 adults in the UK and US. Half followed video-based instructions in lovingkindness meditation, completed questionnaires, and used both online diaries and forums; the control half participated in a light physical exercise course.

At the end of the study, which involved 10-minute daily sessions of lovingkindness meditation for 20 days, participants were assessed on a variety of outcomes: satisfaction with life, depression, empathic concern, and altruism. Both the lovingkindness participants and those who took the light exercise course experienced an increased and generally similar boost in their sense of well-being, but those who underwent lovingkindness training described a richer variety of experiences, both personally and in dealing with others.

"Do I feel I am changing?" wrote one study participant. "A little. Not great Eureka moments, but I do find that I look around me more when I am out, and I notice more. As I pass people in the street, I really look at them and think about their lives. If they look ill, I word-lessly send them wishes for good health. Or if they look cold, I wish them warmth. Because of this, I now feel more involved in the local community and am beginning to see that I do belong here."

Self-compassion is just as important as compassion for others. We all make mistakes. We all fail from time to time. Failure is usu-ally a better teacher than success. But when failure happens, you need to give yourself a break occasionally to better keep issues in perspective and your eye on the greater prize. Self-compassion can be learned too.

In a 2014 study by researchers at the University of Texas at Austin and in Germany, 52 female college students were randomly assigned to either an intervention designed to teach skills of self-compassion or an active control group intervention in which general time man-agement skills were taught.

The self-compassion intervention consisted of three weekly group sessions learning how to be less judgmental about oneself, how to better connect with others, and how to become more mind-ful. Between sessions, participants had "homework" in which they tried to practice what they had learned.

At the end of the study, a variety of measures showed that the self-compassion intervention group displayed significantly greater increases in self-compassion, mindfulness, optimism, and self-efficacy than the active control group. They were also less prone to negative rumination, a cognitive process linked to depression.

More recently, New Zealand scientists looked at self-compassion in treating patients with diabetes. Mood difficulties are common among patients with the disease and are, in fact, linked to poor blood glucose control and increased complications.

So, in a randomized clinical trial, the researchers divided patients with type 1 or type 2 diabetes into one group that received an eight-week mindful self-compassion program (weekly sessions that included mediation and ways to soothe and comfort oneself when distressed) and a control group on a waiting list with no intervention effort. All of the participants were measured for levels of self-compassion, depressive symptoms, diabetes-specific distress, and biological markers of their disease.

At the end of the study, the participants who received self-compassion training were deemed kinder to themselves (rather than being harshly self-critical). They reported less depression and distress, and there was a statistically meaningful decrease in hemoglobin A1c (HbA1c), a protein that binds to glucose in blood. The higher the level of HbA1c in your blood, the more likely you have diabetes or may develop it.

Nowhere is the need for greater empathy and compassion more evident than in health care—on both sides of the equation. When physicians are able to connect personally with their patients, to feel compassion and empathy, everybody benefits. Patients tend to have better outcomes, and doctors are better healers and feel happier and less burned out.

This isn't exactly a new idea, to be sure. People have long talked about improving compassion and empathy in the teaching and practice of medicine, but there have always been more words than action. One place trying to change that dynamic, I'm happy to say, is my own university.

In 2019, UC San Diego announced the creation of T. Denny Sanford Institute for Empathy and Compassion, launched with a $100 million gift from businessman and philanthropist T. Denny Sanford. The institute's mission is threefold: (1) Use the latest and most innovative brain imaging technologies to establish the neurological basis of compassion; (2) use that research to design a new compassion-focused curriculum for training medical students; and (3) take what's learned to also develop new methods to protect and promote the well-being of current doctors and medical professionals, who suffer from appalling high rates of burnout, depression, and suicide.

Over the next few years, the institute's founding researchers hope to make significant, measurable strides in these areas, but already UC San Diego School of Medicine and other institutions are trying to make a difference. For example, UC San Diego medical students can currently take an art class that begins with sketching live nude models, then real human skeletons, and finally cadavers. The class reinforces the idea that patients are whole people of many layers, dimensions, and stories. Drawing helps reveal that, as students take note of little things like bruises from IV lines put in during a last stay in the hospital, tattoos, or old surgical scars. They begin to imagine what the cadavers' life stories and experiences might have been.

In a different class, medical school students get a firsthand taste of how older patients experience the world. They wear goggles and gloves to impair their vision and sense of touch and then are asked to read a prescription bottle or pick up a pill. They put pebbles in their shoes or attach splints to their legs to mimic the pain and difficulty some seniors have simply walking and getting around.

Again, the idea is to expose 20-something medical students to the reality of older patients and their lives, to help them make a closer connection because, at least for a moment, they feel their pain and walk in their shoes.

There are even more elaborate ways to experience old age. An age-simulation suit, dubbed GERT, looks a bit like the protective armor that bomb-disposal teams wear. Once all of its elements have been donned, the wearer's field of vision has been narrowed and made more opaque. They can't hear high-frequency sounds or move their head as freely. Joints are stiff. Strength is reduced. Coordination is less. GERT, which is used in empathy programs and in developing better services and tools for older or physically impaired people, lets one feel old before one's time, and hopefully a little more empathetic for those who actually are.

Compassion training may change not just behavior, but the brain itself. In a 2013 study, published in the journal *Cerebral Cortex*, German and Swiss scientists measured functional neural and subjective responses of healthy adults watching a video of others struggling to perform a task.

Brain scans showed that some participants' initial empathic responses to the task were marked by negative affect and activations in the anterior insula and anterior medial cingulate cortex—a core neural network underlying empathy for pain. In other words, the part of the brain designed to produce feelings of empathy in response to perceived pain responded, but only with negative emotions, or more specifically, with indifference to the struggles of others.

After undergoing compassion training, brain scans of these participants showed increased positive affective experiences. At the neural level, compassion training appeared to elicit greater activity in the medial orbitofrontal cortex, putamen, pallidum, and ventral tegmental area—all brain regions previously associated with positive affect and affiliation. In other words, empathy.

Interventions to boost empathy work in both directions. In a Canadian study, for example, when staff at long-term facilities for people with dementia shared life stories with their charges and vice versa, treatment and care improved. Staff members came to better know their patients as people and not just as collections of symptoms and problems. Patients saw their caregivers as people with their own sets of concerns, dreams, and more. It made a difference for both.

Mindfulness

An ancient Eastern concept that has been gaining increasing attention in the modern Western world is mindfulness. Mindfulness is the ability to achieve moment-by-moment awareness of your thoughts, feelings, bodily sensations, and the surrounding environment. It means paying attention without judgment; without believing, for example, that there's a "right" or "wrong" way to think or feel in a given moment.

I describe mindfulness and its manifestations here because it is a recurring element in much research and in many of the efforts to better understand and improve wisdom.

Mindfulness has its roots in Buddhist meditation. "The past is already gone. The future is not yet here. There's only one moment for you to live." In recent years, mindfulness has entered mainstream secular thinking, thanks to work by scientists like Jon Kabat-Zinn, a professor emeritus of medicine at the University of Massachusetts Medical School and student of many Buddhist teachers and Zen masters.

Almost 40 years ago, Kabat-Zinn created the mindfulness-based stress reduction (MBSR) program that combines mindfulness meditation, body scanning, and simple yoga postures to achieve greater mental clarity and insight. Body scanning involves lying on your back and focusing attention on various regions of the body. For example, focusing on your toes at first, then mentally moving up through the rest of your body.

In various forms, MBSR is now used by many hospitals, health organizations, retreats, companies, and other entities. It is associated with both physical and mental health benefits, from reduced depression and anxiety to improved immune system functioning.

Some studies of Buddhist monks, who have spent years practicing and perfecting the art, describe actual physical changes in the brain.

In a 2011 New York University experiment, researchers put monks under fMRI machines to track blood flow to the brain while they were meditating. The study found that the parts of the monks' brains that were involved in meditation were more robust and active than in people who did not meditate. There was also evidence of increased neuroplasticity, of the brain reforming itself to improve performance. Structures like the prefrontal cortex were reorganized to increase connections between neurons and between circuits, boosting meditative powers. The effect was not unlike a professional tennis player whose years of practice foster better-than-average hand-eye coordination. As they say, practice makes perfect. Or at least closer to it.

There is perhaps no greater or more mysterious entity in the known universe than the brain inside your skull. It contains 100 billion neurons and ten thousand times as many connections, maybe 125 trillion synapses in just the cerebral cortex alone.

Your brain is a vibrant, living, changing entity, and it possesses a singular ability—the capacity to understand, heal, and improve itself. Mindfulness is one of its methods, and it is frequently used in several types of wisdom-improving interventions.

For example, I am collaborating with Ariel Lange, a professor of psychiatry at UC San Diego School of Medicine and a clinician-scientist with the US Department of Veterans Affairs. She and colleagues have studied the use of "compassion meditation" among veterans with PTSD and found that it appears to assist in psychological healing and recovery. The group is now working to see if compassion meditation can help other people grappling with the problems of advanced age.

Prosocial Activities

Numerous studies have shown that acts of kindness promote happiness. Volunteering, for example, is one of the most meaningful prosocial activities a person can do, and it is strongly associated with life satisfaction. People who donate their time feel more socially connected, are happier, and live longer.

A seminal 2015 study by researchers at the University of Southern California and Johns Hopkins University in Baltimore looked at the Experience Corps, a decades-old effort in which older adults were paired with elementary schools to help kids improve their academic, social, and behavioral well-being.

The researchers found that older adults benefited as well as their young charges. They experienced greater generativity, which is the care and concern for others, especially those in younger generations. Older adults were able to share the lessons they had learned in life and felt that their past would make a difference in the future.

This study was the first-ever, large-scale experimental demonstration that participation in an intergenerational civic engagement program can positively alter self-perceptions of generativity in older adulthood. But evidence abounds of beneficial impact at smaller scales. Remember the grandmother hypothesis? There is indisputable value in the shared experiences of different generations living in close proximity, each giving and receiving lessons in life, hope, optimism, tolerance, humor, generosity, and the other hallmarks of wisdom.

"To see how motivated elders are to be involved and give back is very affirming," said the study's senior author, Tara Gruenewald at USC. "We have a segment of the population that has a lot to give, and failure to tap into that resource is quite concerning. [A program such as Experience Corps] really is a win-win; we help our communities and help elders in the process."

Life also tends to be less stressful when shared with others. When you enjoy high-quality relationships, the perception of everyday events can be altered. A negative event appears not so bad. Challenges are more easily confronted and overcome. There are more shoulders to bear the burden. In one study, participants were told they would need to climb a hill. For those asked to do it alone, the task seemed daunting. For those who could climb the hill with a friend, the hill seemed less steep.

In a study of pain perception, the presence of a loved one reduced the awareness of physical pain in response to a stimulus. When researchers looked at brain scans, they found that holding a person's hand while experiencing pain reduced the sensation at the neural level.

Humans are social animals. We do not do well in isolation.

A few years ago, Zak Kelm, James Womer, Jennifer Walter, and Chris Feudtner, all affiliated with Children's Hospital of Philadelphia, published a systematic review of interventions to cultivate physician empathy, which clearly is associated with better treatment, relationships, and outcomes for all concerned. Of 1,415 articles identified, 64 studies met their criteria as efforts to quantitatively assess and improve physician empathy.

Given the topic, there were significant challenges in study design and execution, but Feudtner reported that eight of the 10 studies with highly rigorous designs found that targeted interventions, everything from group discussions and role-playing to personal coaching, did increase empathy.

In the book I coedited, *Positive Psychiatry*, contributors Samantha Boardman, a clinical instructor in psychiatry and assistant attending psychiatrist at Weill Cornell Medicine, and P. Murali Doraiswamy, professor of psychiatry and behavioral sciences at Duke University School of Medicine, describe this clinical vignette:

Lawrence is a 72-year-old retired librarian in good physical health who lost his wife to cancer 10 years ago. His children and grandchildren live across the country. He has a history of depression and mild anxiety. He presented to a psychiatrist six months ago in the midst of a depressive episode; symptoms included poor sleep, reduced appetite, low energy, lack of interest in life, passive suicidal ideation, low mood, and difficulty concentrating. He was prescribed a selective serotonin reuptake inhibitor. He noticed a remarkable improvement overall but still does not feel like "himself." Lawrence's therapist recommended the following positive interventions: 1) taking a half-hour walk every morning to pick up the newspaper rather than driving, 2) joining a book club at the local senior center, and 3) volunteering to work with high school juniors and seniors on their college essays.

Lawrence felt better while taking the medication, but he continued to experience residual symptoms. By engaging in these positive interventions, he began to feel more connected to his community, and he made new friends and renewed old friendships. He found working with the high school students to be particularly meaningful and invigorating.

Emotional Regulation

Elizabeth Gilbert, author of the popular novel (and 2010 film) *Eat Pray Love*, once noted that "your emotions are the slaves to your thoughts, and you are the slave to your emotions." True enough, perhaps, but emotions aren't fixed facts. They are flexible. It's all about how you interpret them and your situation that gives them power.

We've all experienced moments driving when another vehicle cuts in front too closely or somehow behaves in a way we find, at a minimum, to be outrageous. What happens next depends on you. Road rage—an act of violent anger provoked by another motorist's irritating driving behavior—is not uncommon. A 2016 survey by the American Automobile Association found that nearly 80 percent of drivers polled admitted to extreme anger or aggression behind the wheel at least once in the past year. Other studies have linked road rage to thousands of accidents annually—and some fatalities.

Road rage is never worth it, and quelling that impulse to anger almost always is. It's a case of mind over what really matters.

Here again are three main strategies we covered in chapter 6 on emotional regulation. You can use these as quick tricks to help keep your cool:

- *Practice cognitive reappraisal. Make a deliberate effort to reinterpret the meaning of a distressing event. Maybe that other driver moving so erratically has a sick child in the back seat and is racing desperately to the hospital? That would be understandable. It doesn't matter whether you actually know the reason for the other driver's behavior, only that you now have a reason to let the perceived offense pass—safely.*

- *Distract yourself. Move your attention and thoughts elsewhere. Turn on the radio. Sing aloud. Comment on the pleasant weather to your passenger. Get your mind off of what irritates you and move on.*

- *Label what's happening. If you're angry, consciously tell yourself (and maybe your passenger) that you are angry and why. Often simply recognizing the emotion at play and giving it a name is enough to exert control over it.*

Remember, the things that make us feel angry happen to everyone. It's not abnormal to become upset. Anger is a fundamental human emotion and useful at times. The trick is to recognize those times and use it—then lose it—appropriately.

These tips don't apply only to annoying motorists, of course. They can be used in myriad situations. And there are many other things you can do to improve your emotional homeostasis, sense of well-being, and resilience—and thus, your degree of wisdom:

PRACTICE OPTIMISM. This doesn't mean that you ignore difficult facts or dire situations, but that you look for ways to flip negatives to positives. "When one door closes, another door opens, but we so often look so long and so regretfully upon the closed door that we do not see the ones which open for us" is attributed to Alexander Graham Bell, who endured much hardship and failure before finding lasting fame and credit as patent holder of the first practical telephone. Bell's older and younger brothers died of tuberculosis; his two sons died in infancy. When he tried to sell the new patent to Western Union, the telegraph company dismissed the telephone as a gimmick. One door closed, but others would open.

REWRITE YOUR STORY. When your personal narrative threatens to spiral out of control, reframe it to fit a better view of the world and yourself. A setback at work can be repurposed as a wake-up call to do things differently or better going forward. One Harvard study, reported the *New York Times*, found that "people who viewed stress as a way to fuel performance did better on tests and managed their stress better physiologically than those taught to ignore stress."

DON'T TAKE THINGS PERSONALLY. When things go sideways, there's a normal tendency to blame ourselves, to ruminate and fulminate on what we should have done differently or better. Problems and crises in the moment often feel like they will never end, but they do. Mistakes occur; it happens. Shift your focus to next steps and solutions.

REMEMBER, YOU'VE BEEN THERE BEFORE. It can be encouraging to recall in times of trouble that others have been through the same thing or worse. You'll get an even bigger resilience boost if you recall past challenges that *you* overcame.

FIND SUPPORT. GIVE SUPPORT. Not surprisingly, there is a lot of empirical evidence to show that strong support networks of family and friends help people cope better with crises. More surprising is that supporting others can build your resilience. "Any way you can reach out and help other people is a way of moving outside of yourself, and this is an important way to enhance your own strength," Steven Southwick, a psychiatry professor at Yale University told the *New York Times*. "As long as what you're involved in has meaning to you, that can push you through all sorts of adversity."

BECOME MORE RESILIENT. The core competencies of resilience are self-awareness, self-regulation, mental agility, character strengths, and connection. Each is important. Self-awareness allows you to identify the thoughts, emotions, behaviors, and patterns that are counterproductive. Self-regulation moderates those impulses, emotions, behaviors, and thinking that hinder your goals. Mental agility means flexible thinking, multiple perspectives, and a willingness to try new strategies. Knowing your character strengths helps you leverage them to overcome challenges and meet goals. Connection builds strong relationships though positive and effective communication. No one can do everything alone. We all need help sometimes, and we should all offer it as well.

The work of George Vaillant and others suggests that you can become stronger as a result of negative experiences. To be sure, severe stress can result in significant problems that require significant responses, such PTSD, but stress can result in post-traumatic growth.

In one of our studies, we've shown how it's possible to improve resilience and wisdom and reduce perceived stress. Working with the Mather Institute, an Illinois-based organization that supports research in older adults residing in senior living communities, we studied 89 adults over the age of 60 living in five different independent senior housing communities in three states (Arizona, California, and Illinois).

We began by conducting a battery of assessments including the SD-WISE scale. The first month was a control period (no intervention), followed by a group intervention program called Raise Your Resilience (RYR), which teaches participants how to cope with or reduce feelings of depression, better manage relationships and adversity, and generally deal with issues that commonly weigh on an aging person. The participants attended weekly group sessions. They talked about problems and solutions and set goals. The assessments were repeated at the beginning and end of the one-month intervention and three months thereafter.

The participants demonstrated significant improvement on measures of wisdom, resilience, and perceived stress. This confirms that traits like wisdom and resilience are potentially malleable.

Gratitude

A grateful heart is the beginning of greatness, said the late clergyman James E. Faust. It's an expression of humility and the foundation of virtues like faith, courage, contentment, happiness, and well-being. We cannot be wiser if we are not wise to the blessings and gifts we already possess.

Among the most common and effective methods used to promote gratitude is to write about people, places, or things for which we are thankful. To be sure, it's not for everybody (more about that in a moment), and it's not the only way to achieve a greater appreciation of the blessings in life, but it is a relatively easy way to focus the mind and become more aware of blessings, which is often the best and fastest way to help them multiply. Following are four ways to do this:

THREE GOOD THINGS. Keep a nightly journal of three good things that happened to you each day. They can be big or small, but they should be specific because research and clinical observations have shown that general observations of gratitude, like "I have great friends," become stale and less effective if repeated too regularly. It's much better to write something like "I had a terrific dinner with my two closest friends. We shared several thoughts and laughs."

This practice has been shown to increase happiness, but it needs to be practiced regularly. You are not obliged to do it daily or meet a quota. Feel free to start slowly, but be steady. Most participants in clinical trials that have used this approach become proficient with practice. And most discover that because they are looking harder for things to write about, they discover more good things to write about.

WRITE A LETTER. Saying thanks can be wonderfully embracing, cathartic, and revelatory. An effective and popular intervention is to write a letter to a person to whom you are grateful but may never have thanked properly. Often, it is even more effective to deliver the letter to the person, preferably reading it aloud or, if that's not possible, over the phone.

Most people imagine this exercise to be embarrassing or at least awkward, but in studies and practice, an overwhelming number of practitioners found the experience to be intensely positive. Indeed, experimental data have found that writing a gratitude letter may produce a larger, more immediate effect than most simple, positive interventions.

WRITE YOUR OBITUARY. It may sound depressing, but it can be revealing to write a one- or two-page essay about your own life and legacy, composed in the voice and perspective of a biographer. Think eulogy or obituary, but without the requisite mortality. Consider the traits, accomplishments, and behaviors that you would like celebrated and remembered. Then after you've finished, think about how you spend your days now and to what extent your current life aligns with the priorities and values described in your essay. An even briefer way is to think about your legacy as a sentence to be etched on your tombstone.

Almost invariably, there's a gap between aspiration and reality. For some, this can seem depressing or cause anxiety, but there's a better perspective: You have created a narrative of the life you hope to live and leave. It's a road map to follow, beginning today. Like Benjamin Franklin said, "You may delay, but time will not."

SAVOR BEING ALIVE. Recall the paper that colleagues and I published in 2018 after interviewing hospice patients in the last months of their lives, first mentioned in chapter 3. We wanted to know how these patients defined wisdom and whether their terminal illnesses had altered their understanding of it.

The study was powerfully moving. Men and women on the cusp of death tend to strip away unnecessary or transient concerns to address fundamental and enduring truths. Illness and looming death changed perspectives, and in their attempt to accept their situation but still seek "galvanized growth," patients found and refined wisdom.

One way was simple and obvious: they learned to savor moments and small things that previously might have gone unnoticed.

"Unfortunately," said one hospice patient in the study, "my body does not keep up with my mind. I'm limited in the things I'd like to do and want to do, but at the same time, you have to make adjustments. I mean, I used to be an avid tennis player, and hiking was a part of my life. I've had to say, 'Well, that's behind you.' I am very fortunate to have a daughter and a wife who take me out places and who take me to watch the seagulls at sunset."

It's not hard to savor the moment or a sight, sound, or sensation. In clinical interventions, it's one of the things patients begin doing with relative ease, though most discover that when asked to do it on a regular basis, maybe a couple of times a day for two or three minutes each, they weren't as adept as they thought. No one ever said wisdom didn't require a little work.

"I held a moment in my hand," wrote the poet Hazel Lee, "brilliant as a star, fragile as a flower, a tiny sliver of one hour. I dropped it carelessly, Ah! I didn't know, I held opportunity."

It can be particularly challenging to savor things that are old habits, like a daily shower or the same breakfast you eat every day. In such cases, change things up. Take a bath. Swap oatmeal for eggs Benedict on occasion. Savor the novelty.

Does chronicling your gratitude always work to your benefit? No. It requires persistence and thought. You need to at least occasionally refocus what you're writing about to keep it interesting and meaningful. A journal filled with daily observations of gratitude for friends and sunsets will quickly become boring, trivial, rote, and a chore. Your ruminations should have significance to you. Regularly alter the sorts of things you write about, not just what you're thankful for, but also what makes you proud, happy, or offended. If you see a behavior in someone else, write about that and why you approve or disapprove. These are moments of reflection that may surprise you in their revelations.

Openness to New Experience

Curiosity doesn't kill; it thrills. Here are five ways to become more curious:

1. *Find what fascinates you. Cast a wide net. Something will catch your mind.*

2. *Do things you don't know how to do.*

3. *Ask questions. There's no such thing as a dumb question.*

4. *Ask questions of people, not just Google.*

5. *Don't let boredom dictate your days. There's always something you can do or learn.*

Some academic psychologists have long argued that wisdom and creativity—the pursuit of original thought and ideas—do not mix well. In his 1953 book *Age and Achievement*, the late psychologist Harvey Lehman observed that "the old usually possess great wisdom and erudition" but at the cost of intellectual rigidity and an inability to look at things differently or anew.

In 1990, Dean Simonton, distinguished professor of psychology at the University of California, Davis, wrote that creativity and wisdom are frequently viewed as having contrary relations with aging. The former is viewed as a privilege of youth, while the latter is seen as a prerogative of old age.

Even Robert Sternberg, whose decades of prolific research on aging and intelligence have profoundly influenced the field of psychology, thought wisdom and creativity required different ways of thinking: "Creative thinking is often brash whereas wise thinking is balanced."

Perhaps in some ways that is true, but I would argue that it is not *absolutely* true. Wisdom can be a source of creativity. Conceptual creativity—the kind that arises uniquely out of individual emotion, experience, and insight—is perhaps best practiced early in life when one cannot see the pitfalls of brashness and there is time to recover. Albert Einstein, Pablo Picasso, Orson Welles, and Bob Dylan are prime examples of youthful, conceptual creative genius.

But there is another kind of creativity—experimental—and it requires time, lessons learned, and wisdom earned before it can be employed. Charles Darwin, Paul Cezanne, Alfred Hitchcock, and Frank Gehry are all creative old(er) masters. Each achieved greatness only in the second half of their lives.

The famed French-American sculptress Louise Bourgeois (1911–2010) produced some of her greatest works in her 80s and 90s. At age 84, she was asked by an interviewer whether she always felt the impetus to do something different.

She replied, "No, not different. Better!"

How is that possible, asked the interviewer.

"You become better," said Bourgeois, "which is . . . the wisdom of the elders."

Creativity arises from inspiration, which can be found anywhere. We are constrained only by our imaginations, desires, and needs. The goal isn't necessarily to write the next great American novel or paint a museum masterpiece; it is to find new ways to express yourself, and in that expression, to discover new things. Becoming involved in the arts, from dance to theater to expressive writing, or simply sitting down with friends for a lively exchange of ideas can decrease the deleterious effects of aging and increase our sense of self and well-being.

Alone Time

Set aside time for yourself. Alone time isn't a sign of loneliness or disconnection. It's needed time to get to know what you're really thinking. Americans (and increasingly much of the rest of the world) spend far too much time paying attention to external distractions, like cell phones and Twitter feeds, rather than listening to their inner monologue. A 2017 survey by the research software firm dscout estimated the average American touched his or her smartphone—every tap, type, click, and swipe—2,617 times a day. Heavy users do it more than 5,400 times per day. That works out, according to some analyses, to roughly three hours per day staring at your phone.

There are better things to do with your time and brain.

Spirituality

Spirituality and religiosity are different things; the former can exist without the latter. Deepak Chopra has described religion as "belief in someone else's experience," while spirituality "is having your own experience."

Religion is obviously personal—a human being and his or her God(s). General themes may be shared with others, but belief boils down to each individual practitioner. Spirituality is even more individualized. It's different in every person.

So the path to greater spirituality and greater wisdom is a unique path of your own making. No one can tell you exactly how to get there. You must find your own way, but science suggests ways to help.

In our 2019 survey, we found 15 spirituality intervention studies, many involving adults with medical illnesses, often involving serious or terminal diseases like cancer. In about half of the studies, the interventions produced significant results, such as one that taught mindfulness exercises and Buddhist meditation practices to people in a drug recovery program. The goal was to increase behaviors that would decrease the contracting of HIV.

In another study, an eight-week mindfulness-based stress reduction intervention, 211 cancer patients participated in weekly sessions of counseling, yoga, meditation, and group discussion. Participants also practiced at home. Compared to people on a waiting list, the subjects reported increased mindfulness and spirituality, especially in paying greater attention to their daily life experiences, internal and external.

But you don't need to find a study to start.

If you are religious, attend your church or synagogue or temple or mosque on a regular basis. Or visit a service or sanctuary unlike your own to open your eyes and mind to new people, thoughts, and experiences.

If you are not religious, go to any place where you can regularly spend time in thoughtful communion with similar souls. The practice may or may not be spiritual in nature, but it should involve opportunities for shared reflection. It can be a book club, a yoga class, a university extension course, or a convivial gathering of minds over drinks and snacks. We often find our inner strengths when we look beyond with others.

Other Psychological Interventions

We all have a use-by date. Everybody and every *body* wears out. Cognitive impairment is an unavoidable part of aging, especially after age 65, but the process is variable. You have some control. Exercise your mind as you do your body. There's no single best way to do this. Crossword puzzles are great, but if that's all you do to keep your mind sharp, the best you will be able to say is that you've become pretty good at crossword puzzles.

ENGAGE ALL OF YOUR BRAIN. Meet new people. Go to dinner with friends. Talk. Tell jokes. Go back to school. Learn how to code computers and crochet comforters. Take up Zen or the art of motorcycle maintenance.

BUILD YOUR VOCABULARY. Good wine critics know a lot of synonyms. They have myriad, sometimes wildly creative, ways to describe the vintage being reviewed. That's why a wine deemed to be rich and less acidic is "buttery," while a wine higher in acidity is "bright," and a wine with no acidity at all is

242

"flabby." These descriptors sometimes seem silly, but they serve distinct, useful purposes. They allow the critic to more evocatively describe a beverage that the reader, at this point, can only imagine.

A large and sophisticated vocabulary is beneficial throughout and in all aspects of life. When you can find exactly the right word for a situation, problem, person, or thing, it can dramatically improve context and perspective. When someone describes another person as "stupid" or "strange," it's an easy dismissal and cop-out. What makes them stupid or strange? What exactly does it mean to be stupid? In what way? Answering these questions by using words that more precisely characterize your thinking can be revelatory. The person may not be stupid at all, just different in a particular way. And once you realize that, you may discover common ground or at least a place to meet.

READ FICTION. Liverpool University researchers have found that reading the works of great writers, such as Shakespeare or Wordsworth, has a particularly beneficial effect on the mind, triggering the brain's self-reflection circuits in ways that more ordinary writing does not.

WATCH MOVIES. The higher the quality, the better. I love watching classics like *West Side Story* or *Moonstruck* or *Mrs. Doubtfire*. They are classic for a reason. These may seem like simple, passing pleasures, but they are also windows into the hearts, minds, and lives of people who may be very much different from you. And you can have these experiences without even getting out of your chair. With insight comes understanding; with understanding comes compassion. Of course, this isn't true of every film, but everything means something to someone. You have to keep searching.

Physical Activity Interventions

Your mind works best when your brain is healthy.

It should come as no surprise that some of the most effective interventions for improving wisdom involve improving the health of the originating organ and of the body. The average weight of a human brain is approximately three pounds. For a 150-pound person, that's just 2 percent of body weight. And yet, the brain uses up to 20 percent of the body's total energy haul, mostly to fuel electrical impulses between neurons, but also for housekeeping and health maintenance.

To remain healthy, the brain relies on the rest of the body to be healthy. Not just as a reliable source of energy and nutrients, but because it just feels better. Exercise has an immediate and positive effect on mood. Even a single, 30-minute walk on a treadmill has been shown to lift the mood of a patient with major depressive disorder. In some cases, exercise is as effective as medication and potentially has longer lasting results.

There are myriad ways to become or remain physically fit. Walk. Run. Swim. Lift weights. Do yoga. Ride your bike to the library. Do what works for you and what you are willing to do regularly and over time. And always consult your doctor if you have questions or concerns.

And later, sleep. When we sleep, our brains take the opportunity to clear away neurotoxins and consolidate the lessons and memories made during the day. Therapists tend to think of sleep problems as symptoms, but sleep problems also contribute to mental health issues. There are numerous physiological reasons, such as apnea (the temporary cessation of breathing), that impact sleep. These are matters to discuss and address with a physician. For most people, there is no medicine that can match the effectiveness of sleep hygiene. This involves some seemingly simple lifestyle and behavioral changes to improve the quality of a night's rest, such as decreasing alcohol, nicotine, and caffeine intake; exercising more; keeping the bedroom dark and free of distractions, such as a nearby cell phone; drinking a glass of milk before retiring; and using the bed only for sleep (and sex, of course!). These things are easier said than done, but with self-discipline, they can be implemented successfully.

You aren't what you eat, but it's a factor. Good nutrition and diet feed the brain and the mind. Junk food, refined sugar, and processed meats can all wreak havoc on the body—and increase mental ills, such as depression. Evidence suggests that a diet high in saturated fat may contribute to attention deficit hyperactivity disorder and impair brain function.

In the village of Acciaroli on the Cilento coast in Italy, UC San Diego scientists are working with colleagues at Sapienza University of Rome to study a large number of citizens, all over age 90 and some over age 100. It is believed, at least by the locals, that part of the reason for their longevity is their favored Mediterranean diet emphasizing plant-based foods including rosemary, and their routine long walks as part of their daily activity.

However, it is not only diet and activity. Attitude plays a critical role too. Our collaborative study has found that these very old adults possess better mental well-being than family members decades younger. They possess a kind of grit, positivity, work ethic, and stubbornness and strong bonds with family, religion, and land that seems to help them not just survive, but flourish and thrive.

"I lost my beloved wife only a month ago, and I am very sad for this," said one study participant. "We were married for 70 years. I was close to her during all of her illness, and I have felt very empty after her loss. But thanks to my sons, I am now recovering and feeling much better. I have four children, 10 grandchildren, and nine great-grandchildren. I have fought all my life, and I am always ready for changes. I think changes bring life and give chances to grow." That is wisdom.

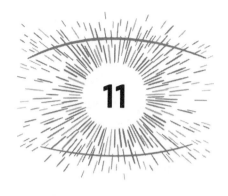

Wisdom Boosters
Drugs, Gadgets, and Artificial Wisdom?

> *One machine can do the work of fifty*
> *ordinary men. No machine can do the*
> *work of one extraordinary man.*
> ELBERT HUBBARD, American author

> *Technology happens. It's not good.*
> *It's not bad. Is steel good or bad?*
> ANDREW GROVE,
> Hungarian-American engineer

IN PREVIOUS CHAPTERS, we traced the emergence of a science of wisdom: the identification of key universal traits and their neuro-biological underpinnings, how to take wisdom's measure, and most importantly to our purposes, how we can use this expanding base of knowledge to become wiser faster.

Now we turn to outside help to enhance wisdom in the form of pharmacology (drugs) and technology (gadgets and artificial intelligence).

For a number of years, a major area of my research was psychopharmacology. I studied antipsychotic drugs for the treatment of schizophrenia. These drugs, discovered in the early 1950s, revolutionized the treatment of patients with serious mental illnesses. Such patients, who used to be institutionalized for decades and treated with electroconvulsive therapy, insulin-induced coma, and even brain surgery, showed little improvement. The antipsychotic drugs markedly reduced these patients' delusions and hallucinations and allowed them to leave the hospital and live in the community.

Unfortunately, the side effects of these drugs over the years, such as irreversible and severe abnormal movements of the body, became a growing problem. A new generation of antipsychotics was introduced in the 1990s. Again, there was a lot of excitement, but a few years later, side effects of these drugs, such as diabetes and obesity, became hazardous. Personally, my research enthusiasm for pharmacotherapy (drug treatment) has progressively diminished.

I published on what I called "the law of a new drug." When a new drug is introduced with considerable fanfare, it is viewed as a panacea for a host of ailments. Slowly, side effects become a growing concern, and in a few years, the drug is thought to be toxic and without much benefit—the exact opposite of a panacea.

In recent years, a massive industry has arisen to develop and promote improvement of our health and life, everything from supplements and drugs to devices and games touted as mind-bending ways to boost brain power. The obvious question is whether they actually work, whether their beneficial effects, if any, translate to real-world activities, tasks, and life in general.

Drugs: Smart and Wise?

There is a whole lot of interest in the so-called smart drugs or brain-boosting drugs, often called nootropics. It's a multibillion-dollar industry presumptively based on neurobiology. Will these drugs increase a person's wisdom?

Aspirin and other analgesics work by blocking pain signals to the brain, disrupting its oversight of a normal immune system response. Selective serotonin reuptake inhibitors (SSRIs), such as Prozac and Zoloft, ease the symptoms of depression by blocking the reabsorption of serotonin in the brain. Serotonin is an important neurotransmitter with many functions, not the least among them being improvement in mood and social functioning. When an SSRI blocks its reabsorption, it means more serotonin is available for use.

If SSRIs can improve mood, the thinking goes, why can't other chemical compounds enhance other brain functions, such as intelligence? It's not a new idea. The ancients expounded all sorts of food-based brain boosters, from the leaves of the maidenhair tree (*Ginkgo biloba*) to lion's mane (*Hericium erinaceus*), a medicinal mushroom. Nootropics in the current sense have been around since at least the early 1970s, albeit in the early days, these were mostly compounds like caffeine and vitamins B6 and B12.

New generations of nootropics are more complex, but largely unproven. Modafinil is one of the most studied. Originally approved by the Food and Drug Administration to treat sleep-related conditions such as narcolepsy, modafinil has been found to sometimes heighten cognitive functioning, including attention and learning, but research data are limited and variable, and there have been no validated tests of modafinil's long-term effectiveness or safety.

For a number of years, college students have turned to prescription stimulants to boost academic performance, especially during exam periods. Developed and intended for people with attention-deficit hyperactivity disorder (ADHD), drugs with names such as Adderall and Ritalin are touted as increasing focus, concentration, and stamina. It's been estimated that as many as one-third of the college students in the US may be using and misusing ADHD stimulants.

That's cause for concern. While these drugs might produce short-term benefits, there is growing evidence that their side effects are worrisome: changes in brain chemistry associated with risk-taking behaviors, sleep disruption, and addiction. Then too, there are ethical considerations: Is it okay to take a brain-enhancing drug to improve one's test scores? Is that cheating? On the other hand, can society justify banning them? Students (and pretty much everybody else) drink copious amounts of coffee and other caffeinated drinks to get a mental boost (real or not). Caffeine changes blood flow in the brain and blocks neural receptors for a molecule called adenosine, a cellular by-product that over time accumulates and produces a feeling of tiredness. Is drinking coffee for its "buzz" unethical too?

In other words, the jury's still out in terms of whether any nootropics or off-label drugs actually boost cognitive function, whether they do it safely over the long-term, and whether we should use them or need them at all.

Our minds are products of our brains, which are products of biology. Biology can be malleable. It can be modified, and thus its product changed as well. The 2011 movie *Limitless* imagined a nootropic drug called NZT-48 that ostensibly allowed users to access "100 percent of their brains." But it is not a question of the amount of access to all parts of our brain. It's more a question of how you use it. As far as I can tell, no one is on the verge of seriously announcing the invention of a foolproof "smart pill," but science fiction like *Limitless* does have a way of becoming science fact, in one form or another.

The most reliable ways to improve cognition right now remain the mostly mundane, things like regular exercise and sleep, a balanced diet and healthy weight, an engaged social life, and no smoking. These won't directly result in greater intelligence, but they will help ensure the necessary precursor—a healthy brain.

If smart drugs are still more fiction than fact, what about the step beyond: wise drugs? Could drugs of the future make a person wiser? This question is not as esoteric (or as far-fetched) as it might first appear. We've seen how brain diseases like frontotemporal dementia (FTD), especially its behavioral variant, can cause a loss of wisdom-related traits. A number of researchers, including my friend and colleague Bruce Miller, professor of neurology at UC San Francisco, are studying genes associated with increased risk of FTD. For example, one form of FTD (as well as amyotrophic lateral sclerosis, or ALS, commonly known as Lou Gehrig's disease) is linked to a mutation in a gene on chromosome 9p. Experts estimate at least 10 percent of patients diagnosed with FTD are known to carry an autosomal dominant genetic mutation. The hope driving such studies is that if and when scientists discover ways to correct these specific mutations—including use of medications—the respective diseases might be cured or even prevented. Does that mean one day we will have wise drugs to treat the loss of components of wisdom, not only in FTD but in other conditions as well? If we do, should we use them to make everyone wiser? Can we do this wisely? These are the kinds of questions that societies might need to ask and debate in the years ahead.

Technology: Games and Gadgets

A few years ago, British researchers published results of a massive study testing the idea that electronic brainteasers and memory games measurably improved mental fitness.

Almost twelve thousand people took part in the six-week study. They were divided into three groups. The first group conducted activities that assessed basic reasoning, planning, and problem-solving, such as picking out the single different object in collections of four. The second group did more complex exercises of memory, attention, math, and visuospatial processing based on popular brainteaser games. The third group spent their time researching online answers to trivia questions.

All of the participants underwent batteries of cognitive tests to assess their overall mental fitness before and after the study. All of the groups showed marginal—and identical—improvement on these benchmark exams.

The findings confirmed researchers' suspicions. When people practice a specific mental task, they get better at that specific task, but it does not translate to improved overall cognition. If you regularly do sudoku puzzles, you will in time improve at logically and quickly figuring out what numbers go where in the grid, but the skill won't carry over to other mental abilities, such as spotting differences in groups of objects or even remembering sequences of numbers.

Nonetheless, these are heady times in the era of physical, mental, and social skill self-improvement. Brain fitness is all the rage, with myriad games, devices, drinks, drugs, and foods on the market, all proclaimed to improve one's cognitive powers faster and better than the old-fashioned method of simply learning.

Do they work? For the most part, I don't think so—at least not to the degree and detail they are marketed or to consumers' enthusiastic expectations. The vast majority of brain-boosting products in stores and online have little, if any, empirical evidence to meaningfully support their claims.

In fact, a 2015 report by the Institute of Medicine (IOM; now called the National Academy of Medicine, a part of the National Academies of Sciences, Engineering, and Medicine, which provide independent, objective analysis and advice to the nation's policymakers) concluded as much. Some cognitive training products were better than others, but persuasive proof was limited, and the IOM advised that makers' claims should be reviewed, evaluated, and considered with care and caution. In other words, there are currently no evidence-based technologies available that will make the brain smarter or wiser.

Yet, research in the last three decades has clearly shown that the brain continues to evolve, even in later life, when a person is active physically, cognitively, and socially. Neurons and synapses in the brain don't stop growing at age 2 or 5 or 20 in people who keep their brains, minds, and bodies fit and active. So, technology or no technology, we can strive to do better for our brains.

Artificial Wisdom?

The last three decades have produced more changes in our daily life than the previous three centuries. It is now hard to think of the time when we did not have email or Facebook or smartphones. Yet all those things appeared just in the last couple of decades.

It is said that we are currently in the fourth industrial age, following the mechanical, electrical, and internet ages. The new age is characterized by a fusion of technology types and is known as the digital revolution. Artificial intelligence (AI) is a leading example of this form of technology. Alan Turing, considered to be a father of AI, wrote a paper in 1950 titled "Computing Machinery and Intelligence," in which he discusses conditions for considering a machine to be intelligent. The term *artificial intelligence* was coined by another computer scientist, John McCarthy, who defined it as the science and engineering of making intelligent machines. As intelligence is traditionally thought of as a human trait, the adjective *artificial* conveys that this form of intelligence describes a machine—a computer.

AI is already present in modern daily life. We use it to access information via Google, develop social interactions through Facebook, and operate security systems at home through various options.

I am not a tech-savvy person and don't care to buy the latest version of laptops or smartphones. Yet, through unplanned circumstances, in 2017 I became codirector of the new Artificial Intelligence for Healthy Living Center at UC San Diego (a collaboration with IBM), which has two components—healthy aging and microbiome. My colleague and renowned microbiome expert Rob Knight is the codirector of the microbiome component, while I head the healthy aging component. IBM is a pioneer in the field of AI.

We are studying more than one hundred people over age 60 who are residing in the independent living section of a senior housing community in San Diego County. Their average age is 84, and the oldest person is 98. We assess these individuals comprehensively, with physical, cognitive, and psychosocial measures along with video- and audiotaping, multiple biomarkers (including microbiome), and sensors on the body and in the environment. The goal is to determine the earliest indicators of cognitive decline using AI. Obviously, one study of this kind is not going to provide the ultimate answer, but this is a proof of concept investigation that will show us the way to do larger and more definitive studies. Once we identify the earliest markers of cognitive decline in later life, we could initiate appropriate interventions long before the symptoms manifest.

One area of AI that has fascinated and intrigued people most is robots. In 2017, a little robot named Jibo made the cover of *Time* magazine—one of its declared 25 best inventions of the year. Jibo represented a new kind of robot: "the world's first social robot," to quote its creator Cynthia Breazeal, a professor at the Massachusetts Institute of Technology (MIT), with whom I have been collaborating in recent months.

The robot, which looks a bit like a couple of large stacked snow-balls with a five-inch round screen and the nonthreatening voice of a young boy, is designed to interact with users. Beyond simply asking it questions like game scores or weather forecasts, which has become ordinary and routine in the age of Siri and Alexa, Jibo is supposed to proactively socialize with you. It tells jokes. It knows your name and celebrates your birthday. Its cute, spherical head rotates up, down, and around as it watches you move about the room, always ready to respond. It apologizes profusely when it "doesn't know" the answer to a question or becomes perplexed by a comment.

Some people love Jibo. He's adorable and fun. Others imagine more therapeutic uses, exploring the possibilities of "compassion-ate" robots. The idea isn't much different from what Jibo does. Imagine a robot designed to be appealing and approachable, some-thing you would be comfortable with living in your home. Now imagine you live alone and that you suffer from loneliness or per-haps depression. A compassionate robot programmed to recognize facial features or interpret emotions in voices might be able to pro-actively respond to detected issues. If you looked or sounded sad, it might suggest a favorite activity or that you call a friend. It could engage you in a game. It might review your medical history and ask if you have forgotten to take a regular medication.

With time, interactions, and machine learning, such a robot would become more attuned to your personality, needs, and desires. It would try to help. These devices already exist in differ-ent forms, in various bits and pieces. Jibo is one example. Sophia is another: a humanoid robot with a mobile face capable of 62 differ-ent expressions and the ability to recognize individuals, crack jokes, and respond to questions (Sophia has done the TV talk show cir-cuit), and seemingly to comprehend what's going on around her/it. In 2017, Sophia even became a citizen of Saudi Arabia, the first robot to receive such status in any country.

Jibo and Sophia are dramatic examples, but machines with varying levels of AI are rapidly populating our lives, from watches that remind you to stand up and take a breath to home systems that assist people who have physical or cognitive problems by turning on lights, adjusting temperatures, and suggesting they take their meds or schedule a doctor's appointment.

Inevitable advances in technology will no doubt allow these systems, devices, and robots to do more and more with increasing human likeness and affinity, but it's hard to imagine robot compassion becoming identical to human compassion. That would seem to require that, first, robots obtain internal analogs of emotions—and be able to reflect on what having emotions means—and that, second, humans and machines would achieve a sort of intellectual, emotional, and moral symbiosis in which we recognize and understand our fundamental natures.

That's asking a lot, though astounding and relentless advances in AI make it imprudent to rule anything out. We are now capable of creating machines and "neural networks" that can learn, which, combined with their vastly greater capacities to store information and their blindingly fast ability to retrieve and process it, promises to alter almost every aspect of the human condition. As with smart drugs, it's natural to wonder if progress in AI might someday lead to the invention of artificial wisdom.

Intelligence, as we know, is not wisdom. Even artificially enhanced and advanced, intelligence will always be just a part of the bigger picture of wisdom. Consider the rapidly moving technology of self-driving cars. Some are already in field tests. There are forecasts of one in four vehicles on the road being autonomous by 2030.

That figure may be too conservative. The technology adoption cycle has been steadily compressing for decades. It took approximately 40 years for telephones to reach 40 percent penetration of the US market and another 15 years to reach 75 percent.

Universal electricity wasn't much quicker. But cell phones did so in just over a decade, and smartphones in half of that. (Some predict smartphones will be rendered obsolete by 2025, replaced by a new technology.)

These technologies have absolutely changed the way we think and behave, not just in affluent countries but in most of the world. Mobile phones are nearly as common on the African savanna as they are on American subways. As always, technology races ahead of our ability to anticipate and prepare for its consequential changes.

Let's look at a perhaps unavoidable scenario in the future: You're in a self-driving car when its brakes fail. The vehicle is speeding toward a crowded crosswalk. To the left, there is a large group of older people. To the right, a woman pushing a stroller. Which direction should the car take?

These are predicaments not unlike classic moral dilemmas used by researchers to study how people make decisions. They present ethically challenging choices with no clear, simple solution. The vast majority of humans would rightfully struggle to make a decision. What would a machine do? How do we teach a machine the moral principles necessary to even attempt to make a wise decision?

The expansion of AI and machine learning has been dazzling, but artificial wisdom is in another realm. As I have discussed numerous times, wisdom is not only a rational activity. It is also emotion driven. Increasingly, machines assist physicians in diagnoses. They can, for example, consider factors such as age, genetics, environment, and socioeconomic status in developing a diagnosis of a specific type of cancer, possible treatments, and likely outcomes. But a machine cannot yet discern the emotions behind and ahead of such a diagnosis and how those might play out or alter consequences.

Human wisdom includes the ability to think critically, to consider all options, and to make the best possible choices with some degree of confidence. I say "choices" because most often in the most difficult situations, there is no single, best choice. A machine can crunch data to produce options, perhaps offering probabilities of success, which is confidence of a sort.

I suspect most of us aren't quite ready for a machine alone to determine something like a cancer diagnosis and then decide our course of treatment and fate. We rely on emotional input too. We want other humans involved, whether trained physicians or family and friends.

None of us is born wise—and to a surprising degree, we must learn about emotions. Fear, anger, and joy are fundamental to our psyche and nature, but how we live with and manage them takes time and teaching.

If humans can learn to experience, express, and control emotions, why can't machines—and in time, acquire something we might call artificial wisdom (AW)? It's certainly not beyond possibility. The 17th-century philosopher and physicist Robert Boyle foresaw human organ transplants, though it would take roughly more than two centuries before that actually happened with a kidney transplant in 1954. Jules Verne predicted the Apollo 11 moon landing in 1865; it happened 104 years later. In 1909, Nikola Tesla opined, "It will soon be possible to transmit wireless messages all over the world so simply that any individual can carry and operate his own apparatus." Go ahead and look it up on your smartphone.

Artificial wisdom is not unattainable, though when it will become reality remains to be seen, and how it will be applied will depend very much on the human equivalent. Wisdom is a uniquely human and wholesome trait that may never be reproducible perfectly in a robot.

However, I believe that wise humans can and will develop wise robots whose primary function will be to serve the humans.

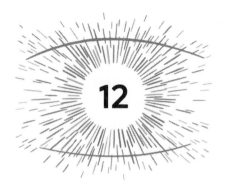

The Future of Wisdom
Moving from Individual to Societal Wisdom

Alone we can do so little; together we can do so much.
HELEN KELLER

None of us is as smart as all of us.
KEN BLANCHARD, *High Five!*

MOST OF THIS BOOK views and discusses wisdom through the prism of the person. We think most often of wisdom in terms of individuals, whether historical figures like Gandhi or Lincoln or Mother Teresa or a contemporaneous grandparent.

There is also wisdom of crowds, of course, the idea that the aggregation of information in groups produces decisions that are better than any made by a single member of the group. It's a popular topic and the subject of other books and debates.

The notion of societal wisdom, however, is much less often discussed—especially in scientific literature—though it seems obvious that some societies and cultures are or have been wiser than others and that improving wisdom collectively benefits them as much as it does individuals.

Culture matters. Although wisdom is a neurobiology-based personality trait that is basically similar across the globe and across the millennia, there are cultural differences in the relative importance of specific components of wisdom. Japanese society places great value on interpersonal harmony and avoidance of conflict; American society not so much. A few years ago, researchers presented a series of stories to random samples of Americans from the Midwest and Japanese from the greater Tokyo area. They wanted to gauge their reactions to these stories describing interpersonal and intergroup conflicts.

The responses showed that wisdom—that is, recognizing multiple perspectives, the limits of personal knowledge, and the importance of compromise—increased with age among Americans but not among Japanese. (Of course, a cross-sectional study can't really prove changes with aging.) Younger and middle-aged Japanese already showed greater use of wise-reasoning strategies than younger Americans because their social norms and expectations required it. The cultural difference weakened with age as older Americans learned through experience what the Japanese had long ago been taught. Obviously, this is just one small study, and the exact findings may not be generalizable.

Similarly, emotional complexity varies by country. Researchers tend to define emotional complexity in two basic ways. There is emotional dialecticism, which means feeling both positive and negative emotions at the same time. And there is emotional differentiation, which happens when a person is able to separate and describe the distinct and different emotions he or she is feeling in the moment.

A research team led by Igor Grossmann and Alex Huynh at the University of Waterloo and Phoebe Ellsworth at the University of

Michigan investigated emotional complexity in different countries by first randomly sampling 1.3 million English-language web pages from 10 countries, tracking how often a positive-emotion word appeared within two words of a negative-emotion word. Sites in Malaysia, the Philippines, and Singapore all had significantly higher rates of mixed emotions than texts from the US, Canada, Australia, the UK, Ireland, and New Zealand. South Africa came in somewhere between the two groups.

Then the researchers looked at collected reports from college students in the US, Japan, India, Russia, Germany, and the UK in which the writers described emotions they had felt during differ-ent experiences, such as enjoying time with a friend or getting hurt during an activity. Students in Japan, India, and Russia were higher in both emotional dialecticism and emotional differentiation.

Grossmann and colleagues attributed the difference to the fact that people from Japan, India, and Russia tend to place higher value on interdependence. They are more aware of the wishes and con-cerns, emotions and desires of other people in their group and consider their emotions to originate through interactions with others. Alternatively, people from Western countries like the US and Canada tend to think of their emotions as coming from within.

Which countries are wiser? That's not easily answered. At present, there are no formal measures of societal wisdom. However, individ-ual societies have often tried to demonstrate their superiority over others by focusing on measures that were considered at those times as being most important for a country's perceived status in the world.

Taking Measure of Societal or National Status

We think most often of modern human societies in the context of countries. American society in the United States is distinct from

British society in the United Kingdom; Chinese from Japanese; Egyptian from South African. Over the course of history, there have been a number of informal, and more recently formal, ways of comparing societies and countries. Let's look at a few.

Bygone Ages

The first and oldest measures are the various religious mythologies that arose to describe the "golden ages" of different cultures. These tended to be recollected periods of relative peace, justice, harmony, stability, and prosperity. Food was abundant; conflict was not. The arts and sciences flourished. People lived long and happy lives. It's not clear to what degree these mythologies accurately reflected real life—they're called mythologies for a reason—but they are invariably viewed as once-upon-better times, golden ages followed by progressively less desirable ones of silver, bronze, and iron.

"The reason people find it so hard to be happy is that they always see the past better than it was, the present worse than it is, and the future less resolved than it will be," noted the French novelist and playwright Marcel Pagnol. That's true of nations as well.

Military Might

During most of human history, societies (usually represented as nations) judged themselves and others by size and military might. Nations and rulers with stronger armies and navies tended to conquer or dominate smaller countries with weaker forces.

Alexander became Great because he created one of the largest empires of the ancient world. At its peak, it stretched more than three thousand miles from Greece to northwestern India. The Mongol army under Genghis Khan, which would dominate the Middle East, China, and Russia during the 13th century, numbered almost one million men. The British Empire at its zenith, supported by an incomparable army and navy, claimed lands, colonies, and outposts around the world and boasted that the sun never set on it.

But with the dawning of the 20th century and the rising cry for independence, former invaders and colonizers gradually or abruptly withdrew to older, original boundaries, and the measure of strength shifted from size and military might to economic prowess.

Economic Indices

Though quite old in concept, the prevailing metric of economic strength since World War II has been gross national product (GNP) and gross domestic product (GDP), measured in US dollars. GNP refers to the work production of all citizens of a country, including those abroad. GDP refers to domestic levels of production. Both have been lauded as key indicators of economic growth and prosperity.

In recent decades, however, the idea that GDP reflects a population's well-being has been challenged. GDP assumes that economic growth "trickles down," spreading benefit across society and diverse demographics. That has not been the case. Economic growth is unequal, and wealth can become highly concentrated. By some estimates, the richest 1 percent of the US population now owns more wealth than the bottom 90 percent.

Such numbers suggest GDP is a poor measure of societal well-being, particularly if you are poor. While GDP is valuable for measuring short-term economic fluctuations, it's not a measure of sustained economic growth. To paraphrase a common saying, a country's money doesn't buy its people's happiness, especially if most of the people don't have most of the money.

The Happiness Index

The GDP does not include other metrics that arguably bear more closely on true well-being, such as health, education, freedom, and the like. New measures attempt to do just that. In 2008, the Himalayan kingdom of Bhutan, squeezed between its much larger and more powerful neighbors China and India, became the first country (and so far, the only country) to promote gross national happiness (GNH) as an index of well-being.

How do you measure collective happiness on a national scale?

Bhutan's government does it by surveying citizens to evaluate how satisfied they are with their lives and correlating that data with other indicators assessing socioeconomic development, environmental conservation, promotion of culture, and good governance. It's a complicated task. Bhutan has conducted two GNH surveys. The latest, in 2015, showed 91.2 percent of Bhutanese reported they were "narrowly," "extensively," or "deeply" happy—a 1.8 percent increase in aggregate happiness from the first survey in 2010.

Two years after Bhutan debuted GNH, the Organisation for Economic Co-operation and Development, an international group of 35 member countries that promotes policies intended to improve economic and social well-being, published its first World Happiness Report (WHR) at a United Nations meeting.

The WHR evaluates six variables over time: income, healthy life expectancy, having someone to count on in times of trouble (social support), generosity, freedom, and trust. The last variable is measured by the absence of corruption in business and government.

The latest report, published in 2019, emphasizes the importance of the social foundations of happiness. The authors say this can be seen in comparing life experiences between the top and bottom five countries.

FIVE HAPPIEST COUNTRIES

1. *Finland*
2. *Denmark*
3. *Norway*
4. *Iceland*
5. *Netherlands*

(The United States is number 19.)

FIVE LEAST HAPPY COUNTRIES

152. *Rwanda*

153. *Tanzania*

154. *Afghanistan*

155. *Central African Republic*

156. *South Sudan*

The happiness gap between these two groups of countries can mostly be explained by the report's six variables, but 80 percent of the variance of happiness around the world occurs within countries. In richer countries, such as the United States, internal variation is not explained primarily by income deficiencies and inequalities—income per person in the United States has increased by roughly three times since 1960, and per capita GDP is still rising—but by differences in physical health, personal relationships, and mental health. The largest single source of unhappiness among Americans is mental illness.

Let's look at mental illness and how it is treated around the world.

First, citizens with mental illness may never get an official diagnosis. My colleague Wael Al-Delaimy at UC San Diego School of Medicine is part of an international effort to boost mental health care in Jordan, which has the largest per capita number of refugees in the world. Victimized by conflict and uncertain lives in overcrowded, underresourced camps, refugees are especially vulnerable to mental health issues, but there is little data and even less care, with just 0.51 psychiatrists per 100,000 Jordanians compared to 12.4 psychiatrists per 100,000 Americans.

Lacking access to treatment, poor people everywhere are instead cared for and sustained by their families and informal support networks, which accept them for who and what they are. What they lack in advanced psychiatric and pharmaceutical aid, they make up in better and longer-term social connectedness, family structure, and support. A famous study conducted globally in the 1970s, called the International Pilot Study of Schizophrenia, led by researchers such as my friend William Carpenter from the University of Maryland, suggested that prognosis for a mental illness like schizophrenia may be somewhat better in developing than in developed countries.

Ironically (or not), these strengths often diminish as countries become more westernized. Once large and extended families took care of their own—often out of sheer necessity. Now families are smaller and more fragmented and must turn to organized (and less personal) forms of care for those in need.

You can see a similar phenomenon with the unfortunate treatment of older people, whose personal and social value may be lost in a fog of declining health and cultural prejudice.

We can all do better—and be happier for it.

The Human Development Index

In 1990, the United Nations Development Programme published its first annual Human Development Report (HDR) and introduced the Human Development Index (HDI), which has become a dominant metric in development circles.

The first HDR posited the concept of human development as progress toward greater human well-being and tabulated a number of country-level indicators. It emphasized outcomes like a reasonable standard of living over strategies such as per capita income. Proxies were used to measure three important elements of well-being: access to health care, education, and goods.

The HDI places greatest emphasis on average life expectancy, education, income, knowledge, and standard of living. These form the centerpiece of the HDR, and most countries are ranked. Norway placed number 1 in the last report (2019), followed by Switzerland, Ireland, Germany, and Hong Kong. The US was number 15. Last in 2019, at number 189, was Niger.

The HDI is useful to policymakers and development profession-als. It allows them to compare the effects of different national policy choices between countries of similar economic status but with different outcomes.

The World Happiness Report and the Human Development Index both represent partial and partially successful efforts to define and compute a societal index, but to create a truly comprehensive measure, one that might arguably reflect a society's state of wisdom, requires many more elements.

Among them could be measures of gender development and equality, poverty, climate, land and water use, public safety, transportation, housing, social and civic participation, community support, recreation and cultural activities, and health services for distinct populations, such as the very young and very old.

Any real and substantial attempt to assess and compute societal wisdom will necessarily be as complex as the topic itself. It will include all of the measures described and more. It will need to look beyond hedonic measures, which define happiness and well-being in terms of materialistic economics, and include a eudaemonic approach that focuses on meaning and self-realization and defines well-being in terms of the degree to which a person or a country is fully functioning as a member of the larger community.

Some researchers have suggested creating criteria to measure *flourishing* in an individual, the state in which people experience positive emotions and positive psychosocial functioning. VanderWeele at Harvard has proposed five broad domains: happiness and life satisfaction, mental and physical health, meaning and purpose, character and value, and close social relationships. He says there are four major and common pathways to flourishing: family, work, education, and religious community.

Unlike single measures, such as GDP, the measures of a flourishing society are infinitely more complicated and nuanced. It requires assessing the sense of wholeness and well-being of all citizens, from overt measures like health and education levels to more ephemeral measures like self-determination, optimism, resilience, civic engagement, vitality, self-esteem, and honesty.

Social policies that promote and improve VanderWeele's major pathways to flourishing—family, work, education, and religious community—will no doubt improve the situation, just as those that harm these pathways harm our chances of flourishing. How we get there and how we measure flourishing are—and always will be— works in progress.

It should be possible to develop an index of societal wisdom analogous to the Jeste-Thomas Wisdom Index for individuals described earlier. Arguably, the components of societal wisdom could be largely similar to those for individuals: prosocial behaviors like compassion and altruism, emotional regulation, self-reflection, tolerance and the ability to deal with uncertainty, and good decision-making skills among them. In many ways though, this is easier said than done. How would we score countries on emotional regulation or self-reflection? Who would make those judgments? Despite such difficulties, I am not willing to give up in this arena. After all, when World War II was raging, few people would have dared to imagine formation of the United Nations or World Health Organization. These organizations are continuing to do invaluable work, although they are still imperfect. We can dream of a day when countries will vie for a Wisdom World Cup!

Individual Versus Societal Wisdom

The precise relationship between individual and societal wisdom is unclear. The two may grow in parallel, a mutually enhancing and reinforcing association in which caring societies foster personal wisdom among all citizens. Conversely, greater societal wisdom may reduce the need for individual wisdom to survive and thrive in later life. Protective environments markedly reduce the risk of mortality from unnatural or avoidable causes. There is less need for individuals to behave wisely if they live within a society governed by wise rules, mores, beliefs, and behaviors.

You can see evidence of this in nature. In 2012, Fraser A. Januchowski-Hartley and colleagues looked at the adaptive behaviors of fish living within the safe confines of an Australian marine reserve (where fishing was prohibited) and those living beyond the reserve's boundaries.

Fish living within the reserve were older and less vigilant because they did not face the same dangers as fish living outside the reserve. Even when they wandered outside, these reserve-dwelling fish displayed reduced vigilance. Something similar can be argued for the behaviors of humans. When a society is protective, individual wisdom is less critical to living longer.

Vaccines become broadly effective through the concept of "herd immunity." If enough people are vaccinated—usually around 80 to 95 percent, depending on the contagiousness of the disease—then the population is generally protected.

No one's suggesting a similar percentage is required for societal wisdom. It's likely impossible to attain and probably unnecessary. Wisdom has a kind of infectious biology all its own. It can be transmitted knowingly and unknowingly via myriad modes, from one person to another to another in bits and pieces, evolving and adapting along the way. It can be incubated, nurtured, and grown in almost anyone, almost anywhere. It can start small but soon transcend all expectations. At the same time, we don't expect every individual to meet all the criteria for wisdom perfectly. A wise society would accept and help them all.

Is Societal Wisdom Increasing or Decreasing?

Is the world becoming wiser or less wise? I make a case for each side of this question.

The Case for Global Society Being Wiser Today

As cognitive psychologist and author Steven Pinker has noted, the number of violent deaths worldwide has fallen from approximately 500 per 100,000 people annually in pre-state societies to just 6 to 8 violent deaths per 100,000 people today. General societal values have arguably improved around the world, both implicitly and explicitly. Authoritarianism was the norm through most of human history. Kings and emperors, sultans and chiefs ruled autocratically, their leadership rarely challenged by the masses they ruled. Today, a majority of countries in the world boast at least some form of democracy, however imperfect.

Humans are generally living longer than ever, even though basic aspects of our underlying biology, such as how long a woman is fertile and able to reproduce, have not changed. On average, menopause occurs around the age of 50. Classical Greek and Roman sources suggest menopausal age two thousand or so years ago was about the same: 40 to 60 years of age.

Average life span is altogether different. In classical Greece and Rome, life expectancy at birth was 20 to 30 years, a decade or two longer if one survived the diseases of childhood. Those numbers have steadily improved over succeeding centuries, albeit variably.

In 2014, my collaborator Andrew J. Oswald and I published a paper in the journal *Psychiatry*, which proposed that the increase in longevity during the past century may be related, in part, to greater societal wisdom, including compassion, which has resulted in a more protective environment and better health care and support for older adults. Medical advances have undoubtedly been critical to longer survival in older adults, particularly those with chronic illnesses such as heart disease and cancer. Indeed, modern medicine has transformed a lot of diseases that were routinely and acutely fatal into chronic lifelong conditions that can be managed for decades, from infections like tuberculosis and syphilis to HIV and AIDS.

At the beginning of the 19th century, no country in the world had a life expectancy longer than 40 years. Over the next 150 years, some parts of the world achieved substantial health improvements with resulting longer average lives. In 1950, for example, life expectancy for newborns was over 60 years in Europe, North America, Oceania, Japan, and parts of South America. But elsewhere, a newborn could expect to live only around 30 years. The gap was enormous. People in Norway had an average life expectancy of 72 years, while that in the West African country of Mali was just 26 years.

Much has changed for the better, globally speaking. Today, most people in the world can expect to live as long as those in the very richest countries did in 1950. The United Nations estimated that global average life expectancy in 2019 was 72.6 years, higher than any country back in 1950. For some countries, such as Japan, Switzerland, Australia, Sweden, and South Korea, life expectancy extends into the 80s. (The United States is on the cusp: 79.3 years on average, a bit higher for women than for men.)

In the 19th and early 20th centuries, increases in life expectancy were driven mainly by improvements in sanitation, housing, and education, which caused a steady decline in early and midlife mortality, which was primarily due to infections. The development of vaccines, antibiotics, and other medical advances continued improvements in the latter half of the 20th century. Now, say experts, the continuing increase is due almost entirely to the decline in late-life mortality—that is, older people with heart disease, stroke, or cancer are living longer.

Once, human compassion seemed limited to immediate kin and tribe, but it has grown with our numbers and contact with others. Slavery, child labor, and sex trafficking are at least not condoned officially by most legal governments. After World War II, organizations like the United Nations, the Red Cross, the World Health Organization, and the International Monetary Fund began helping disadvantaged people across the globe. In the aftermath of a devastating earthquake, fire, tsunami, or distant national crisis, we act as individuals and in larger groups to provide aid and succor, even if we never see any benefit for ourselves or even know those whom we've helped.

Value systems are changing too. Gender equity was not even a serious point of discussion until the middle of the 20th century. Today, the concept is spreading across nations, albeit slowly and incompletely, with occasionally appalling revelations of how far we must still go. The same applies to issues like child marriage and child soldiers that persist in some parts of the world but are increasingly challenged, resisted, and amended. Similarly, there is increasingly greater acceptance of diversity in sexual preferences and greater condemnation of domestic violence.

Globalization and rapid growth in technology and communication have served to reduce disparities among countries and within countries. When I was growing up in India, having a telephone at home was an expensive luxury. Many middle-class households did not have a phone or a refrigerator. If we had applied for a phone, we probably would have had to wait for 15 years or longer because of the lack of the necessary cable network. Today even a person in a Mumbai ghetto is likely to own a cell phone. Social media like WhatsApp are helping people from different continents communicate with one another in seconds.

The Case for Global Society Being Less Wise Today

In contrast to the positives mentioned above, new crises have evolved. The centuries-long threats to health and well-being, such as plague, cholera, smallpox, and polio, have been replaced in much of the world today with a new set of epidemics: opioid abuse, suicides, stress, and loneliness. These are behavioral epidemics that afflict all ages, young and old, and for the first time in decades, the average life span is not lengthening in some places but shrinking as a result.

Every 12 minutes, someone in the United States commits suicide. Every 11 minutes, someone in the US dies from an opioid overdose. Annual rates of deaths from opioid overdose and suicides have been increasing rapidly for more than a decade. As a result, the average life span in the United States has declined for the first time in half a century—for two years in a row at the time of this writing. To stem this public health crisis, there is a movement to "pharmacolize" these epidemics, focusing on development and approval of drugs to prevent deaths.

Unfortunately, this line of thinking is overly simplistic. Vaccines and antibiotics have eradicated numerous past epidemics like plague and cholera, caused by bacterial and viral infections. The modern epidemics of opioid abuse and suicides, however, are fundamentally different. Underlying them is not a pathogenic microbe, but the stealthy and lethal *behavioral* toxin of loneliness. Let me mention a couple other signs of concern for societal well-being before elaborating on loneliness.

Another indicator of worsening societal wisdom is a declining level of public education in the US. Chronic financial crises and shifting trends have imperiled or eliminated many aspects of public education once considered essential to a broad, liberal arts–based curriculum, the old and enduring effort to discover "those universal principles which are the condition of the possibility of the existence of anything and everything," to quote Nigel Tubbs in *Philosophy and Modern Liberal Arts Education: Freedom Is to Learn.*

In classrooms across the country, there is less art and music, less physical education and time spent outside. Courses in civics or even history may now seem quaint or archaic, to the extent they exist at all. We expect more and more of our children but in increasingly narrower fields of inquiry. I think it's safe to say more schools are adding classes on computer coding than those on the rights and responsibilities of citizenship or lessons to be learned from failed or fallen societies and cultures, from Easter Island to the Roman Empire to the former Soviet Union. I am all for increases in education in computers and technology, but it should be supplemented by education and training in well-being and compassion.

In recent years, I have devoted much of my research to investigating loneliness. Though we feel it personally—it is an intimate angst—loneliness is common to the human condition, perhaps now more than ever.

Loneliness is as dangerous to health as smoking and obesity. The US Agency for Healthcare Research and Quality reported that an astounding annual death toll of 162,000 could be attributed to social isolation, exceeding the number of deaths due to cancer or stroke. In the UK, the economic impact of loneliness for businesses was estimated to be over $3 billion annually, and this led to the appointment of a new Minister for Loneliness in 2018.

Multiple studies and surveys suggest more people today feel lonely more often and more deeply than in the past. Indeed, Fay Bound Alberti, a historian and cofounder of the Centre for the History of the Emotions at Queen Mary University of London, notes that prior to the end of the 18th century, there was little mention of loneliness. The term used then was *oneliness*. It carried minimal ideological or psychological weight. It did not have any particular or notable negative connotations. It simply meant a condition of

being alone, apart from people, an unavoidable and often necessary aspect of life. Solitude had its benefits.

And besides, in those days, observes Alberti, most people
believed they were never truly alone. "People lived in small communities, they tended to believe in God (which meant they were
never really alone, even when they were physically isolated), and
there was a philosophical concept of the community as a source
of common good. There was no need for a language of loneliness,"
said Alberti, who published *A Biography of Loneliness* in 2019.

Industrialization beginning in the 1800s reduced social connections and spawned loneliness. The problem has worsened, with the
prevalence of loneliness doubling over the last 50 years.

Loneliness is modestly heritable (37 to 55 percent). Some people
are simply more genetically predisposed than others. Loneliness is
also fundamentally part of life, and valuable in its own way. It can
prompt self-reflection and assessment. It can fuel creativity and,
most importantly, prompt one to get out into the world to seek
people and greater intimacy.

Loneliness is not the same as social isolation. Loneliness is
subjective—a person *feels* anxious, distressed, and fearful because
he or she doesn't have as many social relationships as desired.
Social isolation, on the other hand, is objective—a measurable lack
of social relationships. The two can coexist or occur separately. A
person can be socially isolated but not feel lonely. Another person
can be surrounded by people and feel quite alone. Both, however, carry significant risks to health and require different kinds of
intervention.

What's worrisome is when loneliness persists, when it becomes
chronic or deeply held. Three-fourths of the participants in a 2018
study I conducted with colleagues reported moderate to high levels
of loneliness across the adult life span—from the 20s to 90s. This was
noteworthy because the participants were not considered at high

risk of moderate to severe loneliness. They didn't have major physical disorders. They didn't suffer from significant mental illness. They were, generally speaking, regular people. Loneliness was associated with worse physical and mental health.

Other researchers too have uncovered troubling findings. The Irish Longitudinal Study on Ageing, conducted by Trinity College Dublin, has been following a representative sampling of more than eight thousand older Irish citizens (aged 50 and over) since 2009, looking at their health, social, and economic status over time; their contributions to society and the economy; and the biological and environmental components of "successful aging."

The findings have often been unsettling. The study found that more than 37 percent of participants reported feeling lonely often or some of the time, a percentage that increased with age—women more often than men, and for longer periods of time since females tend to live longer than males. That epidemic of loneliness led to increased reports of chronic health problems, a phenomenon that no doubt was self-feeding: loneliness begets health issues begets depression and greater feelings of loneliness and despair.

In a 2017 study, S. B. Rafnsson and colleagues followed 6,677 dementia-free adults in the United Kingdom for six years, chronicling aspects of their lives such as marital status, number of close relationships, and social isolation, which means contact with family and friends and participation in organizations.

After six years, 220 study participants had developed dementia. Participants who had shown greater levels of loneliness during the study were more likely to suffer dementia than those who had enjoyed a number of close relationships or who were married. Dementia risk was associated with loneliness in later life.

Why this unprecedented rise in loneliness, suicides, and opioid use in the recent years? The rapid growth of technology, social media, and globalization has improved the quality of life in many ways. But it has also upended social mores and produced unprecedented social disconnection. Information overload, 24-hour connectivity, countless but superficial and often adverse social media relationships, and heightened competition from globalization have escalated the level of stress in modern society. A new Gallup poll reported a 25 percent increase in self-reported stress and worry in the US over the past dozen years.

Notably, this stress level affects youth much more than older adults. A study of more than six hundred thousand Americans published in the *Journal of Abnormal Psychology* in 2019 found that stress level was inversely related to age. Twenty-year-olds reported twice as much stress as 40-year-olds and four times as much stress as 70-year-olds. It should not be surprising, then, that increase in the rates of suicides and opioid-related deaths is greater among youth than among seniors. Millennials are among those hardest hit.

Half Empty or Half Full?

In sum, society has made considerable progress in several areas over the centuries; however, in other areas things have worsened. It is the typical glass half empty versus glass half full story. But I am optimistic. I strongly believe that people can and will improve societal wisdom, though it will always be a bumpy path with ups and downs. We must do our best because failure is not an option for the survival and thriving of *Homo sapiens.*

The modern behavioral epidemics of loneliness, suicides, and opiate abuse are the result of increasing stress levels and require behavioral vaccines or antidotes. Herein lies the good news: a surprising finding from our studies is that loneliness is strongly but inversely associated with level of wisdom. We have replicated this finding in three different studies in three different populations: 340 San Diegans across the adult life span, over 3,000 adults from across the United States, and 250 older adults (including 50 over age 90) from Cilento, a region in Southern Italy. Indeed, wisdom (measured with our San Diego Wisdom Scale) emerged as the most significant correlate (albeit in the opposite direction) of loneliness.

Thus, my research suggests an antidote for the toxin of loneliness: wisdom. The wiser one is, the less likely to be afflicted by loneliness. And that's a tidy way to come back to the message of this book: there are things you can do to become wiser—and so, less likely to feel lonely.

Wiser Faster: Individuals and Society

Socrates once bemoaned that the invention of books would "create forgetfulness" in the soul. He fretted that readers would blindly trust external written words, rather than what they knew and remembered for themselves. It's a complaint and caution that echoes throughout human history, repeated with the appearance of the printing press, telegraph, radio, TV, and cell phone. Many believe the internet is making us stupid today.

But there is a theory called the law of amplification, which basically says that the primary effect of environmental factors such as technology is to amplify human forces, to augment already existing powers, capacities, and intentions within people. That's consoling in the sense that I believe wise people would use, say, brain-boosting drugs or technology wisely. But even as we explore these possibilities, we can and must do more to promote its natural development within ourselves as individuals and as a society.

But how do we do that? This book offers a modest step, at least in the sense that I hope it has prompted you to think about the nature of wisdom and how you might become wiser faster. More broadly, though, we must consciously teach, reinforce, and promote the components of wisdom I have described.

Societal compassion—a critical component of wisdom—is part of the remedy. It allocates resources to the care of people, young and old. Just as survival of premature newborns is far more likely when committed, prolonged care is provided, so too is survival and thriving of older adults despite afflictions like drug abuse and social isolation or worsening physical, cognitive, and reproductive functions when societies emphasize care fueled by compassion, empathy, and altruism. More-civilized societies have greater societal compassion and wisdom, including safety nets and better care for the old, disabled, mentally ill, and those who are simply different or in need.

How do we make a society wiser? Through education. John Dewey, the American philosopher, psychologist, and reformer, once said, "Education is not preparation for life. Education is life itself."

Everything begins—and ends—with education. As parents, we try to guide and educate our children in what we believe is right, true, good, and correct. Then we send them to school, where once upon a time we simply expected them to learn the three Rs: reading, 'riting, and 'rithmatic. Over time, however, the public education system assumed additional duties. Physical education courses were added to build healthy bodies. Sex education emerged to provide needed, tempered knowledge. Art and music instruction nurtured creative souls.

We must find ways to infuse the education of our young with lessons that promote the elements of wisdom: compassion and other prosocial behaviors, self-reflection, emotional regulation, openness to divergent perspectives, and ability to make good decisions.

As a society, we talk a lot about remedies. We propound, advocate, and support, but our words are too often not followed by broad, persistent action. There is no surfeit of good ideas to consider and debate. But whatever they are, they should be defined and driven by some basic principles: Our children's education should teach them how to live well, not just make a living. It should be about knowledge, not information; about how to think, not what to think. Is it unreasonable to suggest children should be taught the value of giving and philanthropy early and often, so that it becomes second nature?

"Wisdom is not the product of schooling, but of the lifelong attempt to acquire it," said Albert Einstein. But it starts with an education that provides those lifelong tools.

It extends, too, beyond the academic years. "Life, Liberty and the pursuit of Happiness," wrote the wise framers of the US Declaration of Independence in 1776. Not just happiness in the hedonic sense—the pleasures of life, like a good job, a home, friends, and comfort—but also in Aristotle's concept of eudaemonia, a virtuous life worth living, a self-awareness that strives for meaning and the degree to which each of us attains our full potential.

Too often, we focus on hedonic and not eudaemonic well-being. It's easier, but unwise.

A wise workplace is productive and creative but also happy in all senses of the word. Businesses that focus entirely on sales or profits would not be considered wise if they require constant and unhealthy competition and pressure among employees.

Our wisest business leaders recognize and reflect several basic precepts: They see strength in being vulnerable and open to those less powerful. They promote reciprocity; leadership is not one-way. They encourage risk-taking to eliminate fear. They think courageously to push beyond limits. They value respect before recognition.

Similar concepts apply throughout life and society. A college sports team that seeks to win at all costs rather than ensure its players labor and learn within an atmosphere of collaboration and cooperation, with empathy toward less gifted opponents, is not a wise team, regardless of how many championships it might win. Ultimately, more is lost than won.

Such notions may sound like simplistic platitudes. They may seem obvious and banal, but they are truisms, and by definition, that means they are fundamentally true. We ignore them at our own peril.

Practical Individual and Societal Wisdom During Crises

In the waning days of 1776, Thomas Paine wrote of times that tried men's souls. The American Revolution was in full swing, but frankly, not going so well for the new American government. Valley Forge still loomed.

But the war would eventually end, and a new country would take shape and prosper. There would be other crises, great and small, natural and manmade. That is the way of things. There will always be a new crisis, sometimes beyond imagination.

In this book I have mostly discussed practical wisdom as a means to stave off personal crises, from road rage to bereavement. But societies too struggle to confront and manage crises, to find a way to the other, better side.

Some crises are regional in nature, such as Hurricane Katrina's devastating appearance in 2005, killing an estimated 1,833 people, leaving millions homeless along the Gulf Coast and in New Orleans and causing more than $125 billion in damage. (Just 12 years later, Hurricane Harvey would inflict similar damage in Texas and Louisiana.)

Some are national crises, such as the terrorist attacks on the World Trade Center in New York City, the Pentagon in Washington, DC, and aboard United Airlines Flight 93, which crashed in a field near Shanksville, Pennsylvania. The events of 9/11 resulted in almost

3,000 fatalities, more than 25,000 injuries, $10 billion in infrastructure and property damage, and irreparable change to the American psyche.

And there are global crises, such as World War II or, arguably, climate change. These are crises no person on Earth can escape. The early stages of the novel coronavirus pandemic felt a lot like that, another global crisis that adversely affected individuals, regions, countries, and the globe. Challenges came from two particular directions.

First, there was—and to some degree, remains—uncertainty and confusion. This particular variety of the coronavirus was new; humans had no previous exposure. There was no existing immunological defense. Not knowing what would happen spawned fear and foreboding at every level: Will I become infected? Will I die? What will happen to my loved ones? My community? The country? Humanity?

The other challenge was in the recommended, sometimes mandated, steps to control the rapid and wide spread of the virus, to flatten the curve: social distancing. Humans are social animals. How do we distance ourselves from our loved ones, from our colleagues, from strangers even who might present us with unexpected joys and interests? These strategies necessary to tame the virus flew in the face of everything we teach our kids—shake hands when you greet, hug someone you care for, eat together, share your toys and gifts with others, play with one another. Social engagement is one of the most evidence-based strategies for health and longevity.

How do we suddenly switch to the exact opposite by distancing ourselves from everyone else except for your parents (for kids) and your significant others, if any (for adults)? Here, the strategies related to each described component of wisdom help us make the transition as smoothly as is humanly possible. They are useful not just to survive a crisis, but also to grow from it. They apply to any and all moments of change or confrontation, dilemma or disaster.

1. *Emotional regulation: Don't panic. Accept the reality but also stay positive.*

2. *Self-reflection: Think about how you've successfully emerged from previous hardships, and plan to use similar strategies.*

3. *Pro-social behaviors: Helping others helps oneself. In my qualitative research on loneliness, several older people said that when they help others who need help, they feel energized, happy, and less lonely. As I have mentioned earlier, the best antidote to loneliness and similar stresses is wisdom, especially its compassion component.*

4. *Accept uncertainty and diversity: See how other people have reacted and learn from their actions and tactics. There is no one-size-fits-all solution. Don't be judgmental.*

5. *Decisiveness: You will need to address various moral dilemmas. During the pandemic, it was questions like when to isolate yourself and from whom. The relative importance of family versus job. Whether to risk infection, perhaps life, to help another. These were dilemmas that confronted many, from first responders and emergency room physicians to grocery store workers. You need to make a decision based on all the information you have at that moment, and hope that it will prove correct in the longer term, but ambivalence won't help anyone.*

6. *Social advising, which requires general knowledge of life: Listen to the experts so you can give better advice.*

7. *Spirituality: We have to care for the entirety of humanity and beyond— animals and plants, too.*

8. *Sense of humor: This helps even in otherwise dark moments.*

9. *Openness to new experience: Staying open makes it possible to turn a crisis into an opportunity to grow.*

These observations apply across the board and at all levels of society, from individual workers and stay-at-home parents to leaders of local, regional, national, and international governments and organizations. The crises they will face may differ in detail and scope, but the tools of wisdom that they employ are the same.

In 1943, as World War II raged, Winston Churchill, prime minister of England, stood before an assembled throng and sought to rally them, to infuse them with common courage and hope, as he had done so many times before and would so many times more. In that speech, he said, "If we are together, nothing is impossible. If we are divided, all will fail."

Eleanor Roosevelt (1884–1962) was a different kind of a wise leader. She transformed the role of First Lady to the US president before, during, and after World War II. She became a recognized power unto herself, shining attention on and promoting civil rights policies to assist the poor, minorities, and women; helping formulate the society-changing New Deal social welfare programs; pushing for creation of the United Nations; and later helping to develop the Universal Declaration of Human Rights and UNICEF. She was a global humanitarian.

Our goal and dream should be to create a society that wisely embraces all of its members, a new and global version of the Shangri-La imagined by James Hilton in his novel *Lost Horizon* and by me in my youth. In this future society, we can find success together.

Getting there will be a trek, but let us embark. The first step is to make ourselves wiser as individuals and then in our numbers make our larger society wiser as well.

It can begin now. Here. With you.

Acknowledgments

THIS BOOK IS THE PRODUCT of the brains and minds of many wonderful people whose labors, insights, and contributions I have relied on heavily. I am most grateful to several younger colleagues, without whom this work would not have been possible: Ellen E. Lee, MD, and Barton W. Palmer, PhD, at UC San Diego, and Michael L. Thomas, PhD, at Colorado State University. I also have had the privilege of coauthoring countless papers on wisdom and related topics with a number of other colleagues at UC San Diego, including Katherine J. Bangen, PhD; Rebecca E. Daly, BS; Colin A. Depp, PhD; Emily C. Edmonds, PhD; Graham S. Eglit, PhD; Lisa T. Eyler, PhD; Danielle K. Glorioso, MSW; Sarah A. Graham, PhD; Jamie Joseph, PhD; A'verria S. Martin, PhD; Thomas W. Meeks, MD; Lori P. Montross, PhD; Alejandra Morlett Paredes, PhD; Tanya T. Nguyen, PhD; Lawrence A. Palinkas, PhD; Martin P. Paulus, MD; Emily B. H. Treichler, PhD; Xin M. Tu, PhD; Elizabeth W. Twamley, PhD; Ryan Van Patten, PhD; and Douglas M. Ziedonis, MD. Additionally, I want to thank Salvatore Di Somma, MD, PhD, at Sapienza University of Rome; James C. Harris, MD, at Johns Hopkins University; Ho-Cheol

Kim, PhD, at IBM Research; and Ipsit V. Vahia, MD, at Harvard University for all of their help.

I would be remiss to not highlight several leaders and collaborators in science more broadly, many of whom I also consider dear friends, especially Dan Blazer, MD, PhD, MPH, professor emeritus and former dean at Duke University; Howard Nusbaum, PhD, professor and director of the Center for Practical Wisdom at the University of Chicago; and Charles F. Reynolds III, MD, distinguished professor of psychiatry emeritus at the University of Pittsburgh School of Medicine. I am also thankful to George Eman Vaillant, MD, professor of psychiatry at Harvard Medical School; Bruce Miller, MD, professor of neurology at UC San Francisco; Monika Ardelt, PhD, professor of sociology at the University of Florida; Igor Grossmann, PhD, associate professor at University of Waterloo in Canada; Judith Glück, PhD, professor of developmental psychology at the University of Klagenfurt, Austria; Robert Sternberg, PhD, professor of human development at Cornell University; and C. Robert Cloninger, MD, professor of psychiatry and genetics at Washington University in St. Louis.

There is a story behind every book, and a cast of characters—all critical to its creation and success. Our thanks to all of them are sincere and unending: Heather Jackson, our literary agent extraordinaire, who rose to many unexpected challenges; Haven Iverson, the editorial director at Sounds True, who saw promise in this book and quite literally made it real; Leslie Brown, managing production editor, for overseeing the process; Marjorie Woodall, for her keen-eyed copyediting skills; Dan Farley, for his early advice and guidance; Paula K. Smith, for her daily, constant support; and to David A. Brenner, MD, vice chancellor for health sciences, UC San Diego, and Sandra A. Brown, PhD, vice chancellor for research, UC San Diego, for their scientific and administrative leadership and support of the research infrastructure that made our work feasible.

And last but not least, we want to express our eternal gratitude to our families and friends for their kindness, love, patience, and just being there.

Notes

Chapter 1. Defining Wisdom

Gail Fine, "Does Socrates Claim to Know That He Knows Nothing?" *Oxford Studies in Ancient Philosophy* 35 (2008): 49–88.

Proverbs 4:7 (King James version).

Hermann Hesse, *Siddhartha* (New York: New Directions Books, 1951).

Robert Heinlein, *Between Planets* (New York: Del Rey Books, 1951).

Ursula Staudinger, "A Psychology of Wisdom: History and Recent Developments," *Research in Human Development* 5, no. 2 (2008): 107–120, doi.org/10.1080/15427600802034835.

H. Sheldon, *Boyd's Introduction to the Study of Disease*, 11th ed. (Philadelphia: Lea & Febiger, 1992).

David P. Folsom et al., "Schizophrenia in Late Life: Emerging Issues," *Dialogues in Clinical Neuroscience* 8, no. 1 (2006): 45–52.

A Beautiful Mind, directed by Ron Howard, 2001.

Sylvia Nasar, *A Beautiful Mind* (New York: Simon & Schuster, 1998).

Erica Goode, "John F. Nash Jr., Math Genius Defined by a 'Beautiful Mind,' Dies at 86," *New York Times*, May 24, 2015, nytimes.com/2015/05/25/science/john-nash-a-beautiful-mind-subject-and-nobel-winner-dies-at-86.html.

R. Van Patten et al., "Assessment of 3-Dimensional Wisdom in Schizophrenia: Associations with Neuropsychological Functions and Physical and Mental Health," *Schizophrenia Research* 208 (June 2019): 360–369, doi.org/10.1016/j.schres.2019.01.022.

M. L. Thomas et al., "Paradoxical Trend for Improvement in Mental Health with Aging: A Community-Based Study of 1,546 Adults Aged 21–100 Years," *Journal of Clinical Psychiatry* 77, no. 8 (2016): e1019–e1025, doi.org/10.4088/JCP.16m10671.

D. V. Jeste et al., "Expert Consensus on Characteristics of Wisdom: A Delphi Method Study," *Gerontologist* 50, no. 5 (October 2010): 668–680, doi.org/10.1093/geront/gnq022.

K. J. Bangen et al., "Defining and Assessing Wisdom: A Review of the Literature," *American Journal of Geriatric Psychiatry* 21, no. 12 (December 2013): 1254–1266, doi.org/10.1016/j.jagp.2012.11.020.

Alvin I. Goldman, "Theory of Mind," in *Oxford Handbook of Philosophy and Cognitive Science*, ed. Eric Margolis, Richard Samuels, and Stephen Stich (Oxford, UK: Oxford University Press, 2012), 402–424.

D. V. Jeste and I. V. Vahia, "Comparison of the Conceptualization of Wisdom in Ancient Indian Literature with Modern Views: Focus on the Bhagavad Gita," *Psychiatry* 71, no. 3 (2008): 197–209, doi.org/10.1521/psyc.2008.71.3.197.

D. V. Jeste, "We All Have Wisdom, but What Is It?" *San Diego Union-Tribune*, April 3, 2015, utsandiego.com/news/2015/apr/02/brain-wisdom-explained/.

Chapter 2. The Neuroscience of Wisdom

Winston Churchill, "The Russian Enigma," BBC, radio broadcast, October 1, 1939. Churchill's quote is as follows: "I cannot forecast to you the action of Russia. It is a riddle, wrapped in a mystery, inside an enigma; but perhaps there is a key. That key is Russian national interest."

T. W. Meeks and D. V. Jeste, "Neurobiology of Wisdom: A Literature Overview," *Archives of General Psychiatry* 66, no. 4 (2009): 355–365, doi.org/10.1001 /archgenpsychiatry.2009.8.

T. W. Meeks, R. Cahn, and D. V. Jeste, "Neurobiological Foundations of Wisdom," in *Wisdom and Compassion in Psychotherapy*, ed. R. Siegel and C. Germer (New York: Guilford Press, 2012), 189–202.

D. V. Jeste and J. C. Harris, "Wisdom—A Neuroscience Perspective," *Journal of the American Medical Association* 304, no. 14 (2010): 1602–1603, doi.org/10.1001 /jama.2010.1458.

E. E. Lee and D. V. Jeste, "Neurobiology of Wisdom," in *The Cambridge Handbook of Wisdom*, ed. Robert Sternberg and Judith Glück (Cambridge, UK: Cambridge University Press, 2019), 69–93.

David Eagleman, *The Brain: The Story of You* (New York: Vintage Books, 2015).

J. Decety and P. L. Jackson, "The Functional Architecture of Human Empathy," *Behavioral and Cognitive Neuroscience Reviews* 3, no. 2 (2004): 71–100, doi.org /10.1177/1534582304267187.

Buddhaghosa, *The Path of Purification (Visuddhimagga)*, 4th ed., trans. Nyanamoli Himi (Kandy, Sri Lanka: Buddhist Publication Society, 2010), IX, 23, accesstoinsight .org/lib/authors/nanamoli/PathofPurification2011.pdf.

Will Rogers, syndicated column, August 31, 1924, as quoted in *The Will Rogers Book*, compiled by Paula McSpadden Love (Indianapolis, IN: Bobbs Merrill, 1961).

Ajit Varki and Danny Brower, *Denial: Self-Deception, False Beliefs, and the Origins of the Human Mind* (New York: Twelve, 2013).

John Van Wyhe, "The Authority of Human Nature: The Schadellehre of Franz Joseph Gall," *British Society for the History of Science* 35, no. 1 (2002): 17–42, doi.org/10.1017 /S0007087401004599.

Charles Darwin, *On the Origin of Species by Means of Natural Selection* (London: John Murray, 1859).

J. C. Flugel, *A Hundred Years of Psychology, 1833–1933* (New York: Macmillan, 1933).

Sam Kean, "Phineas Gage, Neuroscience's Most Famous Patient," *Slate,* May 6, 2014, slate.com/technology/2014/05/phineas-gage-neuroscience-case-true-story-of -famous-frontal-lobe-patient-is-better-than-textbook-accounts.html.

H. Damasio et al., "The Return of Phineas Gage: Clues About the Brain from the Skull of a Famous Patient," *Science* 264, no. 5162 (1994): 1102–1105, doi.org/10.1126 /science.8178168.

J. D. Van Horn et al., "Mapping Connectivity Damage in the Case of Phineas Gage," *PLoS ONE* 7, no. 5 (2012): e37454, doi.org/10.1371/journal.pone.0037454.

John Fleishman, *Phineas Gage: A Gruesome but True Story About Brain Science* (New York: Houghton Mifflin, 2002).

M. A. Cato et al., "Assessing the Elusive Cognitive Deficits Associated with Ventromedial Prefrontal Damage: A Case of a Modern-Day Phineas Gage," *Journal of the International Neuropsychological Society* 10, no. 3 (2004): 443–465, doi.org/10.1017/S1355617704103123.

R. Adolphs et al., "Impaired Recognition of Emotion in Facial Expressions Following Bilateral Damage to the Human Amygdala," *Nature* 372, no. 6507 (1994): 669–672, doi.org/10.1038/372669a0.

A. Aftab et al., "Meaning in Life and Its Relationship with Physical, Mental, and Cognitive Functioning," *Journal of Clinical Psychiatry* 81, no. 1 (2020): 19m13064, doi.org/10.4088/JCP.19m13064.

Chapter 3. Wisdom and Aging

Susan Heller Anderson and David W. Dunlap, "New York Day by Day; A New Job?" *New York Times,* April 25, 1985, nytimes.com/1985/04/25/nyregion/new-york-day -by-day-a-new-job.html.

Adele M. Hayutin, Miranda Dietz, and Lillian Mitchell, "New Realities of an Older America," Stanford Center on Longevity, 2010, longevity3.stanford.edu/wp -content/uploads/2013/01/New-Realities-of-an-Older-America.pdf.

"Living to 120 and Beyond: Americans' Views on Aging, Medical Advances and Radical Life Extension," Religion and Public Life, Pew Research Center, August 6, 2013, pewforum.org/2013/08/06/living-to-120-and-beyond-americans-views -on-aging-medical-advances-and-radical-life-extension/.

Daniel Goleman, "Erikson, in His Own Old Age, Expands His View of Life," *New York Times,* June 14, 1988, nytimes.com/1988/06/14/science/erikson-in-his-own-old -age-expands-his-view-of-life.html.

Erik H. Erikson and Joan M. Erikson, *The Life Cycle Completed: Extended Version* (New York: W. W. Norton, 1998).

L. M. Forster, "The Stereotyped Behavior of Sexual Cannibalism in Latrodectus-Hasselti Thorell (Araneae, Theridiidae), the Australian Redback Spider," *Australian Journal of Zoology* 40, no. 1 (1991): 1–11, doi.org/10.1071/ZO9920001.

NOTES

George C. Williams, "Pleiotropy, Natural Selection, and the Evolution of Senescence," *Evolution* 11, no. 1, (1957): 398–411, doi.org/10.1111/j.1558-5646.1957.tb02911.x.

K. Hawkes and J. Coxworth, "Grandmothers and the Evolution of Human Longevity: A Review of Findings and Future Directions," *Evolutionary Anthropology* 22, no. 6 (2013): 294–302, doi.org/10.1002/evan.21382.

M. Lahdenpera et al., "Fitness Benefits of Prolonged Post-Reproductive Lifespan in Women," *Nature* 428, no. 6979 (2004): 178–181, doi.org/10.1038/nature02367.

M. A. Barnett et al., "Grandmother Involvement as a Protective Factor for Early Childhood Social Adjustment," *Journal of Family Psychology* 24, no. 5 (2010): 635–645, doi.org/10.1037/a0020829.

F. Schwarz et al., "Human-Specific Derived Alleles of CD33 and Other Genes Protect Against Post-Reproductive Cognitive Decline," *PNAS* 113, no. 1 (2016): 74–79, doi.org/10.1073/pnas.1517951112.

Heather Buschman, "Newly Evolved, Uniquely Human Gene Variants Protect Older Adults from Cognitive Decline," Newsroom, UC San Diego Health, November 30, 2015, health.ucsd.edu/news/releases/Pages/2015-11-30-Human-Gene-Variants -Protect-Older-Adults-from-Cognitive-Decline.aspx.

M. Ardelt, "How Similar Are Wise Men and Women? A Comparison Across Two Age Cohorts," *Research in Human Development* 6, no. 1 (2009): 9–26, doi.org/10.1080 /15427600902779354.

William Shakespeare, *As You Like It*, act 2, scene 7.

Mark Twain, *Following the Equator* (Chicago: American Publishing Company, 1897).

Joseph Demakis, *The Ultimate Book of Quotations* (Raleigh, NC: Lulu Enterprises, 2012).

Bruce Grierson, "What if Age Is Nothing but a Mind-Set?" *New York Times Magazine*, October 22, 2014, nytimes.com/2014/10/26/magazine/what-if-age-is-nothing -but-a-mind-set.html.

D. V. Jeste, "Aging and Wisdom," *Samatvam* (magazine from the National Institute of Mental Health and Neuroscience, Bengaluru, India), August 2015.

L. P. Montross-Thomas et al., "Reflections on Wisdom at the End of Life: Qualitative Study of Hospice Patients Aged 58-97 Years," *International Psychogeriatrics* 20, no. 12 (2018): 1759–1766, doi.org/10.1017/S1041610217003039.

Alzheimer's Association, alz.org.

Utpal Das et al., "Activity-Induced Convergence in APP and BACE-1 in Acidic Microdomains via an Endocytosis-Dependent Pathway," *Neuron* 79, no. 3 (2013): 447–460, doi.org/10.1016/j.neuron.2013.05.035.

Scott LaFee, "Why Don't We All Get Alzheimer's Disease?" UC San Diego News Center, August 7, 2013, ucsdnews.ucsd.edu/pressrelease/why_dont_we_all_get _alzheimers_disease.

Suzanne Norman et al., "Adults' Reading Comprehension: Effects of Syntactic Complexity and Working Memory," *Journal of Gerontology* 47, no. 4 (1992): P258–P265, doi.org/10.1093/geronj/47.4.P258.

Sara Reistad-Long, "Older Brain Really May Be a Wiser Brain," *New York Times*, May 20, 2008, nytimes.com/2008/05/20/health/research/20brai.html.

292

S. Ackerman, *Discovering the Brain* (Washington, DC: National Academies Press, 1992).

F. H. Gage and S. Temple, "Neural Stem Cells: Generating and Regenerating the Brain," *Neuron* 80, no. 3 (2013): 588–601, doi.org/10.1016/j.neuron.2013.10.037.

Adam C. Roberts and David L. Glanzman, "Learning in Aplysia: Looking at Synaptic Plasticity from Both Sides," *Trends in Neuroscience* 26, no. 12 (2003): 662–670, doi.org/10.1016/j.tins.2003.09.014.

L. T. Eyler et al., "A Review of Functional Brain Imaging Correlates of Successful Cognitive Aging," *Biological Psychiatry* 70, no. 2 (2011): 115–122, doi.org/10.1016/j.biopsych.2010.12.032.

H. Schwandt, "Unmet Aspirations as an Explanation for the Age U-Shape in Human Wellbeing" (discussion paper no. 1229, Centre for Economic Performance, London School of Economics and Political Science, July 2013).

Jonathan Rauch, "The Real Roots of Midlife Crisis," *The Atlantic*, December 2014, theatlantic.com/magazine/archive/2014/12/the-real-roots-of-midlife-crisis/382235/.

Chapter 4. Measuring Wisdom

Jeffrey Dean Webster, "An Exploratory Analysis of a Self-Assessed Wisdom Scale," *Journal of Adult Development* 10, no. 1 (2003): 13–22, doi.org/10.1023/A:1020782619051.

"The Smartest Celebrities," Entertainment, Ranker, ranker.com/list/smartest-famous-people/celebrity-lists.

Shane Frederick, "Why a High IQ Doesn't Mean You're Smart," Center for Customer Insights, Yale School of Management, November 1, 2009, som.yale.edu/news/2009/11/why-high-iq-doesnt-mean-youre-smart.

Kevin Dutton, *The Wisdom of Psychopaths: What Saints, Spies, and Serial Killers Can Teach Us About Success* (New York: Scientific American/Farrar, Straus and Giroux, 2012).

Scott O. Lilienfeld and Hal Arcowitz, "What 'Psychopath' Means," *Scientific American*, December 1, 2007, scientificamerican.com/article/what-psychopath-means/?redirect=1.

J. L. McCain and W. K. Campbell, "Narcissism and Social Media Use: A Meta-Analytic Review," *Psychology of Popular Media Culture* 7, no. 3 (2018): 308–327, doi.org/10.1037/ppm0000137.

P. Reed et al., "Visual Social Media Use Moderates the Relationship Between Initial Problematic Internet Use and Later Narcissism," *The Open Psychology Journal* 11 (2018): 163–170, doi.org/10.2174/1874350101811010163.

E. T. Panek, Y. Nardis, and S. Konrath, "Mirror or Megaphone? How Relationships Between Narcissism and Social Networking Site Use Differ on Facebook and Twitter," *Computers in Human Behavior* 29, no. 5 (2013): 2004–2012, doi.org/10.1016/j.chb.2013.04.012.

J. Stuart and A. Kurek, "Looking Hot in Selfies: Narcissistic Beginnings, Aggressive Outcomes?" *International Journal of Behavioral Development* 43, no. 6 (2019): 500–506, doi.org/10.1177/0165025419865621.

Isaac Newton, *Delphi Collected Works of Sir Isaac Newton*, illustrated (Hastings, UK: Delphi Classics, 2016).

Daniel Doyle MacGarry, ed. and trans., *The Metalogicon of John Salisbury: A Twelfth-Century Defense of the Verbal and Logical Arts of the Trivium* (Berkeley: University of California Press, 1955).

Robert K. Merton, *On the Shoulders of Giants: A Shandean Postscript*, the post-Italianate edition with a foreword by Umberto Eco (Chicago: University of Chicago Press, 1993).

Richard William Southern, *Making of the Middle Ages* (New Haven, CT: Yale University Press, 1952).

M. Ardelt, "Empirical Assessment of a Three-Dimensional Wisdom Scale," *Research on Aging* 25, no. 1 (2003): 275–324, doi.org/10.1177/0164027503025003004.

Charles Cassidy, Evidence-Based Wisdom: Translating the New Science of Wisdom Research (website), evidencebasedwisdom.com/.

Elisabeth Kubler-Ross, *Death: The Final Stage of Growth* (New York: Simon & Schuster, 1975).

Jeffrey Dean Webster, "An Exploratory Analysis of a Self-Assessed Wisdom Scale," *Journal of Adult Development* 10, no. 1 (2003): 13–22, doi.org/10.1023/A: 1020782619051.

M. L. Thomas et al., "Development of a 12-Item Abbreviated Three-Dimensional Wisdom Scale (3D-WS-12): Item Selection and Psychometric Properties," *Assessment* 24, no. 1 (2015): 71–82, doi.org/10.1177/1073191115595714.

M. L. Thomas et al., "A New Scale for Assessing Wisdom Based on Common Domains and a Neurobiological Model: The San Diego Wisdom Scale (SD-WISE)," *Journal of Psychiatric Research* 108 (January 2019): 40–47, doi.org/10.1016/j.jpsychires.2017 .09.005.

Chapter 5. Cultivating Compassion

"Karaniya Metta Sutta: The Discourse on Loving-Kindness" (sn 1.8), translated from the Pali by Piyadassi Maha Thera, Access to Insight (BCBS edition), August 29, 2012, accesstoinsight.org/tipitaka/kn/snp/snp.1.08.piya.html.

Christina Johnson, "Teaching the Art of Doctoring," *Discoveries* (2016): 24–25, https:// view.publitas.com/ucsd-health-sciences/discoveries-2016-uc-san-diego-health /page/26-27.

R. C. Moore et al., "From Suffering to Caring: A Model of Differences Among Older Adults in Levels of Compassion," *International Journal of Geriatric Psychiatry* 30, no. 2 (2014): 185–191, doi.org/10.1002/gps.4123.

"How Having Smartphones (or Not) Shapes the Way Teens Communicate," Fact Tank, Pew Research Center, August 20, 2015, pewresearch.org/fact-tank/2015/08/20 /how-having-smartphones-or-not-shapes-the-way-teens-communicate/.

Aaron Smith, "Americans and Texting," Internet & Technology, Pew Research Center, September 19, 2011, pewresearch.org/internet/2011/09/19/americans-and-text -messaging/.

Donald W. Pfaff with Sandra Sherman, *The Altruistic Brain: How We Are Naturally Good* (New York: Oxford University Press, 2015).

V. Gallese et al., "Action Recognition in the Premotor Cortex," *Brain* 119, no. 2 (1996): 593–609, doi.org/10.1093/brain/119.2.593.

J. Decety et al., "Brain Response to Empathy-Eliciting Scenarios Involving Pain in Incarcerated Individuals with Psychopathy," *JAMA Psychiatry* 70, no. 6 (2013): 638–645, doi.org/10.1001/jamapsychiatry.2013.27.

Scott O. Lilienfeld and Hal Arcowitz, "What 'Pyschopath' Means," *Scientific American*, December 1, 2007, scientificamerican.com/article/what-psychopath-means /?redirect=1.

James Fallon, *The Psychopath Inside: A Neuroscientist's Personal Journey into the Dark Side of the Brain* (New York: Penguin, 2013).

Joseph Stromberg, "The Neuroscientist Who Discovered He Was a Psychopath," *Smithsonian*, November 22, 2013, smithsonianmag.com/science-nature/the -neuroscientist-who-discovered-he-was-a-psychopath-180947814/.

Mike McIntyre, *The Kindness of Strangers: Penniless Across America* (New York: Berkley Books, 1996).

National Kidney Foundation, kidney.org/.

K. M. Brethel-Haurwitz and A. A. Marsh, "Geographical Differences in Subjective Well-Being Predict Extraordinary Altruism," *Psychological Science* 25, no. 3 (2014): 762–771, doi.org/10.1177/0956797613516148.

Sanober Khan, *Turquoise Silence* (Kalindipuram, India: Cyberwit, 2014).

E. Smeets et al., "Meeting Suffering with Kindness: Effects of a Brief Self-Compassion Intervention for Female College Students," *Journal of Clinical Psychology* 70, no. 9 (2014): 794–807, doi.org/10.1002/jclp.22076.

John Emerich Edward Dalberg, Lord Acton, to Bishop Mandell Creighton, 5 April 1887, Acton-Creighton Correspondence, Online Library of Liberty, oll.libertyfund.org /titles/acton-acton-creighton-correspondence#lf1524_label_010.

J. Hogeveen et al., "Power Changes How the Brain Responds to Others," *Journal of Experimental Psychology* 143, no. 2 (2013): 755–762, doi.org/10.1037/a0033477.

S. M. Rodrigues et al., "Oxytocin Receptor Genetic Variation Relates to Empathy and Stress Reactivity in Humans," *PNAS* 106, no. 50 (2009): 21347–21441, doi.org/10 .1073/pnas.0909579106.

A. Kogan et al., "A Thin-Slicing Study of the Oxytocin Receptor (OXTR) Gene and the Evaluation and Expression of the Prosocial Disposition," *PNAS* 108, no. 48 (2011): 19189–19192, doi.org/10.1073/pnas.1112658108.

S. W. Cole et al., "Social Regulation of Gene Expression in Human Leukocytes," *Genome Biology* 8, no. R189 (2007), doi.org/10.1186/gb-2007-8-9-r189.

Emiliana R. Simon-Thomas, "Are Women More Empathic Than Men?" *Greater Good Magazine,* Greater Good Science Center, UC Berkeley, June 1, 2007, greatergood .berkeley.edu/article/item/women_more_empathic_than_men.

Y. Moriguchi et al., "Sex Differences in the Neural Correlates of Affective Experience," *Social Cognitive and Affective Neuroscience* 9, no. 5 (2013): 591–600, doi.org/10.1093/scan/nst030.

Poncie Rutsch, "Men and Women Use Different Scales to Weigh Moral Dilemmas," Shots, Health News from NPR, April 3, 2015, npr.org/sections/health-shots /2015/04/03/397280759/men-and-women-use-different-scales-to-weigh -moral-dilemmas.

R. Friesdorf et al., "Gender Differences in Responses to Moral Dilemmas," *Personality and Social Psychology Bulletin* 41, no. 5 (2015): 696–713, doi.org/10.1177/0146167215575731.

D. W. Muir and S. M. J. Hains, "Infant Sensitivity to Perturbations in Adult Facial, Vocal, Tactile, and Contingent Stimulation During Face-to-Face Interactions," in *Developmental Neurocognition: Speech and Face Processing in the First Year of Life*, ed. B. de Boysson-Bardies et al. (New York: Kluwer Academic/Plenum Publishers, 1993), 171–185.

Jeffry J. Iovannone, "Lady Di Destroys AIDS Stigma," Medium, May 23, 2018, medium .com/queer-history-for-the-people/lady-di-destroys-aids-stigma-a631e2c67f2c.

Roisin Kelly, "Princess Diana's Legacy of Kindess," *Parade*, August 11, 2017, parade .com/593773/roisinkelly/princess-dianas-legacy-of-kindness/.

Simon Perry, "Prince Harry Shares How His Mom Princess Diana, at 'Only 25 Years Old,' Fought Homophobia," *People*, October 12, 2017, people.com/royals /prince-harry-shares-how-his-mom-princess-diana-at-only-25-years-old -fought-homophobia/.

T. Vishnevsky et al., "The Keepers of Stories: Personal Growth and Wisdom Among Oncology Nurses," *Journal of Holistic Nursing* 33, no. 4 (2015): 326–344, doi.org /10.1177/0898010115574196.

E. O'Brien et al., "Empathic Concern and Perspective Taking: Linear and Quadratic Effects of Age Across the Adult Life Span," *Journals of Gerontology, Series B* 68, no. 2 (2012): 168–175, doi.org/10.1093/geronb/gbs055.

H. Y. Weng et al., "Compassion Training Alters Altruism and Neural Responses to Suffering," *Psychological Science* 24, no. 7 (2013): 1171–1180, doi.org/10.1177 /0956797612469537.

J. Galante et al., "Loving-Kindness Meditation Effects on Well-Being and Altruism," *Applied Psychology: Health and Well-Being* 8, no. 3 (2016): 322–350, doi.org/10.1111 /aphw.12074.

K. J. Kemper and N. Ra, "Brief Online Focused Attention Meditation Training: Immediate Impact," *Journal of Evidence-Based Complementary & Alternative Medicine* 22, no. 2 (2016): 237–241, doi.org/10.1177/2156587216642102.

S. Konig and J. Glück, "'Gratitude Is with Me All the Time': How Gratitude Relates to Wisdom," *Journals of Gerontology, Series B* 69, no. 5 (2013): 655–666, doi.org/10.1093 /geronb/gbt123.

"Brain Can Be Trained in Compassion, Study Shows," University of Wisconsin-Madison News, May 22, 2013, news.wisc.edu/brain-can-be-trained-in-compassion -study-shows/.

H. Y. Weng et al., "Compassion Training Alters Altruism and Neural Responses to Suffering," *Psychological Science* 24, no. 7 (2013): 1171–1180, doi.org/10.1177 /0956797612469537.

J. Gonzalez, "Reading *Cinnamon* Activates Olfactory Brain Regions," *NeuroImage* 32, no. 2 (2006): 906–912, doi.org/10.1016/j.neuroimage.2006.03.037.

S. Lacey, R. Stilla, and K. Sathian, "Metaphorically Feeling: Comprehending Textural Metaphors Activates Somatosensory Cortex," *Brain & Language* 120, no. 3 (2012): 416–421, doi.org/10.1016/j.bandl.2011.12.016.

Gertrude Stein, *The Making of Americans* (New York: Albert & Charles Boni, 1926).

R. A. Mar et al., "Exposure to Media and Theory-of-Mind Development in Preschoolers," *Cognitive Development* 25, no. 1 (2010): 69–78, doi.org/10.1016/j.cogdev.2009.11.002.

M. Levine et al., "Identity and Emergency Intervention: How Social Group Membership and Inclusiveness of Group Boundaries Shape Helping Behavior," *Personality and Social Psychology Bulletin* 31, no. 4 (2005): 443–453, doi.org/10.1177/0146167204271651.

T. Singer and M. Bolz, eds., *Compassion: Bridging Practice and Science* (Leipzig, Germany: Max Planck Institute, 2013).

S. L. Valk et al., "Structural Plasticity of the Social Brain: Differential Change After Socio-Affective and Cognitive Mental Training," *Science Advances* 3, no. 10 (2017), doi.org/10.1126/sciadv.1700489.

Chapter 6. Emotional Regulation with Happiness

J. Hilton, *Goodbye Mr. Chips* (New York: Little, Brown, 1934).

Goodbye, Mr. Chips, directed by Herbert Ross, 1969.

W. James, *The Principles of Psychology*, vol. 2 (New York: Cosimo Classics, 2007).

Luke Dittrich, *Patient H.M.: A Story of Memory, Madness, and Family Secrets* (New York: Random House, 2016).

Scott LaFee, "H.M. Recollected," *San Diego Union-Tribune*, November 30, 2009, sandiegouniontribune.com/sdut-hm-recollected-famous-amnesic-launches -bold-new-br-2009nov30-htmlstory.html.

L. D. Kubzanski et al., "Angry Breathing: A Prospective Study of Hostility and Lung Function in the Normative Aging Study," *Epidemiology* 61 (2006): 863–868, doi.org /10.1136/thx.2005.050971.

E. Harburg et al., "Marital Pair Anger-Coping Types May Act as an Entity to Affect Mortality: Preliminary Findings from a Prospective Study (Tecumseh, Michigan, 1971–1988)," *Journal of Family Communication* 12, no. 4 (2008): 44–61, doi.org /10.1080/15267430701779485.

Charles Darwin, *The Expression of the Emotions in Man and Animals* (New York: D. Appleton and Company, 1897).

P. Ekman and W. V. Friesen, "Constants Across Cultures in the Face and Emotion," *Journal of Personality and Social Psychology* 17, no. 2 (1971): 124–129, doi.org/10.1037 /h0030377.

L. T. Eyler et al., "A Review of Functional Brain Imaging Correlates of Successful Cognitive Aging," *Biological Psychiatry* 70, no. 2 (2011): 115–122, doi.org/10.1016/j .biopsych.2010.12.032.

E. Jauk et al., "Self-Viewing Is Associated with Negative Affect Rather Than Reward in Highly Narcissistic Men: An fMRI Study," *Scientific Reports* 7, no. 5804 (2017), doi .org/10.1038/s41598-017-03935-y.

W. Mischel et al., "Cognitive and Attentional Mechanisms in Delay of Gratification," *Journal of Personality and Social Psychology* 21, no. 2 (1972): 204–218, doi.org/10.1037 /h0032198.

S. Bellezza et al., "'Be Careless with That!' Availability of Product Upgrades Increases Cavalier Behavior Toward Possessions," *Journal of Marketing Research* 54, no. 5 (2017): 768–784, doi.org/10.1509/jmr.15.0131.

Phyllis Korkki, "Damaging Your Phone, Accidentally on Purpose," *New York Times*, April 7, 2017, nytimes.com/2017/04/07/your-money/iphones-upgrades -carelessness-neglect.html.

C. E. Wierenga et al., "Hunger Does Not Motivate Reward in Women Remitted from Anorexia Nervosa," *Biological Psychiatry* 77, no. 7 (2015): 642–652, doi.org/10.1016 /j.biopsych.2014.09.024.

Martin Luther King Jr., "'I Have a Dream,' Address Delivered at the March on Washington for Jobs and Freedom," The Martin Luther King, Jr. Research and Education Institute, Stanford University, kinginstitute.stanford.edu/king-papers /documents/i-have-dream-address-delivered-march-washington-jobs-and -freedom.

Wikipedia, s.v. "Women's Tennis Association," last modified February 21, 2020, en.wikipedia.org/wiki/Women%27s_Tennis_Association.

Stephanie Kang, "Questions for: Billie Jean King," *Wall Street Journal*, October 28, 2008, wsj.com/articles/SB122522657604277313.

Sam Laird, "Tony Romo Gets Emotional in Speech About Losing Starting Job to Dak Prescott," Mashable, November 15, 2016, mashable.com/2016/11/15/tony-romo -speech-dak-prescott/.

Jonathan Rauch, *The Happiness Curve: Why Life Gets Better After 50* (New York: Thomas Dunne, 2018).

D. G. Branchflower, "Is Happiness U-shaped Everywhere? Age and Subjective Well-Being in 132 Countries" (working paper no. 26641, National Bureau of Economic Research, January 2020), doi.org/10.3386/w26641.

The Simpsons Movie, directed by David Silverman, 2007.

Daniel Freeman and Jason Freeman, "Is Life's Happiness Curve Really U-Shaped?" *Guardian*, June 24, 2015, theguardian.com/science/head-quarters/2015/jun/24 /life-happiness-curve-u-shaped-ageing.

"Antidepressant Use on the Rise," American Psychiatric Association, November 2017, apa.org/monitor/2017/11/numbers.

A. Weiss et al., "Evidence for a Midlife Crisis in Great Apes Consistent with the U-Shape in Human Well-Being," *PNAS* 109, no. 49 (2012): 19949–19952, doi.org/10.1073/pnas .1212592109.

M. L. Thomas et al., "Paradoxical Trend for Improvement in Mental Health with Aging: A Community-Based Study of 1,546 Adults Aged 21–100 Years," *Journal of Clinical Psychiatry* 77, no. 8 (2016): 1019–1025, doi.org/10.4088/JCP.16m10671.

E. E. Lee et al., "Childhood Adversity and Schizophrenia: The Protective Role of Resilience in Mental and Physical Health and Metabolic Markers," *Journal of Clinical Psychiatry* 79, no. 3 (2018): 1–9, doi.org/10.4088/JCP.17m11776.

A. J. Lamond et al., "Measurement and Predictors of Resilience Among Community-Dwelling Older Women," *Journal of Psychiatric Research* 43, no. 2 (2008): 148–154, doi.org/10.1016/j.jpsychires.2008.03.007.

Ajit Varki and Danny Brower, *Denial: Self-Deception, False Beliefs, and the Origins of the Human Mind* (New York: Twelve, 2013).

K. Bangen et al., "Brains of Optimistic Older Adults Respond Less to Fearful Faces," *Journal of Neuropsychiatry and Clinical Neurosciences* 26, no. 2 (2014): 155–163, doi.org/10.1176/appi.neuropsych.12090231.

"Emotional Fitness in Aging: Older Is Happier," American Psychological Association, November 28, 2005, apa.org/research/action/emotional.

"The Second Bush-Dukakis Presidential Debate," Commission on Presidential Debates, October 13, 1988, debates.org/index.php?page=october-13-1988-debate-transcript.

W. Mischel et al., "'Willpower' Over the Life Span: Decomposing Self-Regulation," *SCAN* 6, no. 2 (2010): 252–256, doi.org/10.1093/scan/nsq081.

S. Jimenez-Murcia et al., "Video Game Addiction in Gambling Disorder: Clinical, Psychopathological, and Personality Correlates," *BioMed Research International* 2014, no. 315062, doi.org/10.1155/2014/315062.

Chapter 7. Balancing Decisiveness with Acceptance of Uncertainty

D. V. Jeste et al., "The New Science of Practical Wisdom," *Perspectives in Biology and Medicine* 62, no. 2 (2019): 216–236, Project MUSE, doi.org/10.1353/pbm.2019.0011.

K. A. Appiah, A. Bloom, and K. Yoshino, "May I Lie to My Husband to Get Him to See a Doctor?" The Ethicist, *New York Times Magazine*, May 20, 2015, nytimes.com/2015/05/24/magazine/may-i-lie-to-my-husband-to-get-him-to-see-a-doctor.html.

A. Bloom, J. Shafer, and K. Yoshino, "How Do I Counter My Sister's Abuse Claims Against Our Father?" The Ethicist, *New York Times Magazine*, June 24, 2015, nytimes.com/2015/06/28/magazine/how-do-i-counter-my-sisters-abuse-claims-against-our-father.html.

K. A. Appiah, A. Bloom, and K. Yoshino, "Can I Hire Someone to Write My Résumé and Cover Letter?" The Ethicist, *New York Times Magazine*, April 8, 2015, nytimes.com/2015/04/12/magazine/can-i-hire-someone-to-write-my-resume-and-cover-letter.html.

William Styron, *Sophie's Choice* (New York: Random House, 1979).

Sophie's Choice, directed by Alan J. Pakula, 1982.

M. L. Thomas et al., "Individual Differences in Level of Wisdom Are Associated with Brain Activation During a Moral Decision-Making Task," *Brain and Behavior* 9, no. 6 (2019): e01302, doi.org/10.1002/brb3.1302.

I. Grossmann, "Wisdom in Context," *Perspectives in Psychological Science* 12, no. 2 (2017): 233–257, doi.org/10.1177/1745691616672066.

I. Grossmann and E. Kross, "Exploring Solomon's Paradox: Self-Distancing Eliminates the Self-Other Asymmetry in Wise Reasoning About Close Relationships in Younger and Older Adults," *Psychological Science* 25, no. 8 (2014): 1571–1580, doi.org/10.1177/0956797614535400.

M. Ardelt and D. V. Jeste, "Wisdom and Hard Times: The Ameliorating Effect of Wisdom on the Negative Association Between Adverse Life Events and Well-Being," *Journals of Gerontology, Series B* 73, no. 8 (2018): 1374–1383, doi.org /10.1093/geronb/gbw137.

K. F. Leith and R. F. Baumeister, "Why Do Bad Moods Increase Self-Defeating Behavior? Emotion, Risk Taking, and Self-Regulation," *Journal of Personality and Social Psychology* 71, no. 6 (1996): 1250–1267, doi.org/10.1037//0022-3514.71.6.1250.

J. S. Lerner, D. A. Small, and G. Loewenstein, "Heart Strings and Purse Strings: Carry-Over Effects of Emotions on Economic Decisions," *Psychological Science* 15, no. 5 (2004): 337–341, doi.org/10.1111/j.0956-7976.2004.00679.x.

David G. Allan, "Good and Bad, It's All the Same: A Taoist Parable to Live By," The Wisdom Project, CNN Health, April 28, 2017, cnn.com/2015/09/02/health/who -knows-whats-good-or-bad-wisdom-project/index.html.

Sewell Chan, "Stanislav Petrov, Soviet Officer Who Helped Avert Nuclear War, Is Dead at 77," *New York Times*, September 18, 2017, nytimes.com/2017/09/18 /world/europe/stanislav-petrov-nuclear-war-dead.html.

Jason Daley, "Man Who Saved the World from Nuclear Annihilation Dies at 77," *Smithsonian*, September 18, 2017, smithsonianmag.com/smart-news/man -who-saved-world-nuclear-annihilation-dies-77-180964934/.

Eryn Grant, Nicholas Stevens, and Paul Salmon, "Why the 'Miracle on the Hudson' in the New Movie Sully Was No Crash Landing," The Conversation, theconversation .com/why-the-miracle-on-the-hudson-in-the-new-movie-sully-was-no-crash -landing-64748.

Robert D. McFadden, "Pilot Is Hailed After Jetliner's Icy Plunge," *New York Times*, January 15, 2009, nytimes.com/2009/01/16/nyregion/16crash.html.

Sully, directed by Clint Eastwood, 2016.

Adam Epstein, "US Aviation Investigators Say They're Unfairly Villainized in Clint Eastwood's Film 'Sully,'" Quartz, September 9, 2016, qz.com/778011/sully -ntsb-investigators-are-not-happy-about-being-made-the-villains-in-clint -eastwoods-film-starring-tom-hanks-as-chesley-sully-sullenberger/.

Daniel Dennett, *Consciousness Explained* (New York: Little, Brown, 1991).

E. P. Seligman and John Tierney, "We Aren't Built to Live in the Moment," *New York Times*, May 19, 2017, nytimes.com/2017/05/19/opinion/sunday/why-the-future -is-always-on-your-mind.html.

D. V. Jeste and E. Saks, "Decisional Capacity in Mental Illness and Substance Use Disorders: Empirical Database and Policy Implications," *Behavioral Sciences and the Law* 24, no. 4 (2006): 607–628, doi.org/10.1002/bsl.707.

L. B. Dunn et al., "Assessing Decisional Capacity for Clinical Research or Treatment: A Review of Instruments," *American Journal of Psychiatry* 163, no. 8 (2006): 1323–1334, doi.org/10.1176/appi.ajp.163.8.1323.

D. V. Jeste et al., "A New Brief Instrument for Assessing Decisional Capacity for Clinical Research," *Archives of General Psychiatry* 64, no. 8 (2007): 966–974, doi.org/10.1001/archpsyc.64.8.966.

R. Van Patten et al., "Assessment of 3-Dimensional Wisdom in Schizophrenia: Associations with Neuropsychological Functions and Physical and Mental Health," *Schizophrenia Research* 208 (2019): 360–369, doi.org/10.1016/j.schres.2019.01.022.

Heather Butler, "Why Do Smart People Do Foolish Things?" *Scientific American*, October 3, 2017, scientificamerican.com/article/why-do-smart-people-do -foolish-things/.

L. T. Eyler et al., "Brain Response Correlates of Decisional Capacity in Schizophrenia: A Preliminary fMRI Study," *Journal of Neuropsychiatry and Clinical Neurosciences* 19, no. 2 (2007): 137–144, doi.org/10.1176/jnp.2007.19.2.137.

D. V. Jeste et al., "Multimedia Educational Aids for Improving Consumer Knowledge About Illness Management and Treatment Decisions: A Review of Randomized Controlled Trials," *Journal of Psychiatric Research* 42, no. 1 (2007): 1–21, doi.org /10.1016/j.jpsychires.2006.10.004.

Chapter 8. Self-Reflection, Curiosity, and Humor

George Dvorsky, "I'm Elyn Saks and This Is What It's Like to Live with Schizophrenia," Gizmodo, io9, February 13, 2013, io9.gizmodo.com/i-m-elyn-saks-and-this-is -what-it-s-like-to-live-with-s-5983970.

Elyn R. Saks, *The Center Cannot Hold: My Journey Through Madness* (New York: Hyperion, 2007).

G. G. Gallup Jr., "Chimpanzees: Self-Recognition," *Science* 167, no. 3914 (1970): 86–87, doi.org/10.1126/science.167.3914.86.

David Goodill, "Moral Theology After Wittgenstein" (dissertation, University of Fribourg, 2017), doc.rero.ch/record/304966/files/GoodillD.pdf.

T. D. Wilson et al., "Just Think: The Challenges of the Disengaged Mind," *Science* 345, no. 6192 (2014): 75–77, doi.org/10.1126/science.1250830.

Stephanie Brown, *Speed: Facing Our Addiction to Fast and Faster—and Overcoming Our Fear of Slowing Down* (New York: Berkeley, 2014).

Kate Murphy, "No Time to Think," *New York Times*, July 25, 2014, nytimes.com/2014 /07/27/sunday-review/no-time-to-think.html.

Fyodor Dostoevsky, *Winter Notes on Summer Impressions*, trans. David Patterson (Chicago: Northwestern University Press, 1988).

Brett McKay and Kate McKay, "Lessons in Manliness: Benjamin Franklin's Pursuit of the Virtuous Life," The Art of Manliness, February 28, 2008, artofmanliness .com/articles/lessons-in-manliness-benjamin-franklins-pursuit-of-the -virtuous-life/.

"Mental Rest and Reflection Boost Learning, Study Suggests," UT News, Health and Wellness, University of Texas at Austin, October 20, 2014, news.utexas.edu/2014/10/20/mental-rest-and-reflection-boost-learning-study-suggests/.

"2015 Global Mobile Consumer Survey: US Edition. The Rise of the Always-Connected Consumer," Deloitte, www2.deloitte.com/content/dam/Deloitte/us/Documents/technology-media-telecommunications/us-tmt-global-mobile-executive-summary-2015.pdf.

C. Kidd and B. Y. Hayden, "The Psychology and Neuroscience of Curiosity," *Neuron* 88, no. 3 (2015): 449–460, doi.org/10.1016/j.neuron.2015.09.010.

R. Golman and G. Loewenstein, "An Information-Gap Theory of Feelings About Uncertainty," Carnegie Mellon University, January 2, 2016, cmu.edu/dietrich/sds/docs/golman/Information-Gap%20Theory%202016.pdf.

C. J. Soto and J. J. Jackson, "Five-Factor Model of Personality," Oxford Bibliographies, February 26, 2013, doi.org/10.1093/OBO/9780199828340-0120.

M. J. Kang et al., "The Wick in the Candle of Learning: Epistemic Curiosity Activates Reward Circuitry and Enhances Memory," *Psychological Science* 20, no. 8 (2009): 963–973, doi.org/10.1111/j.1467-9280.2009.02402.x.

Dilip Jeste, "Seeking Wisdom in Graying Matter," TEDMED, YouTube video, 16:43, June 14, 2016, youtube.com/watch?v=pKaLWePrhhg.

Opie Percival Read, *Mark Twain and I* (Chicago: Reilly & Lee, 1940).

Richard Wiseman (website), richardwiseman.com/LaughLab/.

E. B. White, *Stuart Little* (New York: Harper Trophy, 1945).

E. B. White, *Charlotte's Web* (New York: Harper & Brothers, 1952).

W. Strunk and E. B. White, *The Elements of Style* (New York: Macmillan, 1959).

E. B. White and K. S. White, "Some Remarks on Humor," preface to *A Subtreasury of American Humor* (New York: Coward McCann, 1941).

O. Amir and I. Biederman, "The Neural Correlates of Humor Creativity," *Frontiers in Human Neuroscience* 10, no. 597 (2016), doi.org/10.3389/fnhum.2016.00597.

N. A. Yovetich et al., "Benefits of Humor in Reduction of Threat-Induced Anxiety," *Psychological Reports* 66, no. 1 (1990): 51–58, doi.org/10.2466/pr0.1990.66.1.51.

Josh Howie, "The Divine Comedy," *Guardian*, February 20, 2009, theguardian.com/commentisfree/belief/2009/feb/19/religion-god-humour.

Chapter 9. Spirituality

"Census Data 2001/Metadata," Office of the Registrar General and Census Commissioner, India, 2001, censusindia.gov.in/Metadata/Metada.htm.

T. J. VanderWeele, "On the Promotion of Human Flourishing," *PNAS* 114, no. 31 (2017): 8148–8156, doi.org/10.1073/pnas.1702996114.

"The Global Religious Landscape," Religion & Public Life, Pew Research Center, December 18, 2012, pewforum.org/2012/12/18/global-religious-landscape-exec/.

S. Li et al., "Association of Religious Service Attendance with Mortality Among Women," *JAMA Internal Medicine* 176, no. 6 (2016): 777–785, doi.org/10.1001/jamainternmed.2016.1615.

S. Li et al., "Religious Service Attendance and Lower Depression Among Women—A Prospective Cohort Study," *Annals of Behavioral Medicine* 50, no. 6 (2016): 876–884, doi.org/10.1007/s12160-016-9813-9.

T. J. VanderWeele et al., "Association Between Religious Attendance and Lower Suicide Rates Among US Women," *JAMA Psychiatry* 73, no. 8 (2016):845–851, doi.org/10.1001/jamapsychiatry.2016.1243.

"The Global Religious Landscape," Religion & Public Life, Pew Research Center, December 18, 2012, pewforum.org/2012/12/18/global-religious-landscape-exec/.

Frank Newport, "Most Americans Still Believe in God," Gallup, June 29, 2016, news .gallup.com/poll/193271/americans-believe-god.aspx.

S. Li et al., "Religious Service Attendance and Mortality Among Women," *JAMA Internal Medicine* 176, no. 6 (2016): 777–785, doi.org/10.1001/jamainternmed.2016.1615.

S. Monod et al., "Instruments Measuring Spirituality in Clinical Research: A Systematic Review," *Journal of General Internal Medicine* 26, no. 1345 (2011), doi.org/10.1007/s11606-011-1769-7.

IKAR (website), ikar-la.org/.

Wikipedia, s.v. "Sharon Brous," last modified November 5, 2019, en.wikipedia.org /wiki/Sharon_Brous.

I. V. Vahia et al., "Correlates of Spirituality in Older Women," *Aging and Mental Health* 15, no. 1 (2015) 97–102, doi.org/10.1080/13607863.2010.501069.

K. Dewhurst and A. W. Beard, "Sudden Religious Conversions in Temporal Lobe Epilepsy," *British Journal of Psychiatry* 117, no. 540 (1970): 497–507, doi.org /10.1016/S1525-5050(02)00688-1.

Oliver Sacks, "Seeing God in the Third Millennium," *Atlantic*, Dec. 12, 2012, theatlantic .com/health/archive/2012/12/seeing-god-in-the-third-millennium/266134/.

Andrew Newberg, "Ask the Brains," *Scientific American*, January 1, 2012, scientificamerican.com/article/askthebrains/.

P. Krummenacher et al., "Dopamine, Paranormal Belief, and the Detection of Meaningful Stimuli," *Journal of Cognitive Neuroscience* 22, no. 8 (2010): 1670–1681, doi.org/10.1162/jocn.2009.21313.

"There Are No Atheists in Foxholes," Quote Investigator, quoteinvestigator.com /2016/11/02/foxhole/.

B. Rickhi et al., "A Spirituality Teaching Program for Depression: A Randomized Clinical Trial," *International Journal of Psychiatry in Medicine* 42, no. 3 (2012): 315–329, doi.org/10.2190/PM.42.3.f.

C. Delaney, C. Barrere, and M. Helming, "The Influence of a Spirituality-Based Intervention on Quality of Life, Depression, and Anxiety in Community-Dwelling Adults with Cardiovascular Disease: A Pilot Study," *Journal of Holistic Nursing* 29, no. 1 (2010): 21–32, doi.org/10.1177/0898010110378356.

Chapter 10. Becoming Wiser Faster

American Psychiatric Association, *Diagnostic and Statistical Manual of Mental Disorders*, 5th ed. (Washington, DC: American Psychiatric Publishing, 2013).

Dilip V. Jeste and Barton W. Palmer, *Positive Psychiatry: A Clinical Handbook* (Washington, DC: American Psychiatric Publishing, 2015).

A. Marck et al., "Are We Reaching the Limits of *Homo sapiens*?" *Frontiers in Physiology* 8 (October 2017), doi.org/10.3389/fphys.2017.00812.

"Humans at Maximum Limits for Height, Lifespan and Physical Performance, Study Suggests," ScienceDaily, December 6, 2017, sciencedaily.com/releases /2017/12/171206122502.htm.

K. J. Bangen et al., "Defining and Assessing Wisdom: A Review of the Literature," *American Journal of Geriatric Psychiatry* 21, no. 12 (2012): 1254–1266, doi.org/10 .1016/j.jagp.2012.11.020.

D. V. Jeste et al., "The New Science of Practical Wisdom," *Perspectives in Biology and Medicine* 62, no. 2 (2019): 216–236.

J. D. Sanders, T. W. Meeks, and D. V. Jeste, "Neurobiological Basis of Personal Wisdom," in *The Scientific Study of Personal Wisdom*, ed. M. Ferrari and M. N. Westrate (New York: Springer, 2013), 99–114.

E. E. Lee et al., "Meta-Analysis of Randomized Controlled Trials to Enhance Components of Wisdom: Pro-Social Behaviors, Emotional Regulation, and Spirituality" (under review).

L. R. Daniels et al., "Aging, Depression, and Wisdom: A Pilot Study of Life-Review Intervention and PTSD Treatment with Two Groups of Vietnam Veterans," *Journal of Gerontological Social Work* 58, no. 4 (2015): 420–436, doi.org/10.1080 /01634372.2015.1013657.

Aristotle, *Nicomachean Ethics*, trans. W. D. Ross (self-pub., Digireads, 2016), classics .mit.edu/Aristotle/nicomachaen.html.

K. D. Vohs et al., "Making Choices Impairs Subsequent Self-Control: A Limited-Resource Account of Decision Making, Self-Regulation, and Active Initiative," *Journal of Personality and Social Psychology* 95, no. 5 (2008): 883–898, doi.org /10.1037/0022-3514.94.5.883.

Christine Hammond, "What Is Decision Fatigue?" The Exhausted Woman, PsychCentral, pro.psychcentral.com/exhausted-woman/2019/02/what-is-decision-fatigue/.

Wikipedia, s.v. "Tim Fargo," last modified October 4, 2019, en.wikipedia.org/wiki /Tim_Fargo.

Jon Meacham, *The Soul of America: The Battle for Our Better Angels* (New York: Random House, 2019).

H. Jazaieri et al. "Enhancing Compassion: A Randomized Controlled Trial of a Compassion Cultivation Training Program," *Journal of Happiness Studies* 14 (2013): 1113–1126, doi.org/10.1007/s10902-012-9373-z.

"Bullying," Fast Facts, National Center for Education Statistics, nces.ed.gov/fastfacts /display.asp?id=719.

"Preventing Bullying," Centers for Disease Control and Prevention, cdc.gov /violenceprevention/youthviolence/bullyingresearch/fastfact.html.

Maite Garaigordobil, "Cyberbullying in Adolescents and Youth in the Basque Country: Prevalence of Cybervictims, Cyberaggressors, and Cyberobservers,"

Journal of Youth Studies 18, no. 5 (2014): 569–582, doi.org/10.1080/13676261.2014 .992324.

Wikipedia, s.v. "Dhammapada," last modified December 27, 2019, en.wikipedia.org /wiki/Dhammapada.

J. Galante et al., "Loving-Kindness Meditation Effects on Well-Being and Altruism: A Mixed-Methods Online RCT," *Applied Psychology: Health and Well-Being* 8, no. 3 (2016): 322–350, doi.org/10.1111/aphw.12074.

E. Smeets et al., "Meeting Suffering with Kindness: Effects of a Brief Self-Compassion Intervention for Female College Students," *Journal of Clinical Psychology* 70, no. 9 (2014): 794–807, doi.org/10.1002/jclp.22076.

A. M. Friis et al., "Kindness Matters: A Randomized Controlled Trial of a Mindful Self-Compassion Intervention Improves Depression, Distress, and HbA1c Among Patients with Diabetes," *Diabetes Care* 39, no. 11 (2016): 1963–1971, doi .org/10.2337/dc16-0416.

Scott LaFee and Judy Piercey, "With Landmark Gift, UC San Diego Will Map Compassion in the Brain, Then Prove Its Power," Newsroom, UC San Diego Health, July 22, 2019, health.ucsd.edu/news/releases/Pages/2019-07-22-landmark-gift-to -create-institute-of-empathy-and-compassion-at-UC-San-Diego.aspx.

Kinsee Morlan, "Innovative UCSD Program Aims to Draw Compassion Out of Future Doctors," Arts/Culture, Voice of San Diego, October 16, 2017, voiceofsandiego.org /topics/arts/innovative-ucsd-program-aims-to-draw-compassion-out-of -future-doctors/.

Paul Sisson, "Med Students Learn the Pains of Aging," *San Diego Union-Tribune*, January 31, 2017, sandiegouniontribune.com/news/health/sd-me-medstudents -aging-20170123-story.html.

"Age-Simulation Suit Gives Insight into How It Feels to Be Old," Engineers Journal, Engineers Ireland, April 24, 2014, engineersjournal.ie/2014/04/24 /age-simulation-suit-gives-an-insight-into-how-it-feels-to-be-old/.

Thich Nhat Hanh, *The Art of Mindfulness* (New York: HarperOne, 2012).

Matt Danzico, "Brains of Buddhist Monks Scanned in Meditation Study," BBC News, April 24, 2011, bbc.com/news/world-us-canada-12661646.

A. J. Lang et al., "Compassion Meditation for Posttraumatic Stress Disorder in Veterans: A Randomized Proof of Concept Study," *Journal of Traumatic Stress* (March 31, 2019), doi.org/10.1002/jts.22397.

Natalie Proulx, "Should Schools Teach Mindfulness?" *New York Times*, February 7, 2019, nytimes.com/2019/02/07/learning/should-schools-teach-mindfulness.html.

V. R. Varma et al., "Experience Corps Baltimore: Exploring the Stressors and Rewards of High-Intensity Civic Engagement," *Gerontologist* 55, no. 6 (2015): 1038–1049, doi.org/10.1093/geront/gnu011.

Beth Newcomb, "Older Adults Find Fulfillment as Volunteers Who Help the Young, USC Study Finds," July 30, 2015, Social Impact, USC News, news.usc.edu/84461 /older-adults-find-fulfillment-as-volunteers-who-help-the-young-usc-study -finds/.

P. Goldstein et al., "Brain-to-Brain Coupling During Handholding Is Associated with Pain Reduction," *PNAS* 115, no. 11 (2018): 2528–2537, doi.org/10.1073/pnas .1703643115.

D. Jeste and E. E. Lee, "The Emerging Empirical Science of Wisdom: Definition, Measurement, Neurobiology, Longevity, and Interventions," *Harvard Review of Psychiatry* 27, no. 3 (2019): 127–140, doi.org/10.1097/hrp.0000000000000205.

Zak Kelm et al., "Interventions to Cultivate Physician Empathy: A Systematic Review," *BMC Medical Education* 14, no. 219 (2014), doi.org/10.1186/1472-6920-14-219.

Dilip V. Jeste and Barton W. Palmer, *Positive Psychiatry: A Clinical Handbook* (Washington, DC: American Psychiatric Publishing, 2015).

Elizabeth Gilbert, *Eat Pray Love: One Woman's Search for Everything Across Italy, India and Indonesia* (New York: Penguin, 2006).

Tamra Johnson, "Nearly 80 Percent of Drivers Express Significant Anger, Aggression or Road Rage," AAA NewsRoom, July 14, 2016, newsroom.aaa.com/2016/07/nearly -80-percent-of-drivers-express-significant-anger-aggression-or-road-rage/.

"Who Said 'When One Door Closes Another Opens'?" Your Dictionary, quotes .yourdictionary.com/articles/who-said-when-one-door-closes-another -opens.html.

Tara Parker-Pope, "How to Build Resilience in Midlife," *New York Times*, July 25, 2017, nytimes.com/2017/07/25/well/mind/how-to-boost-resilience-in-midlife.html.

George E. Vaillant, *The Wisdom of the Ego* (Cambridge, MA: Harvard University Press, 1998).

Michael Winnick, "Putting a Finger on Our Phone Obsession," dscout, June 16, 2017, blog.dscout.com/mobile-touches.

E. B. H. Treichler et al., "A Pragmatic Trial of a Group Intervention in Senior Housing Communities to Increase Resilience: Intervention for Resilience in Older Adults," *International Psychogeriatrics* (February 2020): 1–10, doi.org/10.1017/S1041610219002096.

L. P. Montross-Thomas et al., "Reflections on Wisdom at the End of Life: Qualitative Interviews of 21 Hospice Patients," *International Psychogeriatrics* (December 2018): 1759–1766, doi.org/10.1017/S1041610217003039.

Harvey Christian Lehman, *Age and Achievement* (Princeton, NJ: Princeton University Press, 1953).

D. K. Simonton, "Creativity and Wisdom in Aging," in *Handbook of the Psychology of Aging*, ed. J. E. Birren and K. W. Schaie (San Diego, CA: Academic Press, 1990).

Robert J. Sternberg, *Wisdom, Intelligence, and Creativity Synthesized* (Cambridge, UK: Cambridge University Press, 2003).

David Galenson, "The Wisdom and Creativity of the Elders in Art and Science," *HuffPost*, December 6, 2017, huffpost.com/entry/the-wisdom-and-creativity_b_2441894.

University of Liverpool, "Reading Shakespeare Has Dramatic Effect on Human Brain," ScienceDaily, December 19, 2006, sciencedaily.com/releases/2006/12 /061218122613.htm.

L. L. Craft and F. M. Perna, "The Benefits of Exercise for the Clinically Depressed," *Primary Care Companion to the Journal of Clinical Psychiatry* 6, no. 3 (2004): 104–111, doi.org/10.4088/pcc.v06n0301.

D. Rosenberg et al., "Exergames for Subsyndromal Depression in Older Adults: A Pilot Study of a Novel Intervention," *American Journal of Geriatric Psychiatry* 18, no. 3 (2011): 221–226, doi.org/10.1097/JGP.0b013e3181c534b5.

P. L. Fazeli et al., "Physical Activity Is Associated with Better Neurocognitive and Everyday Functioning Among Older Adults with HIV Disease," *AIDS Behavior* 19, no. 8 (2015): 1470–1477, doi.org/10.1007/s10461-015-1024-z.

"Diet and Attention Deficit Hyperactivity Disorder," Harvard Mental Health Letter, Harvard Health Publishing, June 2009, health.harvard.edu/newsletter_article /Diet-and-attention-deficit-hyperactivity-disorder.

Michelle Brubaker, "Remote Italian Village Could Harbor Secrets of Healthy Aging," UC San Diego News Center, March 29, 2016, ucsdnews.ucsd.edu/pressrelease /remote_italian_village_could_harbor_secrets_of_healthy_aging.

Michelle Brubaker, "Researchers Find Common Psychological Traits in Group of Italians Aged 90 to 101," Newsroom, UC San Diego Health, December 11, 2017, health.ucsd.edu/news/releases/Pages/2017-12-11-researchers-find-common -psychological-traits-in-group-of-italians-aged-90-to-101.aspx.

Chapter 11. Wisdom Boosters

A. M Owen et al., "Putting Brain Training to the Test," *Nature* 465 (2010): 775–778, doi.org/10.1038/nature09042.

D. Blazer, K. Yaffe, and C. Liverman, eds., *Cognitive Aging: Progress in Understanding and Opportunities for Action* (Washington, DC: Institute of Medicine, 2015).

K. Benson et al., "Misuse of Stimulant Medication Among College Students: A Comprehensive Review and Meta-analysis," *Clinical Child and Family Psychology Review* 18 (2015): 50–76, doi.org/10.1007/s10567-014-0177-z.

Limitless, directed by Neil Burger, 2011.

M. DeJesus-Hernandez et al., "Expanded GGGGCC Hexanucleotide Repeat in Noncoding Region of C9ORF72 Causes Chromosome 9p-Linked FTD and ALS," *Neuron* 72, no. 2 (2011): 245–256, doi.org/10.1016/j.neuron.2011.09.011.

M. R. Turner et al., "Genetic Screening in Sporadic ALS and FTD," *Journal of Neurology, Neurosurgery & Psychiatry* 88 (2017): 1042–1044, doi.org/10.1136 /jnnp-2017-315995.

Alan Turing, "Computing Machinery and Intelligence," *Mind* 59, no. 236 (1950), abelard.org/turpap/turpap.php.

"The 25 Best Inventions of 2017," *Time*, November 16, 2017, time.com/5023212 /best-inventions-of-2017/.

Dave Gershgorn, "My Long-Awaited Robot Friend Made Me Wonder What It Means to Live at All," Quartz, November 8, 2017, qz.com/1122563/my-long-awaited -robot-friend-made-me-wonder-what-it-means-to-live-at-all/.

Jaden Urbi and MacKenzie Sigalos, "The Complicated Truth About Sophia the Robot—An Almost Human Robot or a PR Stunt," Tech Drivers, CNBC, June 5, 2018, cnbc.com/2018/06/05/hanson-robotics-sophia-the-robot-pr-stunt -artificial-intelligence.html.

Dominic Walsh, "Citizen Robot Marks a World First for Saudi Arabia," *Times* (UK edition), October 27, 2017, thetimes.co.uk/article/citizen-robot-marks-a-world-first-for-saudi-arabia-vjvmmtx3s.

Olivier Garret, "10 Million Self-Driving Cars Will Hit the Road by 2020—Here's How to Profit," *Forbes*, March 3, 2017, forbes.com/sites/oliviergarret/2017/03/03/10-million-self-driving-cars-will-hit-the-road-by-2020-heres-how-to-profit/#51ffa24b7e50.

Michael DeGusta, "Are Smart Phones Spreading Faster Than Any Technology in Human History?" *MIT Technology Review*, May 9, 2012, technologyreview.com/s/427787/are-smart-phones-spreading-faster-than-any-technology-in-human-history/.

John Brandon, "Why Smartphones Will Become Extinct by 2025," *Inc.*, October 16, 2017, inc.com/john-brandon/why-smartphones-will-become-extinct-by-2025.html.

"Mobile Phones Are Transforming Africa," *Economist*, December 10, 2016, economist.com/middle-east-and-africa/2016/12/10/mobile-phones-are-transforming-africa.

Ian Sample, "Robert Boyle: Wishlist of a Restoration Visionary," *Guardian* (US edition), June 3, 2010, theguardian.com/science/2010/jun/03/robert-boyle-royal-society-wishlist.

M. Hatzinger, "The History of Kidney Transplantation," *Urologe* 55 (2016): 1353–1359, doi.org/10.1007/s00120-016-0205-3.

Jules Verne, *From the Earth to the Moon* (Paris: Pierre-Jules Hetzel, 1865).

Nikola Tesla, *Popular Mechanics* (quoting the *New York Times*), October 1909, mentalfloss.com/article/51617/13-nikola-tesla-quotes-his-birthday.

Chapter 12. The Future of Wisdom

I. Grossmann et al., "Aging and Wisdom: Culture Matters," *Psychological Science* 23, no. 10 (2012): 1059–1066, doi.org/10.1177/0956797612446025.

I. Grossmann et al., "Emotional Complexity: Clarifying Definitions and Cultural Correlates," *Journal of Personality and Social Psychology* 111, no. 6 (2016): 895–916, doi.org/10.1037/pspp0000084.

"Marcel Pagnol Quotations," Quotetab, accessed February 22, 2020, quotetab.com/quotes/by-marcel-pagnol#HMghWzT6z7XScOUi.97.

Joseph E. Stiglitz, "Of the 1%, by the 1%, for the 1%," *Vanity Fair*, March 31, 2011, vanityfair.com/news/2011/05/top-one-percent-201105.

"Bhutan's Gross National Happiness Index," Oxford Poverty & Human Development Initiative, University of Oxford, ophi.org.uk/policy/national-policy/gross-national-happiness-index/.

A Compass Towards a Just and Harmonious Society: 2015 GNH Survey Report (Thimphu, Bhutan: Centre for Bhutan Studies & GNH Research, 2016), grossnational happiness.com/.

Wikipedia, s.v. "World Happiness Report," last modified February 16, 2020, en.m.wikipedia.org/wiki/World_Happiness_Report.

"World Happiness Report 2019," United Nations Sustainable Development Solutions Network, March 20, 2019, worldhappiness.report/.

Gabrielle Johnston, "Mental Health Is a Casualty of War," ThisWeek@UCSanDiego, UCSD News Center, December 7, 2017, ucsdnews.ucsd.edu/feature/mental-health-is-a-casualty-of-war.

N. Sartorius et al., "The International Pilot Study of Schizophrenia," *Schizophrenia Bulletin* 1, no. 11 (1974): doi.org/10.1093/schbul/1.11.21.

"Human Development Report 2019," United Nations Development Programme, hdr.undp.org/.

"Human Development Reports: 2018 Statistical Update," United Nations Development Programme, hdr.undp.org/en/content/human-development-indices-indicators-2018-statistical-update#:~:text=Human%20Development%20Indices%20and%20Indicators%3A%202018%20Statistical%20update%20is%20being,trends%20in%20human%20development%20indicators.

T. J. VanderWeele, "On the Promotion of Human Flourishing," *PNAS* 114, no. 31 (2017): 8148–8156, doi.org/10.1073/pnas.1702996114.

D. V. Jeste and A. J. Oswald, "Individual and Societal Wisdom: Explaining the Paradox of Human Aging and High Well-Being," *Psychiatry* 77, no. 4 (2014): 317–330, doi.org/10.1521/psyc.2014.77.4.317.

M. Roser, E. Ortiz-Ospina, and H. Ritchie, "Life Expectancy," *Our World in Data* (October 2019): note 2, ourworldindata.org/life-expectancy#note-2.

F. A. Januchowski-Hartley et al., "Spillover of Fish Naivete from Marine Reserves," *Ecology Letters* 16, no. 2 (2012): 191–197, doi.org/10.1111/ele.12028.

L. Scholl et al., "Drug and Opioid-Involved Overdose Deaths—United States, 2013–2017," *MMMR Morbidity and Mortality Weekly Report* 67, no. 51–52 (2019): 1419–1427, doi.org/10.15585/mmwr.mm675152e1.

H. Hedegaard, S. C. Curtin, and M. Warner, "Suicide Rates in the United States Continue to Increase," *NCHS Data Brief* no. 309 (Hyattsville, MD: National Center for Health Statistics, 2018), cdc.gov/nchs/products/databriefs/db309.htm.

E. Arias and J. Q. Xu, "United States Life Tables, 2017," *National Vital Statistics Reports* 68, no. 7 (Hyattsville, MD: National Center for Health Statistics, 2019), cdc.gov/nchs/data/nvsr/nvsr68/nvsr68_07-508.pdf.

S. Galea et al., "Estimated Deaths Attributable to Social Factors in the United States," *American Journal of Public Health* 101, no. 8 (2011): 1456–1465, doi.org/10.2105/AJPH.2010.300086.

D. McDaid, A. Bauer, and A. L. Park, "Making the Economic Case for Investing in Actions to Prevent and/or Tackle Loneliness: A Systematic Review," (briefing paper, London School of Economics and Political Science, 2017).

F. Alberti, "Loneliness Is a Modern Illness of the Body, Not Just the Mind," *Guardian* (US edition), November 1, 2018, theguardian.com/commentisfree/2018/nov/01/loneliness-illness-body-mind-epidemic.

E. E. Lee et al., "High Prevalence and Adverse Health Effects of Loneliness in Community-Dwelling Adults Across the Lifespan: Role of Wisdom as a Protective Factor," *International Psychogeriatrics* 31, no. 10 (2018): 1–16, doi.org/10.1017 /S1041610218002120.

"Gallup 2019 Global Emotions Report," Advanced Analytics, Gallup, April 18, 2019, gallup.com/analytics/248909/gallup-2019-global-emotions-report-pdf.aspx.

Steven Pinker, *The Better Angels of Our Nature: Why Violence Has Declined* (New York: Penguin, 2011).

D. W. Amundsen and C. J. Diers, "The Age of Menopause in Classical Greece and Rome," *Human Biology* 42, no. 1 (1970): 79–86, jstor.org/stable/41449006.

D. V. Jeste and A. J. Oswald, "Individual and Societal Wisdom: Explaining the Paradox of Human Aging and High Well-Being," *Psychiatry* 77, no. 4 (2014): doi.org/10.1521/psyc.2014.77.4.317.

"Global Health Observatory," World Health Organization, accessed March 11, 2020, who.int/gho/en/.

"Suicide Facts," Suicide Awareness Voices of Education, accessed March 11, 2020, save.org/about-suicide/suicide-facts/.

H. Hedegaard et al., "Drug Overdose Deaths in the United States, 1999–2017," *NCHS Data Brief* no. 329 (Hyattsville, MD: National Center for Health Statistics, 2018).

Mark Gold, "The Surprising Links Among Opioid Use, Suicide, and Unintentional Overdose," Addiction Policy Forum, March 12, 2019, addictionpolicy.org/blog/tag /research-you-can-use/the-surprising-links-among-opioid-use-suicide-and -unintentional-overdose.

Lenny Bernstein, "U.S. Life Expectancy Declines Again, a Dismal Trend Not Seen Since World War I," *Washington Post*, November 29, 2018, washingtonpost.com /national/health-science/us-life-expectancy-declines-again-a-dismal-trend -not-seen-since-world-war-i/2018/11/28/ae58bc8c-f28c-11e8-bc79 -68604ed88993_story.html?utm_term=.5bb1881925a2.

S. Veazie et al., "Addressing Social Isolation to Improve the Health of Older Adults: A Rapid Review," Rapid Evidence Product, Agency for Healthcare Research and Quality, February 2019, doi.org/10.23970/ahrqepc-rapidisolation.

Ceylan Yeginsu, "U.K. Appoints a Minister for Loneliness," *New York Times*, January 17, 2018, nytimes.com/2018/01/17/world/europe/uk-britain-loneliness.html.

Ellie Polack, "New Cigna Study Reveals Loneliness at Epidemic Levels in America," Cigna, May 1, 2018, cigna.com/newsroom/news-releases/2018/new-cigna -study-reveals-loneliness-at-epidemic-levels-in-america.

Claudia Hammond, "The Anatomy of Loneliness," episode 3, BBC Radio 4 (2018), bbc.co.uk/programmes/m0000mj9.

Scott LaFee, "Serious Loneliness Spans the Adult Lifespan but There Is a Silver Lining," Newsroom, UC San Diego Health, December 18, 2018, health.ucsd.edu /news/releases/Pages/2018-12-18-Serious-Loneliness-Spans-Adult-Lifespan-but -there-is-a-Silver-Lining.aspx.

D. V. Jeste, "Is Wisdom an Antidote to the Toxin of Loneliness?" Quartz, March 27, 2018, qz.com/1235824/you-can-actually-learn-to-be-wise-and-it-can-help -you-feel-less-lonely/.

Fay Bound Alberti, *A Biography of Loneliness* (Oxford, UK: Oxford University Press, 2019).

Morlett Paredes et al., "Qualitative Study of Loneliness in a Senior Housing Community: The Importance of Wisdom and Other Coping Strategies," *Aging and Mental Health* (2020): 1–8, doi.org/10.1080/13607863.2019.1699022.

Jianjun Gao et al., "Genome-Wide Association Study of Loneliness Demonstrates a Role for Common Variation," *Neuropsychopharmacology* 42 (2017): 811–821, doi.org/10.1038/npp.2016.197.

E. E. Lee et al., "High Prevalence and Adverse Health Effects of Loneliness in Community-Dwelling Adults Across the Lifespan: Role of Wisdom as a Protective Factor," *International Psychogeriatrics* 31, no. 10 (2018): 1–16, doi.org /10.1017/S1041610218002120.

"The Irish Longitudinal Study on Ageing (TILDA)," Trinity College Dublin, updated February 12, 2020, tilda.tcd.ie/.

S. B. Rafnsson et al., "Loneliness, Social Integration, and Incident Dementia Over 6 Years: Prospective Findings from the English Longitudinal Study of Ageing," *Journals of Gerontology, Series B* 75, no. 1 (2017), doi.org/10.1093/geronb/gbx087.

Julie Ray, "Americans' Stress, Worry and Anger Intensified in 2018," Gallup, April 25, 2019, news.gallup.com/poll/249098/americans-stress-worry-anger-intensified -2018.aspx.

J. M. Twenge et al., "Age, Period, and Cohort Trends in Mood Disorder Indicators and Suicide Related Outcomes in a Nationally Representative Dataset, 2005–2017," *Journal of Abnormal Psychology* 128, no. 3 (2019): 185–199, doi.org/10.1037 /abn0000410.

"Alcohol and Drug Misuse and Suicide and the Millennial Generation—a Devastating Impact," *Pain in the Nation: Building a National Resilience Strategy*, Trust for America's Health, June 13, 2019, tfah.org/report-details/adsandmillennials/.

Nigel Tubbs, *Philosophy and Modern Liberal Arts Education: Freedom Is to Learn* (New York: Palgrave Macmillan, 2014).

Plato, *Phaedrus*.

J. Dewey, *Experience and Education*, vol. 10 (New York: Macmillan, 1938).

Helen Dukas and Banesh Hoffman, eds., *Albert Einstein, The Human Side: Glimpses from His Archives* (Princeton, NJ: Princeton University Press, 2013).

Index

About the Authors

DILIP V. JESTE, MD, is the senior associate dean for healthy aging and senior care, Estelle and Edgar Levi Chair in Aging, Distinguished Professor of Psychiatry and Neurosciences, director of the Sam and Rose Stein Institute for Research on Aging, director of the Center for Healthy Aging, and codirector of the Artificial Intelligence for Healthy Living Center, all at the University of California San Diego.

SCOTT LAFEE is a former science writer and editor at the *San Diego Union-Tribune* and is currently the director of communications and media relations for University of California San Diego Health and Health Sciences.

About Sounds True

SOUNDS TRUE is a multimedia publisher whose mission is to inspire and support personal transformation and spiritual awakening. Founded in 1985 and located in Boulder, Colorado, we work with many of the leading spiritual teachers, thinkers, healers, and visionary artists of our time. We strive with every title to preserve the essential "living wisdom" of the author or artist. It is our goal to create products that not only provide information to a reader or listener but also embody the quality of a wisdom transmission.

For those seeking genuine transformation, Sounds True is your trusted partner. At SoundsTrue.com you will find a wealth of free resources to support your journey, including exclusive weekly audio interviews, free downloads, interactive learning tools, and other special savings on all our titles.

To learn more, please visit SoundsTrue.com/freegifts or call us toll-free at 800.333.9185.

sounds true
WAKING UP THE WORLD